CELEBRITY CULTURES
IN CANADA

Cultural Studies Series

Cultural Studies is the multi- and inter-disciplinary study of culture, defined anthropologically as a "way of life," performatively as symbolic practice, and ideologically as the collective product of varied media and cultural industries. Although Cultural Studies is a relative newcomer to the humanities and social sciences, in less than half a century it has taken interdisciplinary scholarship to a new level of sophistication, reinvigorating the liberal arts curriculum with new theories, topics, and forms of intellectual partnership.

Wilfrid Laurier University Press invites submissions of manuscripts concerned with critical discussions on power relations concerning gender, class, sexual preference, ethnicity, and other macro and micro sites of political struggle.

For more information, please contact:

Siobhan McMenemy
Senior Editor
Wilfrid Laurier University Press
75 University Avenue West
Waterloo, ON N2L 3C5
Canada
Phone: 519-884-0710 ext. 3782
Fax: 519-725-1399

Email: smcmenemy@wlu.ca

CELEBRITY CULTURES IN CANADA

*Katja Lee and
Lorraine York, editors*

Foreword by P. David Marshall

WILFRID LAURIER UNIVERSITY PRESS

Wilfrid Laurier University Press acknowledges the support of the Canada Council for the Arts for our publishing program. We acknowledge the financial support of the Government of Canada through the Canada Book Fund for our publishing activities. This work was supported by the Research Support Fund.

Library and Archives Canada Cataloguing in Publication

Celebrity cultures in Canada / Katja Lee and Lorraine York, editors.

(Cultural studies series)
Includes bibliographical references and index.
Issued in print and electronic formats.
ISBN 978-1-77112-222-1 (paperback).—ISBN 978-1-77112-224-5 (epub).—
ISBN 978-1-77112-223-8 (pdf)

1. Celebrities—Canada. 2. Fame—Canada. 3. Popular culture—Canada. 4. Celebrities in mass media.
5. Mass media and culture. 6. Mass media—Social aspects—Canada. 7. Fame—Social aspects—Canada.
I. York, Lorraine M. (Lorraine Mary), 1958–, editor II. Lee, Katja, 1977–, editor III. Series: Cultural studies series (Waterloo, Ont.)

HM621.C44 2016   306.4   C2015-908734-1
                                        C2015-908735-X

Cover design by David Drummond. Text design by Daiva Villa, Chris Rowat Design.

This book is printed on FSC® recycled paper and is certified Ecologo. It is made from 100% post-consumer fibre, processed chlorine free, and manufactured using biogas energy.

Printed in Canada

RECYCLED
Paper made from
recycled material
FSC® C103567

Contents

Foreword: The Celebrity Nation

P. David Marshall

Perhaps one of the most annoying habits that I have when watching a film or television program is to lean over to whoever has deigned to watch with me and whisper, "You know, she's Canadian." It might be a more recent incarnation of stardom and celebrity via Rachel McAdams or Ryan Gosling. Or maybe it is pulling a slightly older recall of fame from the likenesses of Jim Carrey, Pamela Anderson, or Ryan Reynolds; or even the deeper hallmarks of the well-known from the latter part of the twentieth century such as Catherine O'Hara, Peter Jennings, Michael J. Fox, William Shatner, Raymond Burr, or Leslie Nielsen. My predilection, I am sure, is not a solo affliction, and it is not simply because I am an expatriate. It is another feature of Canadianness, a way in which Canadians work to self-identify. Famous Canadians in the American context almost blend into the American scene and are therefore hidden from clear view except for the work of the cognoscenti (a.k.a Canadians) who regularly and often proclaim their "real" provenance.

Reading celebrity in the Canadian context is complex. The production of public visibility in Canada has had its own patterns that are related to a very intriguing manufacturing of culture. There are intrinsically identifiable figures – that is, the famous who are only really known within the borders of Canada. These are further subdivided into the long-standing linguistic boundaries of French and English; but even these divides end up producing another group of well-known Canadians who have somehow worked to transcend these limits. Politicians, hockey players, musicians, and the occasional other famous athlete can sometimes navigate between the two quite distinct celebrity cultures. Equally of interest are those celebrities who have emerged from what could be called the public production of culture perhaps best articulated through the CBC and Radio-Canada. It is hard to identify this distinctiveness beyond a sensibility that privileges the comfort with a culture not necessarily produced entirely from com-mercialization, but a hybridity of popularity buttressed by national and government-supported systems of media and culture.

As much as there is an internal system of celebrity operating in the various cultural industries, there is a strong determination in the Cana-dian scene to an extrinsic fame and to transcend that Canadian status and locale. Canadian celebrity also is an appeal to validation from cul-tural industries external to Canada that are perceived to be more economi-cally and culturally significant, like the American film and popular music industries, and, to a lesser extent, French film and popular culture. More-over, Canada's privileging of its multicultural mosaic has even led to con-nections to other centres of international production, from Bollywood to Hong Kong, Korea, and China. All of these efforts to attach to extrinsic and transnational fame have been instrumental in shaping the fame industry within Canada.

This appeal outwards, however, is certainly not unique to the Canadian system of celebrity. On some levels, the very idea of celebrity is somewhat alien and foreign to smaller cultural systems and countries like Canada. The definition of celebrity is derived from the work of larger industries that have laboured extensively to ensure the reach of celebrity systems such as Hollywood has done for more than a century. Indeed, it is more accurate to identify that Canada has gone through a somewhat limited "celebritiza-tion" (Dreissens) process in the last forty years: in other words, increas-ingly, Canadian cultural systems have used the celebration of the public individual as a technique to attract attention, organize cultural produc-tion, and maintain the interest of the audiences of the nation. These prac-tices predate this period, but they have certainly intensified and become more homegrown and strategic in recent history.

If this celebritization has in fact expanded and developed in Canadian culture over the last forty years, it is interesting to read whether it has devel-oped in patterns similar to the American system or whether it has begun producing a slightly different attention economy. For instance, one of the key elements of the American celebrity system is an extensive and intrusive investigation of the private lives of the famous. Conceptually, celebrity is a term that is focused on the "extra-textual" dimensions of the well known; that is, the private stories, scandals, and gossip about the famed become a way to maintain the visibility, attention, and allure of celebrities as they become valuable cultural commodities beyond the cultural forms they produce (Marshall, *Celebrity and Power*). However, with the major exception of the well-established and intrinsic celebrity gossip system of fame in Quebec (which needs a much closer look as to how it reproduces

American celebrity-style culture), English-Canadian celebrities are rarely [handwritten annotation]
represented as revealing hidden and inner truths by the Canadian media
system. What has emerged through an expanding celebrity system is something somewhat different and deserving further study.

It is these very dimensions of the particularities and peculiarities of a *the book*
Canadian celebrity system that are explored in this book. *Celebrity Cultures* *is better*
in Canada represents a very valuable intervention. The editors and authors *titled*
have developed an incredibly nuanced reading of how celebrity operates in *English-*
Canada. From its explorations of existing institutions and forms of gover- *Canada*
nance and privilege and how they can shape a public personality system,
this book provides the material and research that can both substantiate
and refute some of the claims that I and others have made about celebrity
in Canada.

One of the clear strengths of this book is its capacity to work through
valuable historical examples. It is this kind of groundwork that begins to
position how celebrity has intersected with the various cultural institutions and media industries within Canada. This historical research also
further identifies how celebrity moves between cultures and nations, which
helps define both what celebrity has become transnationally and within the
Canadian context.

Augmenting the historical dimensions of *Celebrity Cultures in Canada*
is an evident interdisciplinarity in the analysis. Although the cultural
industrial/institutional origins of each celebrity explored has often defined
the home discipline and the editors themselves have certain affinities to
both literary studies and biographical research, the connection to wider
literatures in the study of celebrity and in the organization of public personalities has clearly informed most of the book's chapters.

From my perspective, the ultimate value of this book is that it estab-
lishes the groundwork for what I would call *comparative celebrity studies*, [handwritten annotation]
which is somewhat different from and challenging to some of the literature
on celebrity and globalization that has been written recently (see Marshall and Redmond, part 4). From at least two perspectives, the study of
Canadian celebrity demands comparative research and thus provides the
tools for its exploration between and among national cultures. The dual
national cultures and celebrity systems that are produced in Canada move
the book's investigation regularly and often into comparative research or
recognizing quite quickly how differences between celebrity systems do
not move transnationally and how a researcher has to circumscribe the
validity of their research claims. In addition, Canadian celebrity culture
also has had a long and close relationship with, and a restructuring by
and through, American culture, which further pushes the analysis into

understanding comparative public personality systems and, once again, the non-movement of certain cultural icons transnationally. From its vantage point, *Celebrity Cultures in Canada* both establishes the intrinsic structures of a celebrity system as well as its extrinsic properties; it helps explore how celebrity functions within Canada as well as what elements of a public personality system are translatable into other cultural systems and structures. What I hope will emerge from this book's important work is a continued development of the study of the public personality system of Canada and a growth in the comparative study of celebrity between and among different nations, nation-states, and cultural and linguistic groups. This book thus serves as a template for the investigation of both specific national celebrity cultures and comparative celebrity studies. I hope that editors, authors, and readers take up this intellectual challenge.

Acknowledgements

Editing a collection of essays is the art of coordinating moving pieces—lots of them. And so we owe a great debt of thanks to our nine contributors—the authors of those moving pieces—who embraced the process of assembling and revising this collection with the utmost in professional generosity. At Wilfrid Laurier University Press, our acquisitions editor Lisa Quinn has shown enthusiasm for this project from the very first, and has handled our queries along the way with good grace and a limitless fund of expertise.

Speaking of expertise, we owe the anonymous readers of the manuscript our appreciation for their time, their detailed feedback, their discernment, and their wisdom. This is work that often goes unpaid and unrecognized in our disciplines, and we are deeply grateful for it. A special thank you to P. David Marshall, Chair in New Media, Communication and Cultural Studies in the School of Communication and Creative Arts, Deakin University, for writing such a thoughtful foreword to this book.

We thank the copyright owners of the various visual images contained in this volume for their kind consideration and permissions.

We are also mindful of the excellent and amiable support we have received from the Department of English and Cultural Studies at McMaster University. Warm thanks in particular to Chair Peter Walmsley for his energetic support of and advocacy for all of our department's work.

Katja wishes to express her thanks and appreciation to the Persona, Celebrity Publics Research Group at Deakin University for their gracious support and mentorship. Much gratitude is also due to Ryan Veenstra for being the most tremendous life partner and best friend, and to Lorraine York for being a most attentive and excellent colleague and co-editor.

Lorraine thanks Michael Ross for his saving wit and constant love, and Anna Ross for being her reporter on the spot in Hollywood. And she is grateful for having a hard-working, astute, and collegial co-editor in Katja Lee.

It has been our great good fortune to work with these many excellent individuals and institutions. This project was made possible because of their support and because they so selflessly and warmly shared their time, labour, and resources. Thank you.

Introduction: Celebrity Cultures in Canada. It's Not a Question

Katja Lee and Lorraine York

A crowd gathered and I heard a woman shout, "Who does she think she is, god-damned Elvis Presley?" That negativity was typically small-town, and it stung me. But it was also the old Canada speaking, the reflexive voice insisting that stardom, and everything it entails, is somehow incompatible with the way we Canadians see ourselves.

—Anne Murray, *All of Me*

According to her 2010 memoir, *All of Me* (co-written with Michael Posner), one of Anne Murray's first and, she claims, very few experiences with hostile responses to her success and celebrity occurred during the filming of her first CBC special in her hometown of Springhill, Nova Scotia. The disgruntled woman's question, "Who does she think she is, goddamned Elvis Presley?" suggests that Murray has lost sight of her identity—perhaps aspired to and been granted too much undeserved attention—whereas Elvis, a "real" celebrity, presumably warrants such treatment. The sting of this encounter is felt both personally—as a slight against her not inconsiderable fame and importance in the Canadian music industry at this time—and patriotically—as a misrepresentation of the vibrant and modern cultural climate of the nation. Celebrity in Canada, Murray insists, warrants the crowds but not the condemnation. While Murray clearly has a vested interest in recuperating the value and significance of celebrity cultures in Canada in general, and the cultural and economic power of her own celebrity in particular, her argument about the necessity of resisting those attitudes that might construct Canada and Canadians as incommensurate with the cultures of celebrity is a valuable one: there is *still* a great deal of popular and critical suspicion about the legitimacy, the value, and the significance of celebrities and celebrity systems in Canada.

With *Celebrity Cultures in Canada* we seek not simply to redress this discursive trend, but to make space for the conversations that are already unfolding in celebrity studies, cultural studies, and other disciplines. Our aim is to bring the study of celebrity cultures in Canada to centre stage, to theorize their histories, their development, and the practices of production, dissemination, and consumption that occur in Canada and/or using Canadians. We would like to see the scope, significance, and impact of these cultures acknowledged and examined; we want celebrity in Canada to be recognized not as an absence, not as an amusing anecdote, and not as a question but as a historical and ongoing presence in the Canadian cultural landscape that wields considerable cultural, political, affective, and economic power. We take as our starting point that Canada has a viable and yet vexed celebrity—one that shares much with other celebrity cultures in this transnational global economy, but one where markers and signals of "Canadianness" are circulated as having some kind of significance. What do such markers mean and what is their cultural and economic value? The essays here address these questions across a range of cultural venues: politics, literature, sport, comedy, television, cinema, bureaucracy, social media, activism, and history. While diverse in scope and focus, taken together they paint a picture of the complexities attending celebrity cultures in Canada.

Looking across these essays, we can see decided trends emerging: an interest in how Canadian celebrity operates locally, internationally, and transnationally, and how it is shaped by government policy, shifts in media formats, and inflected by the workings of race, class, gender, sexualities, ability, and disabilities. The first of these interests—the concern with transnationality—coexists with an awareness that nation and locale continue to produce specific iterations of and conditions for the emergence of celebrity culture. In her paper on *Bon Cop, Bad Cop*, for example, Liz Czach shows how the star images of Colm Feore and Patrick Huard, which are crucially inflected by their positions in English-Canadian and Quebecois celebrity systems, seep into their roles in the film. Danielle Deveau, studying Canadian stand-up comedians, reveals how they nervously perform their ambivalent relationship to the Canadian and American markets. Katherine Ann Roberts formulates a theory of Canadian spectatorship, refining the scholarship of Charles Acland, in her study of actor Callum Keith Rennie; she argues that Canadian spectatorial recognition of Canadian artists in non-Canadian productions is a vital part of Canadian celebrity. Katja Lee agrees, finding in the careers of singer Emma Albani, dancer

Maud Allan, and actor Mary Pickford evidence of earlier transnational anxieties; the transnational, she maintains, is "neither an anomaly of nor an obstacle to a better understanding of the contours of Canadian celebrity culture, but a critical, perhaps even characteristic, component of the complex historic processes of celebrity in this country." In her historical study of these transnational celebrity processes, in specific reference to silent film actor Nell Shipman, Amy Shore, like Lee, assesses the problems of the various claims that nations make on these early transnational Canadian celebrities; identifying such claims as part of the broader cultural heritage movement, she argues that they highlight the desired variable in the star text of the celebrity who is to be claimed, while ignoring others (in Shipman's case, her later racism and pro-American xenophobia).

At the same time, many of our contributors, though they are aware of the dangers of national "claiming," show how material, historical, legislative, and bureaucratic conditions in Canada have inevitably influenced the celebrity phenomena that have taken shape within these (contested) borders. Ira Wagman examines the ways in which the labour of administration, including the nitty-gritty of grant applications in the arts world, can reveal much about the working of Canadian celebrity culture from a perspective that is little studied: the relationship between the cultural labourer and the state. Owen Percy takes this concern with arts bureaucracy into the arena of literary prize culture, comparing three Canadian poetry prizes and the way in which they exploit, deny, or refashion celebrity culture. Julie Rak situates sports commentator Don Cherry's celebrity firmly within the history of the nation's public broadcaster, the CBC, showing how Cherry "exists as a Canadian celebrity who could not be exported to the United States because the apparatus which supports him requires him to perform a melancholic nationalist narrative." Valerie Millar examines Terry Fox, another Canadian celebrity attached to nationalist—and capitalist—narratives that fail to disclose "an unremarked, hetero-normative, white, male body and ableist ideology."

This imbrication of the nation within various relations of power—class, gender, sexualities, race, ability, and disability—forms another marked thread in these essays. All of these variables, for Valerie Millar, continue to produce the celebrity myth of Terry Fox, for instance. Class, race, and sexuality become intertwined, as well, in the celebrity of Don Cherry; Julie Rak ponders the working-class mythos of Don Cherry—a mythos that is, she notes, in direct contradiction with his sizeable salary and economic bargaining power with the CBC and, more recently, Rogers, and visually incommensurate with his dandyish mode of dress. That mode—the loudly coloured suits and ties, the high collars, the fedoras—provides Rak with further occasion to probe the ruptures within Cherry's performance of hockey masculinity, seeing in this rupture a melancholic performance of a supposedly more authentic hockey past, and denying its current hyper-capitalist functioning. And Cherry's embrace of the "redneck" to describe himself is equally caught up in melancholic performances of whiteness as a lost, diminished source of social power. Other essays that look to raced performances of celebrity include Katherine Ann Roberts's brief case study of Colm Feore's star text as a model of norms of white English-Canadian propriety. In so doing, she takes some inspiration from Michele Byers's argument that Canadian men whose celebrity travels beyond our borders perform a "safe and sanitized...'whiteness'." Like the interventions of feminist scholars Su Holmes and Diane Negra in their co-edited volume *In the Limelight and Under the Microscope: Forms and Functions of Female Celebrity* (2011), or in Negra's *Off-White Hollywood* (2001), these essays interrogate the intersections of whiteness and sexuality in celebrity culture.

In her essay on indigenous celebrity, Lorraine York, while acknowledging the history of differential access to mainstream media that has produced the privileged celebrity whiteness that Roberts, Rak, and Millar examine, argues that other public spheres that do not privilege whiteness are also active, especially at this time of media and consumer proliferation. She argues for a concept of indigenous celebrity that may be, on some occasions and in some venues, oppositional to non-indigenous media cultures and an indigenous public sphere that is busy independently producing celebrity and publics across a whole range of media.

This present moment of media diversification, with its attendant multiplying of public spheres, signals another discernible trend in many of these essays: a thoroughgoing awareness of the ways in which shifts in media produce celebrity in complex, changing ways. Indeed, studies of early twentieth-century Canadian/transnational celebrity by Katja Lee and Amy Shore show how this has long been the case; as Lee points out, Mary Pickford knew that the coming of the "talkies" restricted the ability of her star image to travel transnationally and translinguistically. In the case of Nell Shipman, Amy Shore explains, in moving from film acting to producing, she was able to leverage her star image as the girl of the wilderness when she co-founded Canadian Photoplays, a company that would specialize in outdoor films. Jennifer Bell's study of the political celebrity of Pierre Elliott Trudeau and Justin Trudeau take us into the mid-twentieth and early twenty-first centuries, and here, too, changes in media form and reflect changes in celebrity, particularly the coming of television in the case of Trudeau *père* and the growth of social media in the case of Trudeau *fils*. Ira Wagman studies the capacity of government-created online representations of the culture industries to rebrand and, at this neo-liberal moment, to monetize those industries.

These intertwining threads—race, gender, sexualities, ability/disability, class, medium, trans/nationality—are notable in this collection for the degree to which the authors of these essays do, indeed, see these variables as multiply constituted, interacting now and throughout the history of Canadian celebrity.

Why Celebrity?

Our commitment to perspectives on celebrity that do not automatically assume a negative cultural critique—what Anne Murray calls "the reflexive voice insisting that stardom and everything it entails is somehow incompatible with the way we Canadians see ourselves" —is founded on our critical reading of the field of celebrity studies. From the beginning, commentary on the phenomenon of celebrity has been haunted by the assumption that celebrity must necessarily be understood to be false, unearned cultural value. As P. David Marshall has shown in his study *Celebrity and Power* (1997), the current understanding of the concept of celebrity as an ambiguous, tenuous cultural power derives from the nineteenth century, and he traces the efforts of thinkers such as William Hazlitt, Thomas Carlyle, and Ralph Waldo Emerson to safeguard the concept of heroism, as a category defining authentic human accomplishment, from its arriviste cousin "celebrity"—flash-in-the-pan social renown (6–8). For those working in cultural studies, this bifurcation finds a parallel expression in the foundational mid-twentieth-century thought of Horkheimer and Adorno, and their by now all-too-familiar critique of the "culture industries." For Edgar Morin, writing in the mid-twentieth century (1957), celebrity is similarly threatening and suspect, but in a psychological rather than a sociological vein; the star is "the product of a projection-identification complex of a particular virulence" (102) and the star is "psychotic: she polarizes and fixes obsessions" (166). As Kate Egan and Sarah Thomas have recently observed, Morin's writings form part of the "close association" that they perceive between theories of stardom and "the terminology of the 'cult.' Edgar Morin's seminal account of stardom phrased the interaction between star and fan as a form of cult appeal, emphasizing the phrase's religious connotations" (2)—and, we would add, its problematically pathologizing ones as well.

In constructing a genealogy of celebrity theory and its negative cultural critical tendencies, a key figure linking the earlier theorists to more recent commentators is Daniel Boorstin, whose 1962 book *The Image* remains a touchstone, even for theorists who are essentially in disagreement with it. Boorstin picks up the strand of thought that Marshall perceives in Hazlitt,

Carlyle, and Emerson, seeing a decline from "greatness" to "fame." In a breathtaking moment of self-contradiction, Boorstin observes that "Of course, there never was a time when 'fame' was precisely the same thing as 'greatness.' But, until very recently, famous men [sic] and great men [sic] were pretty nearly the same group" (46). The mantra that has haunted decades of celebrity analysis, though, is Boorstin's endlessly quotable "*The celebrity is a person who is known for his* [sic] *well-knownness*" (57; emphasis in original). And ever since Boorstin figured the celebrity as a content-less tautology, a "pseudo-event" (57), the idea of ideological emptiness has continued to haunt the field of celebrity studies, even after Richard Dyer's trenchant ideological critique of this assumption in *Stars* (1979).

Moving away from a knee-jerk negativity is an as yet unfinished project in celebrity studies: a project to which the present volume consciously contributes. To turn away from that negativity, while remaining mindful of the role of manufacture and industry, it is salutary to return to the work of Richard Dyer. Unlike many of the celebrity theorists who were to follow his lead, he has consistently refused the notion of celebrity as morally bankrupt or bereft of cultural value. First in *Stars* (1979), then in *Heavenly Bodies* (1987), he explored the way in which "star images function crucially in relation to contradictions within and between ideologies, which they seek variously to 'manage' or resolve" (*Stars* 34). The question of whether the image of Marilyn Monroe is "good" or "bad" is neither here nor there for Dyer; what is of interest is the way in which her star text (the sum total of the star's representations in culture) mediates conflicting ideas in the 1950s and 60s about women's sexuality and labour. In *Only Entertainment* (2002), Dyer meditates explicitly on his refusal to mine celebrity texts for what Joshua Gamson calls the "depths" of their "superficialities" (6). Reintroducing the element of pleasure itself as worthy of analysis (rather than the superficial, naive response that must be set aside for a serious analysis of textual depths), Dyer radically refuses the "this-is-bad-for-you" school of cultural critique.

A related, growing movement in celebrity studies to which this volume also contributes is the increasing attention to the power of fans to produce celebrity or, at least, to intervene in its production. In his conclusion to *Stars*, Richard Dyer noted that in the study of stardom, "the audience has been conspicuous by its absence" (162). Audience study has long been seen to be methodologically slippery, existing at a complex juncture of empirical research and reception theory. For cultural studies scholars, Stuart Hall's 1973 encoding/decoding model has inspired a shift toward the recognition of audiences as much more than passive victims of hegemonic will, setting the stage for John Fiske's much-quoted observation that "the art of popular culture is the art of making do," and so it is significant that Dyer references Hall's foundational concept in his conclusion as one of several "signs...that this absence is beginning to be made up by new theoretical developments" (160). Since 1979, much has, indeed, been done to fill that absence, not least the burgeoning field of fandom studies. In 2012, the *Journal of Fandom Studies* published its first issue, and several influential monographs have appeared in the first decade of the twenty-first century (Matt Hills's *Fan Cultures* in 2002, Cornel Sandvoss's *Fans: The Mirror of Consumption,* and Steve Bailey's *Media Audiences,* both in 2005). The fact that much recent fan activity takes place online is highlighted by the work of David Gauntlett, who argued in the 1990s that the new interactive media were rapidly blurring the lines between audiences and producers. In celebrity studies, where several of the major books in the field are structured according to the concepts of "production" and "consumption" (Dyer, Turner), the implications of this paradigm shift are immense. In this volume, essays that meditate on fan/viewer investments, like Rak's study of Don Cherry's classed, gendered, raced appeal to fans, or Roberts's study of Canadian spectatorship practices for consuming Canadian stars in American vehicles, respect and seek to know more about these acts of consumption.

So far, we have used the term "stardom" interchangeably with "celebrity," but our title for this volume consciously embraces the latter term, as one that signals performances of public individualism across a whole range of media and cultural activities, from sport, politics, and cinema to academia, music, and online communities. Our contributors productively vary in their terminological choices, film scholars Czach and Shore, for instance, using film historian Richard deCordova's influential distinction between "picture personalities" and "stars," Czach to argue that Quebec produces "stars" while English Canada produces "recognizable actors," and Shore to trace early cinematic actor Nell Shipman's transition from "picture personality" in early silent film to "star," a figure whose (represented) private life is a source of interest.

The relationship between the terms "star" and "celebrity" has been the cause of much academic meditation and argument; there is a growing debate in contemporary studies of celebrity culture over whether distinctions among terms such as "fame," "stardom," and "celebrity," not to mention others such as "notoriety," "renown," or "reputation," are methodologically useful. (Indeed, an entire session of the 2009 Modern Language Association of America's annual conference was devoted to the question of the relationship among the terms "stardom," "celebrity," and "fame.") This is not an empty semantic debate; as Su Holmes and Sean Redmond maintain, in the

introduction to their collection *Framing Celebrity* (2006), the act of nam-
ing celebrity phenomena is anything but neutral; in their words, it "raises
the issue of terminology—the categories used to explore and conceptualize
fame" (10). When we survey the important books that have been written
on celebrity, this concern with taxonomy is widespread. Many commen-
taries are heavily invested in drawing distinctions among fame, celebrity,
and stardom, though these categories tend to spin off other subcategories in a kind of taxonomical infectiousness. Chris Rojek, for instance,
in his valuable book *Celebrity* (2001), begins, as others do, with etymol-
ogy, pointing out that "the Latin root of the term" celebrity "is *celebrem*,
which has connotations with both 'fame' and 'being thronged'" (9). From
there, Rojek spawns a host of categories, arguing, first of all, that "notoriety
is a sub-branch of celebrity culture" (10). He quickly adds, though, that
"a distinction should be made between celebrity, notoriety and renown"
(12). Renown, for Rojek, is what other critics would call niche-celebrity
(Orth): celebrity within a specific, restricted sphere. Celebrity, already
thus divided, is headed for further mitosis, like a cell gone exponential:
there is also, Rojek continues, ascribed, achieved, and attributed celebrity (ascribed—by birth, like monarchy; achieved, in competition; and
attributed, not through skill but by some social intermediary's say-so).
The mitosis intensifies; Rojek further theorizes the celetoid, what he calls
a "compressed" version of attributed celebrity (the one-hit wonders of the
celebrity world, so to speak). No sooner established than subdivided: the
subcategory of the celetoid is the "celeactor," a celebrated fictional character who performs a satirical function (think Rick Mercer's ranter or Mary
Walsh's Marg Delahunty). Already, we can see how realms of cultural value
inform these taxonomies; the ascribed celebrity could be described, somewhat cynically, as the celebrity of whom we do not approve, and the further
category of celetoid seems to mark a deepening of that disapproval. Rojek's
categories of ascribed and achieved celebrity uneasily reproduce the heroic
theory of Carlyle, Hazlitt, and Emerson.

Of course, the term "stardom" signals the considerable influence of
studies of cinematic celebrity on subsequent theories of social visibility,
and so it is meaningful for film scholars in this volume, like Roberts, Czach,
and Shore, to draw upon this rich history and theory. The positioning of
Dyer's *Stars* in all major surveys of the field confirms this genealogical fact.
Graeme Turner, in his 2004 book *Understanding Celebrity*, pays tribute to
that history, calling "the development of the film star…the most elaborate and socially grounded instance of the broad phenomenon of modern
celebrity" (14). As a category, stardom has also held the power to hierar-
chize and exclude; one example would be John Langer's 1981 article "Tele-

vision's Personality System," in which he argued that stardom was specific to the film medium; television, on the other hand, created "personalities" who "play themselves," in Langer's words, "whereas stars emanate as idealizations or archetypal expressions to be contemplated, revered, desired and even blatantly imitated, stubbornly standing outside the realms of the familiar and the routinized" (Marshall, *The Celebrity Culture Reader* 185). In this volume, Roberts, in particular, surveying the transtextual production of the Canadian-born actor Callum Keith Rennie in his Canadian and American television and film roles, nuances Langer's strict categorizations to show how fans may consume Rennie's meanings intertextually and transnationally.

Indeed, several contributors to this volume, like Roberts, engage with televisual celebrity as its own distinctive category that is shaped, in large part, by the particularities of the medium. In this, they engage with more recent television theory such as that of James Bennett, who breaks away from the critical tendency for televisual fame to be forever chained to its cinematic cousin "stardom." In *Television Personalities: Stardom and the Small Screen* (2010), Bennett directs our attention to television stars who work in non-fictional roles—the Simon Cowells, the Jamie Olivers, in the case of the British programming that attracts Bennett's attention. He argues that although "Television personalities only ever play themselves, emphasizing the continuousness and authenticity of their ordinary persona" (2), this performance constitutes intense labour, and needs to be read in the context of ideological currents and contexts. In this collection, Rak's reading of Don Cherry's performance of a melancholic self, Deveau's study of Canadian comic personalities (whose monologues present a performed self commenting on the conditions of their labour), Bell's study of how the televisual medium was implicated in Pierre Elliott Trudeau's political celebrity, and Millar's analysis of Terry Fox's raced, classed, abled persona all emphasize the crucial importance of television as a means of producing and disseminating a public image in Canada.

The work in this collection extends, as well, to those venues of celebrity that are less likely to be disseminated mainly through visual media like television or cinema. Frequently, these more specialized venues produce a version of celebrity that critics are increasingly referring to as "niche" celebrity (or, in the case of online presentations of self, "microcelebrity"; Senft). Owen Percy's essay on prize culture in Canadian poetry, for instance, takes as its subject a field that is often associated with small-scale production: literature. Not surprisingly, scholars in Canadian literary celebrity like Percy, Joel Deshaye, Faye Hammill, and Lorraine York have often felt the need to justify bringing together celebrity and the literary field at all. (The introduction to York's *Literary Celebrity in Canada* [2007] is entitled "Literary Celebrity?" An early working title for that chapter was "Canadian? Literary? Celebrity?") Such anxiety usefully poses the question, how much public visibility makes for a "celebrity"? Rather than positing an answer, or an inevitably arbitrary line in the sand, *Celebrity Cultures in Canada* points to the ways in which some of these assumptions about what constitutes celebrity continue to be mobilized as reasons for disregarding the labour of Canadians in the field of celebrity culture.

[margin note: anxiety about discussing celebrity culture in Canada ↓]

As we have staunchly argued, by our very act of refusing to phrase the subject of celebrity cultures in Canada as a question, celebrity and stardom in (and in transnational contact with) Canada is a form of labour that requires and richly rewards deeper study. Whether our contributors mobilize the term "fame," "celebrity," "stardom" or other markers of heightened social presence, each with its own historical and ideological contexts, our volume title's embrace of the broad term "celebrity" welcomes all, not to homogenize, but to signal a variegated field within which these various epistemologies mix and mingle. As Su Holmes and Sean Redmond argue, the very term "celebrity" and its "currently ubiquitous use" in the field of celebrity studies signal how the other terms that find a home under its sign "cannot be viewed as autonomous academic constructs, divorced from the wider historical and cultural contexts in which they circulate" (*Stardom and Celebrity* 8). The term "celebrity" invites us to explore other "wider historical and cultural contexts" in which Canadian celebrity subjects and fans circulate, as discursive but also materially lived phenomena that reach across borders, media, disciplines, and cultural fields, while also being crucially inflected by those same borders, media, disciplines, and cultural fields. This commitment to the material conditions and histories of celebrity is one that *Celebrity Cultures in Canada* performs and reaffirms.

[margin note: this book resists the anxiety in important, significant ways.]

Why Canada?

To use the nation as an organizing and filtering device for thinking about celebrity phenomena might seem counterintuitive: in today's cultural climate where global markets, transnational corporations, and digital modes/systems of dissemination structure the vast majority of celebrity production and consumption practices, the nation often seems like a somewhat antiquated and irrelevant construct. And yet it is not. Nations still play a critical role in shaping both local and global celebrity cultures, and critics in Canada and around the world are taking note of its effects. Institutions of production are still located in and governed by regional and national bodies. Whether the state monitors and controls the flow of information or just the modes and methods by which corporate bodies and individuals profit from these systems, the production of celebrity culture is almost always in some form or another operating under the administration of the nation. Practices of dissemination and consumption are also often shaped by state policy, most noticeably through the regulation and/or funding of broadcasting content, networks, corporations, and technologies. The boundaries of nation are even felt in how we use and access the internet and social media: geo-blocking, for example, has been effectively used by political and corporate bodies alike to limit the access and flow of online cultural products, and online activities are still monitored and prosecuted by state bodies. Bureaucracy is, as Wagman and Percy argue in their chapters, a critical, often contested, component of the celebrityscape of Canada.

While the effects of a nation's policy and policing on its celebrity cultures are important and far reaching, they are rarely the cause of the rise or fall of particular trends or celebrity phenomena: Beatlemania and the British Invasion in the 1960s would have occurred regardless of what bureaucratic infrastructures were in place and Wayne Gretzky would still have become "The Great One" with or without Canadian content regulations. However, tracing and articulating how cultures circulate and consume celebrity in national contexts is a far more challenging task and can just as easily overestimate the scope of consumption as underestimate the importance of regional differences and the effects of circulating in smaller but, often, more cohesive public spheres. (See, for example, Czach's work on Québécois star systems and York's investigation of indigeneity and celebrity in this volume.) Moreover, as Bill New has pointed out, borders "neither require nor guarantee fixed differences, or inevitably commit to the erasure of difference" (27); celebrity cultures inevitably seep (or sometimes leap) beyond national borders and the specificity of a celebrity's cultural references or language are often no guarantee of the limits of his or her circulation and consumption. (We might recall, for example, the extraordinary national and international success of Innu folk-rock band Kashtin in the late 1980s and early 1990s and their popular Innu-aimun-language singles "E Uassiuian" and "Tshinanu.")

Sometimes, however, there are expressions and experiences of celebrity culture that are more or less contained within a nation; the ways in which celebrated individuals are mobilized in or manufactured in nationalistic frameworks, whether beer commercials or the Olympics, often constitute celebrity phenomena that circulate more or less within national boundaries. While our television programs, radio shows, newspapers, and magazines can make their way out of the country, they are more often instruments of celebrity production and dissemination within our borders than without. Indeed, as the chapters that follow demonstrate, there are a great deal of celebrity phenomena that are specific to Canada and to Canadians whether in terms of our practices of consumption as Shore, Lee, and Roberts investigate and our practices of production and dissemination as Percy, Rak, Wagman, Deveau, York, and Czach explore, or whether as a function of a specific political and cultural climate, as Bell and Millar suggest.

There is also a great deal of affective potential bound up in the construction, circulation, and consumption of a star's national identity: such identities might be contested, perhaps a site of dispute that allows multiple nations to lay claim to the individual (Anna Paquin); such identities may make the individual a metonym for the nation, rendering the individual shorthand for the perceived opportunities (Celine Dion) or failings (Celine Dion, again) of a region or nation; or such identities may precede the individual, enabling (Pierre Trudeau) or precluding (Don Cherry) them from pursuing some projects or promoting their cultural products in certain places or amongst particular demographics. Regional and national identities, however they are constructed and disseminated, can be mobilized to produce cultural or economic capital but they might also prove to be, most especially in times of political crisis, liabilities (Rob Ford). In short, the cultural and political identities of famous people matter: these identities matter to the star, to the fans, to the industries that attempt to capitalize or mitigate the effects of these identities, and to the nations that administer these individuals and industries. The regional and national identities of fans matters too: such identities can, as Roberts explores, shape patterns of consumption and the forms and activities of fandom that in turn might influence the content of the celebrity's cultural products and how they are produced and disseminated. Certainly the national identity of the industries managing these relationships matters: although much celebrity industry is now both transnational and vertically integrated, the difference between a US-based company and a branch plant significantly affects the process of cultivating celebrity. Even when we consider the individual cogs in this industry—the agents, producers, publicists, etc.—their location and connections shape not only their own access to celebrity industries but their capacity to further the careers of their clients.

In the study of celebrity, then, the nation is more than simply a space wherein production and consumption of celebrity occurs: as critics have increasingly noted in the last two decades, the cultural and political logistics of the nation play a critical role in organizing and structuring those celebrity experiences and cultures. Moreover, critics are increasingly engaged with examining these trends as they occur inside nations that are not usually recognized as *the* global forces in the celebrity culture industries. One of the first texts to pursue this avenue of inquiry was

Graeme Turner, Frances Bonner, and P. David Marshall's *Fame Games: The Production of Celebrity in Australia* (2000). In a text that examined the players, institutions, and trends of Australian media outlets and the growing visibility of celebrities (including Australian celebrities) in that media, the authors demonstrated in no uncertain terms that the nation is a meaningful construct for investigating celebrity phenomena. Within a decade, several more English-language monographs and edited collections began to appear, some additionally organized by the consideration of particular time periods or forms of celebrity: *Stardom in Postwar France* (2007), edited by John Gaffney and Diana Holmes; *Celluloid Deities: The Visual Culture of Cinema and Politics in South India* by Preminda Jacob (2009); *Seeing Stars: Sports Celebrity, Identity, and Body Culture in Modern Japan* (2010) by Dennis Frost; *Celebrity in China* (2010), edited by Louise Edwards and Elaine Jeffreys; *Shocking Chic: Celebrity and Glamour in Contemporary Russia* (2011), edited by Helena Goscilo and Vlad Strukov; *Idols and Celebrity in Japanese Media Culture* (2012), edited by Jason Karlin and Patrick Galbraith; and *Latin American Icons: Fame Across Borders* (2014), edited by Dianna C. Niebylski and Patrick O'Connor.

Even more numerous and diverse in scope are the articles and chapters exploring celebrity in specific national contexts. In these rich works we might find not only useful models for our own studies of Canadian celebrity cultures but also rich sites of comparison. In New Zealand and Wales, for example, there is an interest in the nature of small nation celebrity and the media systems in which it is produced and circulated. In "'We look after our own': The cultural dynamics of celebrity in a small nation," Jeremy Olds and Lyn Barnes determine that New Zealand magazines represent national and global celebrities differently and typically foster a more benevolent attitude to their more "down-to-earth" compatriots. Ruth McElroy and Rebecca Williams, in "Remembering Ourselves, Viewing the Others: Historical Reality Television and Celebrity in the Small Nation," coin the term "localebrity" to characterize localized regional or small nation celebrity and note the distinctive ways in which audiences interact with these individuals whether through media or on the street. As McElroy and Williams rightly point out, small nations like Wales often struggle to make their media and celebrity cultures visible outside their own borders but, within their borders, reality television programming has played a critical role in promoting and affirming national celebrity. Consider, for example, a program like "I'm a Celebrity! Get Me Out of Here" which has, to date, been taken up by eleven nations from the UK and Denmark to Romania and The Netherlands, and which depends upon "localebrities" to take up the mantle of celebrity in a program that is, typically, almost impossible to export. Although this particular program does not exist (yet) in Canada, it is certainly entertaining to imagine which cast of characters we could populate such a show with (Margaret Trudeau, Tie Domi, Tanya Tagaq, Ian Hanomansing, Hazel McCallion, etc.). Like other national iterations of international franchises, such a program clearly functions to affirm and consolidate celebrity and national identities for very specific national audiences, but what difference does the specific nation make to these functions? We might also look to how other nations manage and negotiate multiple celebrity systems such as the Latino/a media and celebrities circulating in the US and the Indigenous television and film cultures in Australia, or how celebrity is produced and consumed within multilingual nations like Hong Kong and India. There is, indeed, much to be learned from such comparative work, the first step of which is our goal here: to better understand the nature of celebrity in Canada.

Celebrity Cultures in Canada thus represents the first edited collection exploring the production, dissemination, and consumption of Canadian celebrity phenomena, but the subject has been probed and explored before in other guises: in 1975, Pierre Berton's *Hollywood's Canada* sought to expose how the nation has been misconstrued in film; and more recently, in equally irreverent tones, the theme of Canadian popular cultures has been taken up by David Flaherty and Frank Manning's *The Beaver Bites Back? American Popular Culture in Canada* (1993) and Geoff Pevere and Greig Dymond's *Mondo Canuck: A Canadian Pop Culture Odyssey* (1996). Biography, as David Marshall has pointed out, has long been a favoured method for lionizing famous Canadians from H.J. Morgan's *Sketches of Celebrated Canadians* (1862) to the memoirs, biographies, and collections that crowd the bookstore shelves today (236). A great deal of critical work has also been done on literary celebrity cultures in Canada, and a robust conversation about the celebrity producing and disseminating mechanisms of Canadian television and film is developing. Additionally, there is a growing body of exceptional work done by both Canadian and non-Canadian scholars using Canadian case studies to examine local and global celebrity phenomena: while the scope and range of that material is too broad to examine here, it is worth noting that many of the contributors in this volume have been part of that conversation and continue to play roles in the development of this field.

Amongst this scholarship, we can trace various attempts at theorizing the broader conditions of celebrity cultures in Canada. In Michele Beyer's "On the (Im)possibility of Canadian Celebrity," she argues that Canadian celebrities are typically one of two types: those that circulate only at home and therein are not "really" celebrities by the standards invoked by US star systems, and those who have passed into the American system. Either way, she suggests, it is difficult, perhaps impossible, to be demonstrably Canadian and a celebrity, a perspective that is frequently endorsed by both the media and celebrities albeit with little evidence, save pithy anecdotes, to buttress such sweeping claims. However, the sheer scope of media, fan, and critical attention to celebrity in Canada belies the ease (and humour) with which this position is often assumed. There certainly *are* celebrity phenomena, celebrity industries, and Canadian celebrities in Canada, and the critical discussions we are having about these phenomena tend to coalesce around either the structures of celebrity in Canada or the discourses of celebrity in Canada (although these are, of course, intimately connected and often acknowledged as such). This latter category, ironically, includes and absorbs those very discourses that question the viability, significance, and/or existence of Canadian celebrity: to disavow Canadian celebrity is to participate and sustain a discourse about the phenomenon. The scope of discourses of Canadian celebrity are, however, far more robust, varied, and positivist than this, although there is often more discord than consensus when it comes to articulating the conditions and expressions of celebrity in Canada. In both popular and critical assessments of celebrity in Canada, it is common to attempt to quantify what makes Canadian celebrity phenomena unique or demonstrably Canadian: the Canada Walk of Fame website suggests that it is the "graciousness of our Canadian personality" ("About Us"); Clarence Karr, looking to the lifestyles of some of our early twentieth-century literary celebrities, has suggested that their unwillingness to change or embrace the excesses enabled by fame could be attributed to their Canadian identities (56); and various individuals from academics to Atwood have characterized Canada's relationship to fame as "uneasy" (York 115–116). Lorraine York, on the other hand, contends there is no "nationally specific performance" (5) or "de facto Canadian characteristic" (116) or approach to fame in Canada, a perspective that informs this current project and our attempt to showcase the breadth of celebrity phenomena occurring under and in the name of Canada.

On the level of discourse, however, it is not difficult to trace certain trends and dominant mythologies that govern how Canadian celebrity is discussed—this desire to quantify "Canadianness," for example, or the prevalence of self-deprecating jokes. The ways in which celebrity is understood, discussed, and mobilized in Canada has had, Sheryl Hamilton convincingly argues, an impact on the distinctive and somewhat muddled approach of our legal system to publicity law. One of the most prominent and consistent elements in Canadian discourses of celebrity is the invocation of the American star system. The ease with which American cultures of celebrity can circulate in Canada and the capacity of our talent, particularly English-Canadian talent, to pass into their systems has prompted discourses that mobilize the US as the yardstick by which to measure ourselves, as the primary source of and influence on celebrity cultures in Canada, and as a critical export market for our talent. The anxiety generated by the flow of culture and capital between our nations and the seeming permeability of our borders nevertheless implicitly affirm the importance and existence of such borders—we are not continuous with the US star system, just very much affected by it. From the flow of print culture material in the nineteenth century to the broadcast signals of radio and television in the twentieth century, the communities closest to our shared border have been consuming American cultures of celebrity for a very long time. The effects of this are felt not only in the fabric of our bureaucratic policies that govern and regulate various industries of celebrity, but also in the very provenance of many such bureaucratic bodies and institutions. The effects are also felt in the rise and fall of various iterations of nationalism in this country and the cultural practices that attend them from Royal Commissions to the maple leafs on our bodies and backpacks. Canada is by no means the only nation to feel the weight of American celebrity cultures shaping and influencing how celebrity is conceived, measured, discussed, produced, and consumed at home, but there is certainly an argument to be made for the long-standing impact of our cultural and geographical proximity to them.

Nevertheless, while the discourses and structures of celebrity in Canada today are often shaped by our proximity to the US, the degree to which this dominates our discourses often obscures the many ways in which celebrity cultures in Canada have developed and operated independent of that shared border. We are, after all, a nation with *two* formally acknowledged star systems, English-Canada and Quebec, and host to several burgeoning public spheres, such as amongst Indigenous, Asian, and South Asian communities, whose media structures, when well-integrated across platforms, have the potential to give rise to celebrities. (These spheres, as York argues in "Celebrity and the Cultivation of Indigenous Publics in Canada," are too often rendered invisible, not unlike how Canadian celebrityscapes in general are often trivialized or even delegitimized when measured by the reach and influence of other star systems.) That Canada's star systems are acknowledged and articulated along these lines reminds us that systems and infrastructures of production, dissemination, and consumption in this nation are shaped by the cultural and political institutions of various regions and language groups and that these institutions are not equally or equitably distributed across the communities of the nation.

Quebec's success in generating a self-sustaining star system in the second half of the twentieth century is more than simply a function of having developed a viable film industry: it is a success built on the marked preference of the Québécois to consume local personalities and programs and a well-integrated system dominated by corporations like Québecor Inc. for cultivating and promoting individuals across multiple media platforms (Dickinson 38–39). That Quebec has been far more successful than English Canada in this project has played a role in shaping government policy: in a 1999 Performance Report, the CRTC called for the active development and promotion of a "home-grown 'star-system' [in English Canada] similar to the one existing in Quebec." The scare quotes accompanying "star-system" in this document betray the CRTC's conflicted and sometimes ambivalent position vis-à-vis Canadian celebrity: while they recognize that Canadian celebrities make Canadian cultural industries sustainable, even profitable, there is a hesitation to characterize the system in which they circulate in Canada (whether in Quebec or English Canada) by the discourses of stardom. Once again, it seems, the ghosts of non-Canadian star systems make themselves felt even in a report that explicitly identifies *Quebec* as the yardstick by which to measure English-Canadian efforts.

Yet the Quebec star system is more than just a model for English-Canadian, Indigenous, and other star systems, it is also a critical instrument in disrupting the assumed primacy of the US as the source of imported celebrity cultures and the site of exported talent in Canada: francophone markets offer a different career trajectory for Québécois stars and the political stakes for performing regional and national identities are typically higher. The very different pressures, structures, trajectories, functions, and ideological investments that shape each star system reminds us that not only does Canada have (at least) two star systems but they are quite different systems: while there is occasional short-term or long-term crossover, they can operate in relative isolation from each other. These conditions might very well help distinguish what makes celebrity cultures in Canada distinctive from celebrity cultures elsewhere, but they also make it challenging to speak of trends across the nation.

To use Canada as an organizing device for thinking about celebrity is thus not an impossibility or even a possibility but, as both popular and academic writers have demonstrated, a rich and ongoing project. This study of celebrity cultures of Canada is a process of articulating, claiming, and defining what is Canadian and examining how it operates inside or outside of our borders, but it also seeks to understand what celebrity phenomena are disseminated and consumed within our borders regardless of their point of origin or production. If *Celebrity Cultures in Canada* is focused exclusively on the former project it is because we think a dedicated space for investigating the celebrity phenomena claimed for Canada and circulating amongst Canadian media and audiences is both long overdue and a critical context for considering the latter project. In sketching the contours of a long history of celebrity in Canada, these eleven essays help us understand what is at stake, culturally, politically, and economically, to be celebrated in Canada and/or as a Canadian. What they showcase is how varied the field is and has been and how much has been masked, forgotten, or overwritten. It is our hope that this text might inspire and perhaps even contextualize further investigations into the workings of celebrity in Canadian contexts for, as Bachman-Turner Overdrive reminds us, we suspect that we "ain't seen nothing yet."

Rediscovering Nell Shipman for Canadian Cultural Heritage

Amy Shore

In the summer of 1977, film historians and movie buffs converged with locals in Priest Lake, Idaho, to memorialize silent film actress, screenwriter, director, and producer Nell Shipman. A jut of land overlooking Priest Lake was renamed "Nell Shipman Point" in honour of the woman who had come to this remote location more than fifty years earlier to produce the feature film *The Grub-Stake* (1923). Like the heroine of the film that brought her to the rural Northwest, Shipman was selected for the honour because she embodied the region's historical mythology of pioneering the American frontier. In his account of early and silent cinema, Kevin Brownlow captured this sense of Shipman's public personality by describing her initiative to film in Priest Lake as emblematic of the "incredibly rigorous conditions" endured by many early filmmakers "for the sake of the picture" (330). Like the pioneers who "civilized" Idaho in the 1800s, Shipman brought modernity—in the form of the movies—to Idaho in the early 1920s and deserved a monument for this pioneering accomplishment.

The creation of "Nell Shipman Point" is one among dozens of efforts in the United States, Canada, and Europe to "rediscover" and celebrate Nell Shipman as part of various cinematic cultural heritages. In 1987, Thomas Fulbright described such cultural heritage activities as emerging from a "cult" dedicated to the Canadian-born "Queen of the Dogsleds," whom Fulbright recalled as "the person we old fans associated with dogsleds, snowshoes, parkas and canoes rushing toward a rushing waterfall" (5). By 1987, the cult described by Fulbright had spread across the United States, Europe, and Shipman's birth country of Canada where "she has been named the First Lady of Canadian Cinema [and] where the Canadian Film Institute has collected and enshrined an impressive amount of Nell

Shipman memorabilia—including prints of the famous and never to be forgotten *Back to God's Country*" (5). Nell Shipman became known to a new generation as the picture personality of her most successful films: "The Girl from God's Country."

The cult of Nell Shipman was—and continues to be—fuelled by various notions of cultural heritage and cinema. Shipman is "rediscovered" over and over again as new audiences are introduced to her work and films. This rediscovery can be attributed in great part to Tom Trusky, a professor at Boise State University who was the main archivist of Shipman's professional career. From 1984 until his death in 2009, Trusky travelled throughout the Pacific Northwest, and then the rest of the United States, Canada, and Europe, to exhibit Shipman's films as they were found and restored. It was this "roadshow" that extended Shipman's rediscovered stardom to other locales and opened up the development of various cinematic cultural heritages. A few quotes from newspapers where Trusky exhibited Shipman's films show how Shipman was "rediscovered" by different locales:

> "Make way for Nell Shipman, queen of the dogsled! Nell who? Don't feel bad if you've never heard the name. For only recently has the pioneering silent-screen writer, director, producer and star been rediscovered." (Musetto)

> "You've probably never heard of actress, writer, director, producer and studio builder Nell Shipman, but hers is one of the fascinating and forgotten stories of the early movies." (Movshovitz)

> "Meet Nell Shipman, A Canadian-born, Seattle-raised film director and star who shocked audiences with her pioneering courage on both sides of the movie camera." (English).

> "Nell, Nell, Nell. Every paper in the region has produced at least some copy of Our Own Nell Shipman this spring, to commemorate the rediscovery and rerelease of some of her films." (Lombardi)

As locations around the United States rediscovered Shipman, her place in American film history crystalized: she was a maverick who could serve as a heroine for film histories outside of mainstream Hollywood film history. Shipman's rediscovered star served as a floating signifier that could point to the value of various "independent" or "alternative" histories of cinema, from national, regional, and local histories to feminist film histories.[1]

The greatest claim to Shipman's rediscovered star, however, was made north of the continental United States in Canada where the mythological legacy of "dogsleds, snowshoes, parkas and canoes rushing toward a rushing waterfall" has come to carry international currency.[2] In the pages that follow, I argue that Canada's cultural claiming of Shipman is made possible by the nature of her original stardom, which embodied ideals of late-nineteenth- and early-twentieth-century Canadian nationalism. Her "picture personality" as a wilderness heroine was reified during the tenure of her stardom from 1911 to 1924 and now is available through artifacts of stardom—posters, promotional materials, and the film images themselves—to be plucked out of their original contexts and repurposed to promote a cinematic cultural heritage for the country that claims authenticity as "God's Country."[3] By focusing exclusively on Shipman's star image, however, Canada's cultural claims elide complex and contradictory aspects of Shipman's career and politics in order to assert an idealized cinematic national heritage. In the end, I hope to show that the "rediscovery" of stars for cultural heritage has its limits and may reproduce the challenges of celebrity for the historical subject (in this case, Shipman) rather than recover the star's subjectivity and larger contributions (or complexities) within film history.

Canada Rediscovers Nell

There they go
Free from woe
Forgetting me
Aw, Gee!

—Nell Shipman[4]

In 2000, Great North Productions of Edmonton, Alberta, produced a documentary on Nell Shipman that borrows its title from the epitaph that Shipman wrote for herself in a letter to a friend. *Ah Gee, Forgetting Me...* presents a story of Shipman's life and work through montages of footage from her movies, still images from archives, and interviews with film historians, archivists, and members of her family. Now distributed with Shipman's 1919 feature *Back to God's Country* on DVD from the Idaho Film Collection, *Ah Gee, Forgetting Me...* is the only documentary currently in circulation that focuses exclusively on Shipman's career and impact on cinema.

A summary of the opening of the documentary presents the key issues at play in Canada's rediscovery and cultural claiming of Shipman. As images of a thoroughly modern building fill the screen, a voice-over names the institution: "The National Archives of Canada, a futuristic steel and glass structure that houses Canada's ghosts." Dissolve to footage from one of Shipman's early films in which she is hiking a rocky wooded area with a brown bear at her side and the voice-over sutures the edit: "Among its many residents is a national treasure rescued from oblivion by a dedicated team of archivists and film restorers." The film then dissolves again to a man walking down the halls of the National Archives, where he swipes a key card that opens up steel doors through which he passes. Dissolve back to a famous scene of Shipman wrapping a blanket around her naked body after having bathed in a remote stream and then dissolve again to our Canadian archivist donning a parka before he opens yet another steel door within the Archives. Dissolve to footage of Shipman trudging through snow in a vast and empty landscape and dissolve yet again back to the archivist walking down one more hallway before he arrives at a row of shelves holding film reels. The two "characters" (Shipman and the archivist) converge through superimposed images at the end of a shelf where we find out that Shipman's films are being preserved. The archivist explains their shared journey: "This is the cold storage vault here at National Film Archives of Canada where we keep our films for preservation purposes. It's at −18 degrees Celsius or 0 degrees Fahrenheit so it's very cold and very dry and what's kind of comforting, perhaps, is the fact that the film is now stored in the same sorts of conditions as it was shot originally up in the tundra." A dissolve to footage of Shipman driving a dogsled across the tundra in the midst of the archivist's explanation drives the point home: the National Archives of Canada is the natural "home" for Shipman's legacy— her "ghost" is most comfortable haunting the country where she was born and "lived" through her films.

This opening scene is a familiar act of cultural claiming that takes place in all sorts of institutions, from museums and archives to libraries, national parks, corporate exhibits, malls, amusement parks, and historical tourist sites in Canada and around the world. The title shot that directly follows this scene makes it clear that Shipman recognized her own absence from history: superimposed over footage of Shipman smiling into the camera is her self-authored epitaph: "Ah Gee, Forgetting Me...." An empty signifier, Shipman is lifted out of oblivion by the National Archives of Canada and made meaningful: she is a pioneer of Canadian Cinema.

As Katja Lee illustrates in her study of Canada's claims on Mary Pickford, Emma Albani, and Maud Allan in this volume, Shipman is not alone in such processes of cultural claiming. However, the process by which Shipman is rediscovered and culturally claimed is unique, I argue, in that it reveals an interesting problematic for such cultural heritage work. The rediscovery in the documentary—as has been the case with other "rediscoveries" of Shipman in Canada and elsewhere—focuses almost exclusively on the years in which she appeared on screen (1911 to 1924). What is rediscovered in these accounts is Shipman's image from the era of her celebrity. The reason for the focus on Shipman's image over her broader contributions to film history—screenwriting, directing, producing—is bound up in the economies of cultural heritage. "Cultural heritage" as a practice transformed in the eighteenth and nineteenth centuries from *private* transfers of goods, land, and holdings through inheritance to *public* collection, organization, and presentation of objects in museums, conservation of land in the form of public parks and heritage sites, and preservation of homes and buildings through historical societies and records. The practice of modern cultural heritage requires an artifact of some sort to which an official entity (town, city, state, nation, or non-governmental organization) can claim authority and transform the artifact into "cultural property." Eisuke Tanaka explains the political economy of cultural property: "The materiality of objects considered 'cultural' plays an important role in providing a concrete image of a particular past, the history of the nation or an ethnic group, and thereby proving their existence and presence. This is one of the central aspects of the relationship between nationalism and the idea of the past. An aspect of this reification of the nation is that the nation can 'own' cultural objects" (64).

For Canada to claim Shipman as the "Girl from [Canadian] God's Country," she must first be turned into an object for cultural claim and then linked to Canada as a site of "origin." Tanaka observes that, "objects considered 'cultural property' acquire a particular symbolic value for their rightful owner, the nation or ethnic group. Those who claim ownership of cultural property must verify their link or continuity with the originators of the objects" (66). In the documentary, Shipman becomes what Kevin Walsh describes as one of the "surfaces" of history upon which cultural heritage becomes inscribed. Shipman is emptied of historical significance by the voiceover and title "Ah Gee, Forgetting Me...." She is then made available for authoring through the practice of cultural heritage, which reflects the desires and needs of the authors, not the objects/surfaces recovered. Laurajane Smith explains: "What makes these things valuable and meaningful—what makes them 'heritage'...—are the present-day cultural processes and activities that are undertaken at and around them, and of which they become part...heritage is heritage *because* it is subjected to the management and preservation/conservation process, not because it simply '*is*'" (3–4, author's emphasis). I argue that this political economy of cultural heritage—the need for a form of cultural property to establish a heritage—results in the historical focus on Shipman's onscreen career and star persona. As image and star, Shipman becomes reified and available for claim as "cultural property."

The conditions and limits of Shipman's "rediscovery" are, ironically, connected to her initial "discovery" as a film star in early Hollywood.

Richard deCordova's seminal study of the star system in early Hollywood provides a road map for understanding how Shipman became the "Girl from God's Country" and, in the process, a commodity available for consumption both during the era of her stardom and in her star's "afterlife." DeCordova explains the nature of the star as commodity: "The star system does not produce stars the way that a factory produces goods. The system is rationalized, but it is not geared toward producing a standardized product in the usual sense of the word. It produces a product that is in fact highly individuated—the individual star" (9). For Shipman, this individuated star persona was the "Girl from God's Country,"[5] which was established first through the logic of what deCordova describes as the "picture personality." The "picture personality" was an actor whose "persona" was established through his or her performance of particular character types across a series of films. From 1911 through 1915, Shipman was one of the stock players who performed in a series of Vitagraph films set in the Canadian Northwest, including *The Half-Breed's Daughter* (1911), *Sons of the Northwoods* (1912), *The Whiskey Runners* (1912), *Pierre of the North* (1913), *Into the North* (1913), *Breed of the North* (1913), and *From Out of the Big Snows* (1915). It was in 1916 that Shipman emerged as a full "picture personality" when she played the lead role in two adaptations of wilderness novels by famous Canadian author James Oliver Curwood. In *God's Country and the Woman* (Vitagraph, 1916) and *Baree, Son of Kazan* (Vitagraph, 1919), Shipman played the melodramatic heroine who had become a staple of cinema by this time but, in her case, with a twist: whereas other melodrama queens of the era often took to the country for adventure and then returned to urban environments for narrative closure, Shipman's heroines stayed firmly planted in the wilderness. In her autobiography, Shipman describes the lure of the first role in *God's Country and the Woman* as well as the discourse that would shape her picture personality:

> Rollin Sturgeon was the director who hired me, not because I could act, in fact he loathed all stage performers, but I was the type: athletic, a swimmer, someone who could get around the wilderness without stubbing her toe on a pinecone. My landing the lead in such a picture to co-star with two Vitagraph favorites, Bill Duncan, who was leading man, and George Holt, the heavy, was my break; the happening for which actresses of today still pray. To me the lure was the fact that we'd spend three months of winter in this then unknown and almost uninhabited mountain resort, that I'd act for an important company and be paid for my fun. I was to drive a team of sled-dogs, paddle a canoe, travel on showshoes [sic], undergo pages of Curwoodian drama in a setting which if not quite like my own Northwest was near it. (47–48)

Promotional materials for *Back to God's Country* clearly illustrate Shipman's status as a "picture personality" tied to the Pacific Northwest, particularly Canada. The *Moving Picture World* multi-page advertisement that announced the film's production on September 20, 1919, emphasized three items: Nell Shipman as the star, James Oliver Curwood as author, and the Canadian Arctic as the set. Throughout Canada, newspapers and film digests claimed Shipman for Canada with *The Canadian Moving Picture Digest* explaining her commitment to her birth country: "As Nell Shipman is Canadian, having been born at Victoria, B.C., of English parentage, she naturally leans toward the making of a story with Canadian life as the background, and a Canadian theme as its motive which, now that Canada has so splendidly won the applause of the civilized world, would find ready and profitable market in all the negotiable markets of the world."

Back to God's Country was wildly successful and is considered Canada's first feature film. It established Shipman firmly as the "Girl from God's Country" in popular culture and is what transitioned Shipman from "picture personality" to "star." DeCordova explains the distinction between "picture personalities" and "stars" as one based in the discourse surrounding the actor:

> The star emerged out of a marked expansion of the type of knowledge that could be produced about the player. The picture personality was defined...by a discourse that restricted knowledge to the professional existence of the actor. With the emergence of the star, the question of the player's existence outside of his or her work in film became the primary focus of discourse. The private lives of the players were constituted as a site of knowledge and truth. (98)

This expansion of knowledge about Shipman to "behind the screen" is evident in the formation of the Shipman-Curwood production company, Canadian Photoplays, Limited, which produced *Back to God's Country*. The marketing of the company indicates the degree to which Canada—culturally and economically—was central to the development of Shipman into a star who signified "independent" or "alternative" cinemas. The prospectus for Canadian Photoplays defines the vision of the company in juxtaposition to the growing centrality of Hollywood in the film industry: "Canadian Photoplays, Limited, does not expect to compete with the already established studios in the United States in the production of studio-made pictures, but in the great pictures of outdoor life, with their intense dramatic interest, no country in the world can surpass Canada." In the first public stock offering announced through the *Calgary Herald*, Shipman's photograph is placed prominently in the centre of the page with a note that her prior films with Fox-Lasky, Famous Players, and Vitagraph had sold "in every country for the last three years" and proved her box-office appeal on an international level. This is juxtaposed with the assertion that the new production company, Canadian Photoplays, Limited, "is an All-Canadian enterprise. Owned exclusively by Canadians exploiting Canadian stories, with a Canadian star under Canadian management." The dual claims made by the production company are clear: Shipman is a Canadian who gained stardom in Hollywood but has left it behind to help build an independent Canadian cinema. As deCordova argues, it is such discourse about the private lives of stars (here, Shipman) that gives stardom its cultural (and economic) power. Shipman's stardom could offer legitimacy to the new production company and convince backers to invest.

After *Back to God's Country*, the Shipmans ended their partnership with Curwood in Canadian Photoplays, Limited (or Curwood ended it, depending on who told the story) and formed their own production company with the goal of producing wilderness stories authored by Nell Shipman and shot on location throughout the Pacific Northwest.[6] The discourse surrounding the launch of their independent production company both produced and leveraged Nell Shipman's star persona as the "Girl from God's Country" who lived and worked independent of Hollywood. A piece in the *Los Angeles Times* from August 4, 1923, exemplifies this use of Shipman's star persona. Entitled "Nell Shipman: One Star Not of Hollywood," the article explains that "Just as Nell Shipman is engaged making a picture unlike all others, so the star and her company live in a manner unlike other players. Miss Shipman and those who act and assist in her productions are not of Hollywood and its film colony, but belong to a bigger world and live a more spacious and wonderful life—they are truly of God's country—the great outdoors." Describing the studio that Shipman established in Priest Lake, Idaho, the reporter focuses on Shipman's own living conditions to note her unique star persona: "And the star of 'Grub-Stake,' which is coming to the Kinema Theater today has no mansion. She lives in a log hut, thick walled and comfortable even in the most rigorous winter."

This status as a Hollywood outsider was reinforced by Shipman herself in the years following the demise of her Idaho studio. In 1925, Shipman published in *Atlantic Monthly* a serial account of the trials and tribulations of shooting *The Grub-Stake* at her Idaho studio that reminded readers of her commitment to making cinema outside of the studio system. In 1930, Shipman published her first serialized novel *M'sieu Sweetheart* in *McCall's Magazine*, where she once again presented a heroine traversing the wintry terrain of northern Canada.[7] Newspaper coverage of the serialized novel emphasized the Canadian setting: "It is a tale of the far north where the great silent men live, such men as made the hero stuff of the cinemas in which Miss Shipman played in the good old silent days when James Oliver Curwood's stories kept the screen filled with the lure and romance of the land of ice and snow where men were men, and all the rest of it" ("Untitled"). Then in 1932, Shipman wrote a "Hollywood novel" of sorts. *Abandoned Trails* is a fictional narrative in which the heroine has markedly similar experiences to those of Shipman when she wrote and starred in *Back to God's Country* in Canada.

While Shipman would continue to publish through the 1930s and wrote the screenplay for *Wings in the Dark* (1935), which starred Myrna Loy and Cary Grant, her "star" declined quickly after 1924. What is left: fading memories among the viewing public and, later, what can be found in collections and archives. The artifacts, which we historians depend upon to make sense of the past, set the stage for Shipman's "rediscovery" in the late 1970s through the early 1990s. Those artifacts that lend themselves to "rediscovery" through cultural heritage practices are those that can most easily be reified: the films (as material objects) and Shipman's star persona as the "Girl from God's Country," which is materialized through her onscreen performances and press coverage of the films.[8] And if the onscreen images of Shipman are the artifacts that are reified, then the landscapes in which she appears provide the geographic links for cultural claims of Canada as her location of "heritage." In *The Uses of Heritage*, Laurajane Smith reminds us that cultural heritage requires "boundedness": "a discrete 'site,' 'object,' building or other structure with identifiable boundaries that can be mapped, surveyed, recorded and placed on national or international site registers" (31). Onscreen Shipman is "bounded" by landscapes that Kay Armatage aptly describes as signifying "Canada": "In Nell Shipman's film and James Oliver Curwood's novels, God's country is always Canada, usually in its most far-flung reaches" (114). As Smith explains, the separation of "nature and "culture" since the rise of the Enlightenment helps support heritage claims to cultural landscapes as these spaces are naturalized within discourses of the nation (31). Just as landscapes of the Western United States code classical Western films as uniquely "American," landscapes of the northern tundra code Shipman's films as "Canadian." Furthermore, when drawn out of the narratives of the films themselves, Shipman's reified image as the "Girl from God's Country" can be used to establish her as a "pioneer" of early cinema and provide Canada with legitimacy in claiming authorship of early cinema, albeit an "alternative" authorship that is outside of the mainstream history of Hollywood cinema. By culturally claiming Shipman and her films as part of Canada's heritage, Canada becomes the "frontier" of early cinema and Nell Shipman a cinematic pioneer.

Forgetting and Remembering: The Limits of Cinematic Cultural Heritage[9]

In March 2014, filmmaker Karen Day of Boise, Idaho, launched a Kickstarter campaign to help fund a new documentary on Nell Shipman, tentatively titled *Girl from God's Country*. The trailer for the documentary focuses on Shipman's time in Priest Lake, Idaho, where she built her independent studio and filmed *The Grub-Stake* (1923) as well as a series of short films before she "vanished" (Day). Day frames the documentary by explaining that "The question of what happened to Nell and why led us all over the country and into the dusty film archives of the silent era. After a year of research, the answers to this mystery have proven to be as fascinating and complicated as this forgotten pioneering woman and her lost films." The trailer includes interviews with Shipman's descendants as well as scholars and archivists matched to present-day footage of Priest Lake and footage from Shipman's films shot there. The interviewees explain how Shipman "disappeared" from the film industry and history but is now being rediscovered. The call to action to fund the documentary ends with this promise: "Finally, in our film, *Girl From God's Country*, Nell Shipman will deservedly be seen as a star among great stars—a role she has played silently for too long" (Day).

In this fundraising campaign, we can see the now familiar narrative of cultural heritage at work by staging the "forgetting" of Shipman so that the filmmaker can then "rediscover" her and place her within a particular bounded landscape, this time Priest Lake, Idaho. In the process of this cultural claiming, Priest Lake takes its place in cinema history as well: "This early film pioneer went to the Idaho wilderness and built her own unique cinematic world called Lionshead Lodge...." The trailer presents Shipman as a highly progressive individual who was a feminist, environmentalist, and animal rights activist—all of which, her granddaughter Nina explains, are terms that can be retroactively attributed to her because she was so far ahead of her time. By "pioneering" in Priest Lake, the location too becomes a space for an alternative, more culturally progressive history for early cinema.

While the documentary itself is still in production, the trailer and marketing for the film end in the same place as the Canadian documentary *Ah Gee, Forgetting Me* as well as numerous other accounts of Shipman's career: at the end of her work in silent cinema with little more than footnotes to the remaining fifty-plus years of her life. In *Ah Gee, Forgetting Me*, the final moment of the documentary presents footage of Shipman lying in the woods with a bear. The voice-over explains what we are seeing: "In her last silent film, *Light on the Lookout*, Nell wakes up in the final scene at dawn on a bed of boughs with a bear" and then cuts to a title card: "The End."

The documentary literally ends with Shipman's final appearance onscreen. Once Shipman left the screen and her status as film star, her role in these cultural heritage narratives ends. The reason is simply this: her value as a "surface" upon which to inscribe a country (Canada) or region's (Idaho) cultural heritage is lost once her reified image "disappears." When the processes of rediscovery are bound by the limits of Shipman's star image, it raises two critical questions: (1) What do the limits of Shipman's star image occlude in terms of her contribution to film history? (2) What is at stake for those of us engaged in these processes of rediscovery and cultural claiming?

First, what is occluded by this focus on Shipman's stardom from 1911 to 1924? In a letter to the editor of the *Idaho Arts Journal*, Frank Thompson identifies the flattening of Shipman's career in rediscovery narratives produced by film reviewers and reporters covering the Shipman "roadshow":

> While I am happy that Nell Shipman has been receiving a great deal of press lately (more than she got during her own checkered career, I'm afraid), few of the writers have been very successful at getting at what makes Shipman so important.... Consequently, we have statements like Jeanette Ross's "(Shipman) has a list of firsts..." Like what? First female writer? Producer? Director? Actress? Nope. The first two decades of American filmmaking saw many women as prolific, adventurous and successful (or more so) than Shipman.... Both Ms. Ross and Ms. Lombardi seem intent on slighting Shipman's work while lionizing its creator as "one of those marvelous, reactionary, independent women forgotten by our history books."[10]

Thompson criticizes Ross and Lombardi—two reviewers of the Shipman "roadshow"—for dismissing Shipman's films as overly melodramatic. Thompson rightly argues that their assessments of the films are anachronistic but more importantly, he points to the limits of the positive feminist reclamation made by Ross and Lombardi. He states, "Sure, it's interesting that she had lots of adventures in the wilds of Canada and Idaho but it's the product of those hardships that exists for us now. Let us judge her as an artist, not merely as a plucky woman who survived a dangerous trek across a frozen lake.... I'm only sorry that Shipman, having gone through incredible hardships, insensitive producers and decades of neglect, must now run a gauntlet of ignorance and condescension."[11] As with other claims of Shipman for a cultural heritage, the aspects of her star image that lend themselves to the claim are highlighted—in Ross and Lombardi's cases, the feminist aspects—and, in turn, eclipse her fuller life and work.

So what might we find should we move beyond the rediscovery of Shipman's star persona and the era to which rediscoveries are typically confined (1911 to 1924)? The answer is complex and not always helpful to the progressive histories advanced by the cultural heritage narratives because a number of Shipman's later works exhibit xenophobic and racist discourses.[12] For example, Shipman didn't stop working in film after the demise of her Idaho studio. Along with writing screenplays for Hollywood productions, Shipman doggedly pursued making independent films for decades. The Nell Shipman archives at Boise State University contain more than 120 stories, plays, scripts, film scenarios, and film treatments all developed after 1925. Among them is a 1947 film that Shipman produced and directed: *The Story of Mr. Hobbs* (also titled *The Clam-digger's Daughter* and *A Tale of the Tidewater*). Shot on location in Cape Charles, Virginia, the film was lost for decades and then found under its current title in the British Film Institute archives. In 1996, the Cape Charles Historical Society screened the film for the public, and Tom Trusky, the main archivist of Shipman's work and papers, attended the event. In an interview following the screening, Trusky remarked that while the film followed the Shipman formula of the wilderness heroine who must save her man from villains, he found himself bothered by the film's treatment of a black house servant and a Latin American ruler. In a 2005 follow-up story about the film, Trusky told a reporter, "It seemed to my '80s or '90s eyes, very racist." The reporter shares the aftermath: "Trusky went home and examined her other films with that in mind. What he concluded was that her stereotyped treatment of Chinese and Hispanics and blacks was based on gender. A woman of any race was basically treated well, he said, 'but if you're male and you're in power, she has an ax to grind with you'" (Tennant).

While Trusky displaces the retrograde representations of non-white characters in Shipman's films onto a feminist politics, Judith Smith, writing for *Cinema Canada* in 1978, finds another troubling aspect of Shipman's post-1920s work that isn't as easily displaced onto one of Shipman's other cultural heritages. Smith offers a standard account of Shipman's rise to stardom with an emphasis on her Canadian-based productions to claim her for Canadian film history. In the midst of this account, Smith differentiates Shipman from her contemporaries as uniquely "Canadian": "In recent years, Nell Shipman has been noted for her profound loyalty to her Canadian homeland, a tendency so rarely exhibited by her compatriots Mary Pickford, Marie Dressler, Mack Sennett and Norma Shearer. She always wanted to make films about Canada in Canada." But when Smith arrives at Shipman's work in later years, she terminates the Canadian claim: "As anti-communist paranoia divided Hollywood during the fifties, Nell became more visibly American in her outlook, and worked on behalf of the right-wing front" (J. Smith 37). During the 1950s and 1960s, Shipman wrote a series of anti-communist, traditionally patriotic screenplays, including *The Fifth American* and *The Fires of Batsto*, which celebrated American history and condemned critiques of American foreign policy. Correspondence from the era in which Shipman tried to gain backing for the productions further exhibits the virulence of her right-wing positions, which are inconsistent with the cultural progressivism at the heart of the many forms of cultural heritage claims that Canadians, Idahoans, feminists, and other authors of alternative film histories made (and continue to make) upon Shipman.[13]

In the case of Canada, I argue that within the midst of the emerging national policies and public discourse on multiculturalism during the late 1970s through the early 1990s, Shipman's post-stardom works contradicted the values of contemporary cultural heritage claims. A Canadian national discourse that depicted the country as a "cultural mosaic" and celebrated difference informed both colloquial and official policies of multiculturalism that were advanced during the first two waves of Shipman's "rediscovery" (1970s and 1990s). The xenophobic and sometimes racist discourses advanced in works such as *The Story of Mr. Hobbs* contradicted such national ideals of cultural identity and, therefore, did not fit neatly into a multicultural history of Canadian cinema. As a woman, Shipman adds to the diversity. As a woman who produced complex and contradictory cultural artifacts, Shipman is problematic.

When limited to her star persona of the "Girl From God's Country," Shipman is able to fit into a celebratory history of Canadian cinema that is aligned with the contemporary ideals of a multicultural Canada. The historiographical logic is based in what Caroline Frick describes as the "socially structured practice" of film preservation. She argues, "A more thorough investigation of the history and context for specific archival decisions and actions reveals how preservation practice, and its commonly invoked heritage rationale, has been employed *at particular moments* and *for particular reasons* over the course of the past century" (Frick 6, my emphasis). In Canada, Shipman was first rediscovered and preserved during the waves of globalization, multiculturalism, and feminism[14] that swept Canada in the 1970s and 1990s. The "particular reason" for her rediscovery seems on the surface to be that Shipman can, as a woman, represent diversity in Canada's film history. But it seems that there is a second, more subtle, set of cultural desires at work in the reclaiming of Shipman. Nell Shipman as the "Girl from [Canadian] God's Country" represents a "lost" form of nationalism that links national identity and landscape. Erin Manning explains:

It has been argued that, while the land provides food and shelter, the land-scape provides ideologies. This is certainly the case in Canada, where the country's "true north strong and free" asserts itself in the national imagi-nary as the link to "Canadian identity." ... This quest for national identity through the image of the landscape recalls the modern desire for authen-ticity, where the unity of states and citizens is constructed on the putative ethnic or racial identity of a nation, which, in turn, is anchored to the rep-resentation of the landscape of the motherland as a nostalgic longing for a lost, presumably less alienated culture. (5–7)

When entombed in the National Archives, the "Girl from God's Coun-try" offers the person experiencing the cultural heritage an opportunity to relive and contain a lost form of nationalism. Like the archivist in the documentary *Ah Gee, Forgetting Me* who passes through locked steel doors and traverses long hallways to arrive at Nell Shipman and her films, those of us engaged in the act of cultural heritage can both enjoy the celebra-tion of a nostalgic territorialized form of Canadian national identity and lock it away to return to our contemporary world of global citizenship and multiculturalism. She becomes a figure of inspiration amidst the Cana-dian tundra—the frontier—that signals a cultural legacy of independence, strength, and vitality. Indeed, Shipman's own subjectivity is contained and the production of her as a Canadian cinema pioneer is naturalized in these rediscoveries. By the time of her first waves of "rediscovery," Shipman was able to serve as both a nostalgic figure of a homogeneous ideal of Canadian national identity *and* a figure representing a diverse, multicultural Canada.[15]

In essence, the many "rediscoveries" of Nell Shipman for the purpose of cultural heritage do not discover Nell Shipman, the person, artist, or agent of history. Rather, they discover exactly what they long for: the "Girl from God's Country" who can let us experience a longed-for (and always already constructed) past. All of these "rediscoveries" of Nell have, iron-ically, resulted in a second *forgetting* of Nell. The question now is this: will we—the curators, historians, documentary filmmakers, and others invested in the "cult" of Shipman—remain, in Nell's words, "free from woe" as we continue to forget her or will we recognize our own complic-ity and find new ways to celebrate and examine the work of Shipman and other pioneers of early cinema?

Notes

1 Kay Armatage has written the most comprehensive biography of Shipman: *The Girl from God's Country: Nell Shipman and the Silent Screen* (University of Toronto Press, 2003). In the traditional histories of Canadian cinema, Ship-man has often been included within an account of her first husband's career, resulting in many of her own contributions to Canadian film being reduced

to onscreen performance prior to the feminist reclamation of her work. See, for example, Peter Morris, *Embattled Shadows: A History of Canadian Cinema: 1895–1939* (McGill-Queen's UP, 1978). Other books by her collaborators document Shipman's import as a performer, director, and producer. See, as examples, Joseph Walker and Juanita Walker's autobiographical account of his work as a cinematographer, *The Light on Her Face* (ASC Press, 1984) and Lloyd Peters's account of his time at Shipman's Idaho studio, *Lionhead Lodge: Movieland of the Northwest* (Ye Galleon Press, 1976).

2 As Sherrill E. Grace explains in *Canada and the Idea of North* (McGill-Queen's UP, 2007), Canada has a long history of claiming signs of northern habitat— extreme weather, pioneering personalities, and treacherous landscapes—as definitive of their culture as a northern people through literature, art, music, drama, history, geography, politics, and popular culture. This discursive legacy, which has circulated internationally, has produced Canada as a quintessential "northern" territory much like Siberia in the Eastern Hemisphere.

3 As Sherrill E. Grace notes in *Canada and the Idea of North*, such a claim of Canada as "God's Country" is closely aligned with international discourses across North American, Europe, and countries of the Eastern Hemisphere that associate "northern peoples" with problematic cultural ideals of purity. Most clearly illustrated in the German Nazi campaign that idealized Aryan culture, such arguments evoke discourses of evolution as well as biblical and mythical origins to claim authenticity as a privileged site. Thus, the term "God's Country" used in the Shipman films refers as much to the idealization of the natural world as untarnished by humans (and thus closer to a kind of Eden) as it does to an idealization of northern cultures as being divinely privileged in the world order. While this problematic cultural claim is never made fully explicit in Shipman's films, it can clearly be recognized in moments of cultural juxtaposition that turn toward Orientalism in films such *Under the Crescent* (1915), *God's Country and the Woman* (1915), and *Back to God's Country* (1919), among others. The notion of "God's Country" did not, however, originate with Shipman and the films but the books of James Curwood from which several of the films with the phrase "God's Country" are adapted.

4 This epigraph has several "lives" in the history of Nell Shipman. Shipman first included this epitaph at the close of a letter dated "April 25" from Old Lyme, Connecticut (the year is not listed but is circa 1925 based on in-text references). The letter is included at the close of her 1968-authored autobiography as a way to explain the outcome of her zoo of animals, which were in peril at the point where she ends her autobiography. It is also quoted in *Variety*, March 27, 1987, as a means to assert the "rediscovery" of Shipman in the 1980s. Part of the epitaph also serves as the title of a documentary about Shipman's career and life: *Ah Gee, Forgetting Me.*

5 It is interesting to note that in 1916, Canadian newspapers emphasized Shipman's origins in Victoria, British Columbia, as a key element of her picture personality. The *Vancouver World* (April 24, 1916) went so far as to dub her the "Victoria Girl" in mimicry of the popular phenomenon of giving the top

female star of a studio the title of the studio plus "Girl," such as the "Bio-graph Girl" (Florence Lawrence). The newspaper subtly claimed Shipman as "produced" by Victoria/Canada and placed her within a history of her stage performances along the Canadian coast in the prior decade under the name of Helen Barham (her maiden name).

6 In the midst of their transition back to the United States, Nell and Ernest Ship-man also ended their personal partnership and filed for divorce.

7 *M'sieu Sweetheart* was later published in book form in the United States and Canada as *Get the Woman* (Dial Press, 1930) and in Great Britain as *Neeka of the North* (Collins, 1931)

8 See Hilary A. Hallett's study of female stars and the rise of early Hollywood for more on how marketing materials and press coverage for films worked to materialize stars and, in turn, leave their images as the relics of their contri-bution to film history. Hilary A. Hallett, *Go West, Young Women: The Rise of Early Hollywood* (Berkeley: University of California Press, 2013).

9 This portion of my essay is inspired by Shelley Stamp's keynote presentation at the 2013 Women and the Silent Screen Conference in Melbourne, Australia, where she borrowed from Richard Koszarski to discuss the "forgetting with a vengeance" that has taken place (and continues to take place) in regards to women in film history.

10 Letter to the Editor from Frank Thompson of Eagle, Idaho. *Idaho Arts Journal* 4.4.

11 Ibid.

12 It is important to note that such tendencies are clearly evident in her earlier work but have frequently been overlooked as symptomatic of broader Orien-talist tendencies in early and silent cinema rather than a sign of "authored" ideology.

13 Boise State University holds extensive correspondence by Shipman to friends and potential backers of her proposed productions in the Nell Shipman Archive (MSS 81).

14 The 1970 report by the Royal Commission on the Status of Women marks the emergence of second-wave feminism into Canadian national discourse and policy. Following this report, the rediscovery of female figures in Canada's national history became part of the broader efforts to generate a multicultural past that corresponded with the new national ideal of a "cultural mosaic." Shipman's rediscovery can be understood as part of that larger national effort to integrate women's history into "Canada's history."

15 Some historical context is necessary to unpack the layers of cultural heri-tage that lie beneath the surface claims of Shipman for Canada's film his-tory. First, consider that in 1971, Canada was the first country to officially adopt multiculturalism as a policy. The 1971 Multiculturalism Policy of Canada confirmed the rights of Aboriginal peoples and the status of Canada's two official languages. This policy, which officially established Canada as the land of "cultural mosaic" (in contrast to the "cultural melt-

ing pot" of the United States), revised earlier forms of Canadian nationalism most clearly embodied in the Canada First Movement of a century prior. While a short-lived political movement, Canada First's "expression of a popular Canadian ideal had enduring significance" (as quoted in the Ontario Heritage Trust plaque that commemorates the building where the movement originated). The national "ideal" of the Canada First Movement was bound up in racial ideology that idealized "The North"—the same "North" that is idealized in Shipman's films. Eva Mackey explains that the Canada First Movement drew from British and other Northern European forms of nationalism that asserted Northern races to be superior to Southern races and used the rugged landscapes of Northern countries as proof for the "energy, strength, self-reliance, health and purity" of the people who inhabited them. The shared boundaries of their Northern landscape gave Canadians (French *and* English) a common cultural identity that differentiated them from the rest of North America. Along with the racialization of North/South that undergirds the Canada First ideology, there is the profound absence of Indigenous cultures in the movement's account of Canadian national identity. In 1971, the Multiculturalism Policy of Canada officially reversed the old form of nationalism and put into question all of the iconography that had supported the geographically bounded form of Canadian identity espoused by the Canada First Movement.

2

"What an elastic nationality she possesses!" Transnational Celebrity Identities in the Late Nineteenth and Early Twentieth Centuries

Katja Lee

In Canada we have a long history of having to move beyond our geopolitical borders and cultural institutions in order to produce and disseminate celebrity. Now, more than ever before, we are dependent on international and transnational cultural, financial, media, and corporate institutions to play some role in the production of celebrity culture, and the result of this new global celebrityscape is that celebrities born in Canada are more and more often crafting public identities that do not necessarily harness them to explicitly or exclusively Canadian identities. These transnational celebrities, celebrities whose identities don't just circulate beyond the boundaries of Canada, but are constructed and received as exceeding the claims of any one nation, often do not deny their connections to Canada but nor do they rely on them to make meaningful contributions to their labour, identity, or celebrity. Hence, whatever claims Canadian cultural and media institutions might lay to the likes of Christopher Plummer, Avril Lavigne, or Jim Carrey often feel slightly disingenuous—after all, there is nothing demonstrably Canadian about them—and reveal an implicit anxiety about the instability of transnational identities and the boundaries of Canadian culture.

As we have seen from other contributions in this volume, such as Katherine Ann Roberts's exploration of Callum Keith Rennie's cross-border career and Danielle Deveau's examination of Canadian comedians in the US, transnational celebrity and its attendant anxieties play a critical role in contemporary Canadian celebrity culture; however, these are not

strictly contemporary phenomena. This chapter seeks to trace their earlier iterations in the celebrity cultures of the late nineteenth century and
early twentieth centuries when a considerable number of Canadians were
leaving Canada in order to pursue their careers. Those apprenticing in
highbrow cultural industries often made their way to Europe while those
in the popular or mass-cultural industries were typically dependent upon
American cultural institutions. This is not to claim, as Nick Mount does,
that "fame was the province of elsewhere" (31); famous Canadians like
L.M. Montgomery, Pierre Berton, and Rick Mercer remind us that one can
stay in Canada, carve out an explicitly Canadian identity, and use Canadian cultural institutions to promote a career. However, at the turn of the
century there were considerably more opportunities for achieving a celebrated career beyond the borders than within them. As people moved
and developed new identities away from their place of birth, discourses of
identity and nationalism that could capture the ambiguities raised by these
conditions were slow to emerge, hampered by lingering investments in the
stability, singularity, and definability of national identity. The failure of
language to keep pace with the growing cultural reality of transnational
identities created an interesting dilemma for those who might be legitimately claimed by multiple nations and yet not exclusively claimed by any
one: how did these celebrities frame themselves and how did they manage
the various competing claims on their national identity?

To answer these questions this chapter looks to three Canadian-born
women who, during the late nineteenth and early twentieth centuries,
sought training and careers beyond our borders and there met with
extraordinary success, international celebrity, and some confusion about
their national identities. They were opera diva and intimate of the royal
households of Europe, Dame Emma Albani (1847–1930);[1] the scandalously
clad dancing sensation of Edwardian London, Maud Allan (1873–1956);
and "America's Sweetheart," Hollywood's first major female superstar,
Mary Pickford (1892–1979). Of all the women who picked up stakes and
sought greener pastures outside of Canada, what makes these particular
women interesting case studies is that they all, in some way, resisted the
claims of various cultural, legal, and media institutions to harness them to
a specific national identity and chose, instead, to mobilize a transnational
identity long before such discourses existed for framing their subjectivity.
Moreover, each woman was able to make such an identity not only desirable, but culturally and economically valuable. As we will see from their
press interviews and autobiographies, each woman had a different strategy
for working with and around the discourses that sought to fix and stabilize her identity: Allan, through conflicting and evasive media strategies,

sought to create an image of herself as artistic and exotic and thereby out-side normative national discourses; Pickford, on the other hand, willingly lent herself to both Canadian and American nationalistic discourses, pre-cluding either one of them from claiming her entirely; and Albani, claimed and marked by many nations but seemingly at home in none, offers, in her memoir, an "elastic nationality" (122), a capacity to stretch and accommo-date the demands and cultures of multiple spaces.

As we trace how these women managed the claims of various Cana-dian cultural institutions, we can unpack the effects of both past and pres-ent attempts to interpolate or, perhaps, annex these women into a history of Canada's contribution to the arts. These acts of claiming/reclaiming/branding to serve nationalistic projects are symptomatic of the conditions of transnational celebrity, but they are also politically fraught practices for they threaten to overwrite other claims and other modes of political and cultural self-identification. For Maud Allan, Mary Pickford, and Emma Albani, Canadian attempts to claim them exclusively for Canada failed in their time (and, in respect to Pickford, continue to fail today), but that failure to consolidate their celebrity under one nationalistic discourse is instructive: not only does it reveal the important role such claims have on producing transnational subjects and the power of celebrity subjects to manage these discourses, but it allows the celebrity image to remain open and dynamic (rather than static and overdetermined) long after the celebrity has passed away. This capacity of celebrities to remain flexible and mobile—in effect, to remain transnational—in the face of the pow-erful practices of national bodies to claim them for their own is neither an anomaly of nor an obstacle to a better understanding of the contours of Canadian celebrity culture, but a critical, perhaps even characteristic, component of the complex historic processes of celebrity in this country.

Transnational Celebrity and the Politics of Claiming

The act of claiming an individual for Canada can occur in any number of ways: we might, as fans and audience members, call them Canadian or suggest that they are "from Canada," we might witness such claims in print, broadcasting, or digital media, or see these individuals mobilized in Cana-dian contexts like Halls and Walks of Fame. Both regional and federal arms of the Canadian government are active in these processes: not only do they possess the legal capacity to tax or issue official identification, but they are powerful shapers of culture in their archiving and commemorative prac-tices. The rationales for these claims are as diverse as the claims themselves: the individual was born here, grew up here, married a Canadian, lived here, worked here, was influenced by something here, visited here, paid taxes here, etc. Contrary to Northrop Frye's suggestion that we are "riddle[d]" by the question "Where is here?" (116), the conditions of transnational celebrity and the politics of claiming suggest that the bigger question is "How much 'here' is enough?" And yet, as with attempts to define what "Canadian" is or what constitutes "Canadianness," there is no satisfactory answer to the question that does not invite further speculation and considerable dissent. Even if we agree that belonging to a nation is imagined, impossible, and governed by arbitrary boundaries with arbitrary points of inclusion and exclusion, the question of nationality has real political, cultural, and affective consequences. Nationality matters. And because it matters we police its boundaries and craft elaborate mythologies to shore them up, a process which inevitably pulls into its wake the names and identities of particular individuals.

Some celebrities are quite easily folded into our mythologies of nationhood—Nellie McClung, Farley Mowat, Pierre Trudeau—not because they harbour or betray some essential Canadianness but simply because their national identities are uncontested. Those with contested national identities, those individuals claimed by the cultural institutions of multiple nation-states,[2] are more numerous and present a more complex challenge to these mythologizing processes: what right do we have to call Emma Albani, Mary Pickford, and Maud Allan Canadian and recuperate them into a history of Canadian achievements in the arts? Arguably, every right, but so too does the US or the UK. To be subject to multiple, overlapping, and sometimes contradictory narratives is what P. David Marshall has suggested is the essence of celebrity. In *Celebrity and Power* he argues that celebrity is a "terrain" that is continually being negotiated by multiple participants:

> The concept of negotiation and struggle provides a metaphor that can aid in the deconstruction of the ideologies around leaders and celebrities. The celebrity is a negotiated "terrain" of significance. To a great degree, the celebrity is a production of the dominant culture. It is produced by a commodity system of cultural production and is produced with the intention of leading and/or representing. Nevertheless, the celebrity's meaning is constructed by the audience. An exact "ideological fit" between production of the cultural icon and consumption is rare. (47)

This negotiation is further complicated when we take into account the movement of the terrain into multiple spaces—no longer is there *a* dominant culture or audience but several, each of which initiates its own negotiation of what the celebrity terrain signifies. These audiences might argue for the legitimacy of their construction of the celebrity and therein lay claim, either politically or culturally, to the individual, and such claims might very well contradict claims made elsewhere.

To be a transnational subject, however, is more than simply having one's national identity subject to contestation: as Aihwa Ong's scholarship demonstrates, the individual gives rise to that condition by appearing to possess or embrace a kind of mobility and flexibility across spaces and cultures:

> *Trans* denotes both moving through space or across lines, as well as changing the nature of something. Besides suggesting new relations between nation-states and capital, transnationality also alludes to the *trans*versal, the *trans*-actional, the *trans*lational, and the *trans*gressive aspects of contemporary behavior and imagination that are incited, enabled, and regulated by the changing logics of states and capitalism.... I am concerned with transnationality—or the condition of cultural interconnectedness and mobility across space—which has been intensified under later capitalism. (*Cultural Logics* 4)

Transnationality, Ong clarifies, is not a function of economics (although it certainly is tied to global markets), but it is above all "situated" in cultural practices that open up new modes for constructing identity (*Cultural Logics* 17–19). Such practices that enable the swift movement of people, culture, and capital not only allow individuals to conceive of themselves beyond conventional national boundaries and to inhabit, mobilize, and benefit from flexibility (Ong, "Chinese Cosmopolitans" 136), but also create the conditions by which others can read and respond to that flexibility by inscribing new meanings onto the transnational subject. Michael Giardina, building on Ong's work, suggests that it is possible for the transnational celebrity to, in fact, "appea[r] as a *tabula rasa* on which local meanings and desires are inscribed" (204). Hence the very condition or appearance of flexibility becomes an opportunity for others to make a claim and turn what appears to be ambiguity into a concrete declaration that serves local or, indeed, national purposes. Taken globally, these multiple, overlapping, and competing discourses of the celebrity create a complex terrain in which the individual might thus appear to exist in, even simultaneously and rationally belong to, multiple national discourses—she has, in effect, become a transnational celebrity.

Further complicating the construction and negotiation of this terrain is, of course, the celebrity herself. Regardless of the global processes at work, she may not self-identify as transnational. What happens if, for example, she seeks to hold onto her Canadian identity or shed it altogether in favour of some other national identity? Marie Dressler (1869–1934), for example, was born in Cobourg, Ontario, and cultivated two extremely successful careers (stage and cinema) in the US. Both of her autobiographies detail her patriotic attachment to the US, and in *My Own Story* (1934) she explicitly claims, "I looked upon myself as an American citizen long before marriage actually made me one" (64). Nevertheless, Dressler has been claimed by various Canadian cultural and media institutions, most recently in 2008 by Canada Post, which featured her, along with Norma Shearer, Raymond Burr, and Chief Dan George, in a "Canadians in Hollywood: The Sequel" stamp series.[3] As Dressler's fate reveals, an individual can resist the construction of herself as transnational and define herself with strong ties to a particular nation, but she does not control the meaning of her celebrity, and her self-definition as Canadian or American or Mohawk or Québécois exists alongside and in competition with the other participants of the celebrity terrain, who might mobilize her differently. Such is the power of fans, the media, and other cultural and government institutions to make the celebrity mean what she does not want to mean.

These acts of claiming, particularly when they attempt to overwrite the individual's self-definition or the claims of less powerful nation-states, can be politically fraught and, at their worst, imperialist extensions of the colonizing project: to claim Pauline Johnson or Chief Dan George or Louis Riel for Canada is to mobilize a cultural juggernaut that can dominate or even efface the presence of other claims. But celebrity culture is rarely a monolithic creature impervious to counter-narrative. By being attentive to the voices of dissent in the celebrity terrain, as we shall do in the final section of this chapter, we can recuperate or make space for these alternate claims and narratives such as those made by an individual about her national identity. There are, of course, limitations to such a project. The celebrity is only one agent negotiating the terrain of their identity and thus their modes of self-definition may not shift the terrain in their favour; in fact, it is far more likely that by making space for a competing narrative of national identity, we increase the likelihood that, instead of consolidating the terrain, it is further fractured and made divisive, creating the conditions by which transnational celebrity can emerge.

Contexts for Canadian Claims

In much work on transnational celebrity—including the scholarship of Ong and Giardiana and the recent collections assembled by *Celebrity Studies* in 2011 and Russell Meeuf and Raphael Raphael in 2013—the focus has been squarely on post–World War II and contemporary examples of transnational subjectivity. However, these cultural practices are not limited to the second half of the twentieth century; they were also present in the late nineteenth and early twentieth centuries, albeit in different forms and shaped by early mass media. The more readily one could move one's name, image, and labour across spaces and cultures, the easier it was for that individual to be at home and make a home wherever mass media had already taken her. In Mary Pickford's autobiography, *Sunshine and Shadow* (1955), she astutely recognized what transnational celebrity meant for her and her work on the silent screen, but also what it allowed audiences to do with her identity:

> I adored the English, and, having been born in Canada under the Union Jack, I felt completely at home with them. But I found this same warmth and friendliness everywhere: Paris, Rome, Alexandria, Moscow, Tokyo.... We of the silent screen enjoyed a unique privilege. Through our voiceless images we were citizens of every country in the world. This world citizenship of the screen we threw away with the advent of talk. (126–127)

Silent film had carried Pickford's image everywhere and intertitles (cards of dialogue or exposition inserted between scenes) written in the audience's language made her an intimate citizen of each culture and nation. As she notes, the "talkies" disrupted that relatively seamless integration of her labour into multiple spaces, but the effects of "world citizenship" were still profoundly felt wherever in the world Pickford travelled.

Few celebrities of Pickford's time experienced the kind of mobility and flexible citizenship that silent screen stardom could enable; however, print media allowed celebrities to move across space and cultures relatively quickly and this created the potential for local populations to develop relationships with a celebrity.[4] These relationships could easily turn into claims should the celebrity and/or her labour ever "touch down" in that space. For individuals whose livelihood necessitated travelling for training or performance, fame and celebrity could forge those relationships in hindsight as exemplified by that perennial refrain so frequently heard in the contexts of Canadian celebrity, "we knew her when..." As technological innovations made it easier and cheaper for the individual to move her name and image (the telegraph, the photograph, etc.) and to move her body (advances in both internal and external combustion engines) across vast distances, the opportunities for making or appearing to make a meaningful connection to multiple spaces exploded. Acting troupes, for example, were no longer confined to the dimensions of their local theatre, but with expanding rail networks could take their show on the road and develop a name, reputation, and celebrity in multiple spaces (Walden 377). In short, modernity heralded new opportunities for developing not just celebrity but transnational celebrity.

The role that Canada might play in the transnational subject's identity, however, was more likely to be as a departure point than as a place where one developed one's labour and/or celebrity (Vance 183, 190). This is not to claim one could not find a mentor or an opportunity to exercise one's talents in Canada, but it was widely acknowledged that one was more likely to find more opportunities to develop a career and celebrity in places with larger populations and more extensive cultural centres.[5] The normative trajectory for those born in Canada was thus to gravitate toward the major cultural centres of Canada—Toronto and Montreal—and from there depart for the US or Europe.[6] Canada as a celebrity training ground for those born outside the country is not unheard of—Martha Black, for example, was born in Chicago and made a name for herself in the Yukon with her gold rush and political activities[7]—but such examples are the exception rather than the rule, and it is an easier task to identify those individuals who brought their celebrity with them to Canada to visit or to stay.

At the turn of the century, then, the transnational celebrity with a connection to Canada was most likely to be an individual who was born in the country and for reasons often, but not always, related to the development of her career and celebrity, moved elsewhere. This basic plot underlies the story of many celebrities' careers including those of Mary Pickford, Maud Allan, and Emma Albani, but what it sketches in general does not account for their very diverse relationships to Canada. The circumstances that took each of these women beyond our borders, for example, vary considerably: Maud Allan was just a child when her family relocated to the US, and from there she moved to Germany to pursue music training. Emma Albani also made her way to Europe for musical training via the US but was almost a decade older than Allan when she left Canada and, unlike Allan, claims strong memories of her place of birth and the US. Mary Pickford also relocated to the US at a young age, but unlike Allan, the move was part of an overall family strategy to keep her and the rest of the family employed in theatre work. All of these women returned to Canada at least once after their careers had taken off, but the reception they received varied from stark indifference to media orgies: Maud Allan's 1916 tour in Toronto, for example, received one note and a few ads but no reviews or images in the *Toronto Star,*[8] portending the obscurity she had fallen into, whereas any return of Pickford to Toronto was well publicized well into the 1930s.[9]

Yet regardless of how much press they generated in Canada during or after the height of their careers, when they did appear in Canadian newspapers, Allan, Pickford, and Albani were consistently claimed for Canada. Sometimes this took the form of a brief nod to their roots or, more often, they were simply declared to be "Canadian," a claim that was, until Canada developed its own citizenship laws in 1946, based on cultural rather than political constructions of nationality (Baldwin 524). It is worth noting as well that until that time, women born in Canada who married non-British subjects, as Mary Pickford did, legally became "aliens" and lost their right to claim British subjecthood (Baldwin 522–524).[10] Regardless of her legal identity, Pickford's relationship to Canada throughout her life was consistently constructed as intimate and ongoing.[11] These claims even persisted posthumously: a sampling of some of the more recent and well-publicized efforts to claim Pickford for Canada include a star on the Canada Walk of Fame in 1999, a Canada Post stamp in 2006, and Peggy Dymond Leavey's 2011 biography, *Mary Pickford: Canada's Silent Siren, America's Sweetheart.*

Compared to the cultural legacies that still attend Mary Pickford's fame, Maud Allan has fallen into obscurity, due in part to the relative brevity of her fame (her popularity was at its height over the 1908–1909 theatre season), the negative effects of a 1918 lawsuit on her image (Medd), and the absence of commemorative efforts by provincial or federal governments (there have been no plaques, statues, or stamps, and few archives). Dance Collection Danse, a Toronto-based archive and publisher that promotes the history of dance in Canada, is one of the few institutions that have taken an interest in Allan's career: not only do they maintain a physical and digital archive on Allan, but they published one of Felix Cherniavsky's two biographical portraits of Allan, and one of their directors published a long piece on Allan, "Willing to Be Thrilling," in *The Beaver* in 2006 (Bishop-Gwyn). As befits the DCD's mandate, Allan is consistently claimed for Canada in all of these works. The posthumous commemoration of Albani's Canadian heritage, on the other hand, has been the work of both private citizens and institutions beginning as far back as 1937, when a government plaque was raised in her hometown, Chambly. These efforts continue today in popular periodicals such as *The Beaver* (now *Canada's History*) and *Maclean's* and, as noted in detail by Robin Elliot, in high school texts and in the scholarship of Québécois writers keen to claim Albani not for Canada but Québec (109–110).[12]

However precarious, spurious, or compelling these claims appear to be, they exist as part of the celebrity legacy attending these women's identities over the twentieth century and, in Albani's case, the nineteenth century as well. These women were aware such claims and qualifications to their identities were being made; indeed, at times they were complicit with these efforts, confirming in their autobiographies, for example, that they were indeed born in Canada. Their strategies of self-representation, however, did not seek to contain their identities under one national flag but to find some way to articulate the transnational condition their celebrity

Left: Canada Post stamp, issued in 1980, commemorating the fiftieth anniversary of Emma Albani's death. *Right:* From Canada Post's "Canadians in Hollywood" series, a stamp issued in 2006 to commemorate Mary Pickford. Reproduced with permission of Canada Post.

had engendered. As we turn now to how and why each woman sought out ways to manage Canadian (and other) claims to her identity, we see that across their diverse strategies, each woman sought to protect the value of her career and celebrity: the production of a transnational identity, it seems, was difficult but also potentially rewarding and lucrative labour.

Maud Allan, Mary Pickford, and Emma Albani: A Few Tactics

The notoriety of Maud Allan's dancing career and her relative lack of training in this field necessitated a great deal of public relations work to safeguard the value of her labour: modern dancing was quite new and, as cosmopolitan as Edwardian London liked to envision itself, Allan was still dancing on stage in sheer shifts and beaded bras, while the women in her audience drew abbreviated breaths through their corsets. Although Allan had secured the patronage and support of several key society figures, she also appears to have been active in promoting her labour in the media. Her autobiography, *My Life and Dancing* (1908), was first serialized in a London newspaper (Cherniavsky, *Salome* 177) and then, in an uncanny anticipation of celebrity autobiography practices of the late twentieth century, issued as a keepsake with full-page photos in a special "Souvenir" edition for her 250th consecutive performance at the Palace Theatre. As Cherniavsky's extensive research reveals, Allan's dancing and celebrity garnered her considerable international media coverage, and in those reports one detects a consistently evasive strategy for addressing the question of her national identity. Claimed as Canadian by Canadian media outlets, American by American media outlets, and either Canadian, American, English, or British by European and Australian papers, the widespread confusion about Allan's identity was not simply the wishful thinking of fans or the failure of reporters to check their facts, but was deliberately aided by Allan's contradictory and confusing answers. In a 1914 interview in the *Perth Daily News*, for example, Allan was reported to have answered the question, "You are a Britisher?" with the following:

> I was actually born in Canada, and my parents are English and Scotch. But, as I have traveled the world, I have become a native of many places. When I was in San Francisco the papers announced it was there that I came into the world. There are three cities in Scotland where I was born, and when I was in the Eastern States I learned for the first time that I left Australia, for a reason, the paper said, 15 years ago. I spent my childhood in California but, though my father is a naturalised American, I am more British than anything. (qtd in Cherniavsky, *Maud Allan* 118)

The brilliance of this response is that, in the guise of appearing to resolve the ambiguity and confusion about her identity, she simply affirms it. Each time a concrete identity is articulated, it is immediately destabilized: she was born in Canada but of English and Scottish extraction and her father is American (by law making her American too), but she claims British cultural identity. Moreover, this last sentence, which appears to make a firm declaration, is not actually distinguishable from the preceding sentences that reported the rumours about her: in this context, this legal identity from one place and a cultural identity from another could be yet another misguided rumour.

Allan's autobiography further complicates efforts to limit her identity to any one space. The text traces a vague portrait of an early childhood in Toronto and offers more detail about her experiences with the music culture of California. The text moves quickly into an "apprenticeship" narrative that takes her throughout Europe until she achieves success in England.[13] In lieu of offering narratives of influential places, she notes important individuals and, because she was trained in music and not dance, considerable energy is expended in rationalizing her career and her success in terms of her capacity to naturally channel the beauty and art of the world around her into movement. One of the more striking arguments she makes to this effect is to position her labour as an expression of the ancient cultures of Greece, thereby giving her risqué career an impeccable providence. However, these discourses of embodiment that she uses for framing her labour also work to position her as a citizen of this faraway time and place:

> When first I came to London, one of my earliest friends, a critic, who was perhaps more poet that [sic] critic, and perhaps more seer than either, said to me: "You danced, I think, in Syracusan groves and on the slopes of Mount Etna, for the pleasure of Dorian and Ionian immigrants, when Sicily was a peaceful colony of ancient Greece. You danced whilst Theocritus read his idylls in the Mediterranean twilights, and then you just went to sleep—and have wakened again just now...."
>
> I think I can see the boats from Argolis, seven hundred years before Christ, landing their companies upon the Trinacrian sands....
>
> Syracuse in Sicily, B.C. 210, London in England A.D. 1908.
>
> What a wild fancy! and yet—I do sometimes think that I was one of those ancient dancers, whose duty in life was to express in motion the hopes, fear, passions, regrets, which rose in men's and women's hearts and found expression in movement when the world was younger, and simpler.... (10–11)

The history of dance she proceeds to offer, heavily referencing classical scholars and tracing the precedents for her own work in early Christian churches and across Europe, lends her an exotic cultural history that also works fiercely hard to legitimize her dancing style, costumes, and lack of professional training. Allan, her text would have us believe, is not so much a creature of Canada or the US or even England but is a being without nation because she is an instrument for the expression of multiple cultures across time. However, Allan's desire to position herself outside the boundaries of conventional citizenship eventually backfired on her, as it did for that other scandalously clad dancing sensation of dubious origins, Mata Hari.[14] In a spectacular and socially devastating public trial in 1918, Allan was portrayed as a dangerous and degenerate foreigner with unsavoury connections to Germany (Medd). Unlike Mata Hari, who was executed as a spy in 1917, Allan survived (it was only a libel suit and had been initiated by Allan), but the trial and attendant publicity made clear that her labour and transnational identity, far from being valuable, were now liabilities (Medd 30).

As Allan's fate reveals, wartime makes it very difficult to appear ambiguous about one's national identity. Mary Pickford, whose extraordinary success on the silent screen had given her, as noted earlier, a kind of "world citizenship" (127), had considerably more success than Allan in managing her transnational identity during World War I. As Beth Zdriluk has examined in detail, Pickford was mobilized by *both* American and Canadian war propaganda and publicity machines and, particularly in the final years of World War I, Pickford "serve[d] as an important, loved, and socially-charged national symbol" for each nation.[15] What warrants emphasis here is not just that Pickford was mobilized by both nations as a symbol of their unique character, but that Pickford willingly lent herself to these projects and that this was part of a lifelong strategy for managing her identity. After all, why pick sides when you can play for both teams? With Canadian media outlets, Pickford encouraged Canadians to claim her as their own: in Arthur Stringer's 1918 *Maclean's* article, for example, she is quoted as suggesting she could never forget she was Canadian (Sept. issue, 22), in a 1934 article with the *Toronto Star* she is quoted, "I belong to Toronto and Toronto belongs to me" (Knowles 3), and as late as 1959 in an interview with CBC she claims she is "very, very proud of being Canadian" ("Mary Pickford Interview"). Meanwhile in the US, Pickford pursued projects that obscured these sentimental proclamations and positioned her as American: as Zdriluk has pointed out, Pickford's starring role in the 1917 film *The Little American* and the Liberty Bonds ad, "100% American," were wartime pieces that mobilized "America's Sweetheart" to stir up nationalistic sentiment. Yet, as early as 1916 and as late as 1979, newspapers quoted Pickford as declaring that she was American ("Mary Pickford Quits," "Star of Silent," Whitfield 339), and various press interviews and speeches reveal that her Canadian roots were effaced as befitting the occasion (such as in her speech to the American Women's Association in 1926 ["Leaders Honored"]).[16] According to one report of her trip to England in 1920, she and Douglas Fairbanks toured England in a car draped in American flags—a tribute no doubt to her American husband, her legal married identity, and her career in the US entertainment industries, but nevertheless a symbolic statement that did not accommodate her much touted attachment to Canada ("Douglas and Mary").

Pickford was, in short, complicit with both nationalistic discourses, a brilliant public relations strategy that endeared her to both Canadian and American audiences without alienating either. This worked in part because she knew her identity was flexible and could support these multiple and simultaneous claims. Occasionally we see Pickford attempt to articulate those ambiguous conditions that allow her this flexibility: in the same CBC interview she claims to be "very very Canadian," for example, she also introduces some instability into that identity, suggesting that "when I'm asked which country do you prefer? [Pause.] I said 'Well, I don't know.' England is my grandmother, Toronto, Canada is my mother and the United States is my husband." The evasiveness of her answer here is strategic for at the same time as it traces real sites of ancestry, it refuses to articulate a specific national identity.[17] In fact, the logic of this family tree makes it impossible for her to do so and allows her to remain intimately connected to several nations and yet embody or belong to none exclusively.

In her memoir, *Sunshine and Shadow* (1955), Pickford also gives Canadians plenty of ammunition for claiming her as their own, but she does so without precluding the possibility that other claims might be made to her identity.[18] Her childhood in Canada, for example, makes its mark on her but certain habits and behaviours (such as table manners and speech patterns) have to be relearned for success in the American market. This same industry transforms her from Gladys, who is "sent back to Canada," into "Mary," who "embark[s] on a great and thrilling career"(65), a tacit acknowledgement of the critical role that American industries played in the production of not just "Mary Pickford" the name, but Mary Pickford, the film star and celebrity. Yet "America's Sweetheart" is not necessarily or exclusively an *American* sweetheart: although her private life and working career are clearly based in the US, the narrative begins and ends with her in Toronto. Moreover, the text continually refers us to the public life that was not confined to any particular geographical space: her films and her celebrity were everywhere, a point driven home with photos of the crowds that greeted her in Japan, France, Denmark, Germany, and Sweden. What is remarkable about these images is that the crowds are indistinguishable from one another—without captions, these images could have been taken anywhere, lending the impression that Pickford fans constitute a kind of nation unto themselves. The other photo inserts in *Sunshine and Shadow* seem designed to interpellate us, as readers, into that nation (if we're not part of it already) by exposing us to those same images that united these international fans—famous publicity shots of her private life, formal studio head shots, and film stills from her most popular works. Thus, unlike Allan and Albani's memoirs, which were written for a British audience, Pickford's autobiography speaks to no particular nation.[19] It is written in English but addressed to her fans and, like her other celebrity texts, offers fans everywhere the opportunity to continue their parasocial relationship with her. All are invited to consume her, and the very openness of this invitation ultimately precludes any one of us from staking exclusive rights to her.

If Allan's strategies of self-representation (at least in terms of her national identity) might be characterized as evasive and Pickford's as often bordering on sentimentality, Emma Albani's are altogether different: she appears to accept Canadian claims to her and identifies Canada as her "native" land several times throughout her memoir, *Forty Years of Song* (1911), but she professes no attachment to this place or, in fact, *any* place. Her memoir instead renders a portrait of international celebrity as a kind of benevolent homelessness necessitated by a career where, like Allan, her training had taken her throughout Europe but her working years kept her continually on the move (unlike Allan, who was, during the height of her success, firmly attached to a particular location). In an opera career that spanned an impressive forty years, Albani toured extensively throughout the world—North America, Europe, Australia, India, South Africa, and elsewhere—sometimes more than once. Her memoir's detailed attention to her success in these places is designed to affirm the cultural value of her labour, but it also, perhaps inadvertently, reveals how a travelling artist is not only by necessity very mobile, but easily adopted by multiple national groups for their own purposes. Much like Giardina's notion of the transnational celebrity as a blank slate upon which local means might be written, Albani finds herself used as a vehicle through which both fans and monarchs can access affective and patriotic attachments to their own culture and home. Her rendition of "Home, Sweet Home," for example, appears to evoke strong sentimental responses, particularly from English-speaking audiences all over the world, and a performance of a French melody, she notes, inspired such patriotic fervour amongst Canadians that the sheet music was issued with her image and sold extremely well (183).[20] In parts of Europe with strong operatic traditions, so pleased are some groups with her capacity to embody certain roles and do justice to their language that she is marked as a kind of honorary accessory to that culture: not only does she receive medals from various monarchs across Europe (photographed for the text), but in parts of Italy, she notes, she became "the daughter of Bellini" or "La Sonnambula" (48) and in Germany, Emperor William I titled her a Royal Court Singer (160).

Albani's ability to slip between nations and embody or channel their cultures inevitably leads to some confusion about her national identity:

> Lady Hooper, writing to the *New York World* from Paris at this time, says of me: "What an elastic nationality she possesses! In American she was an American, and hailed from Albany. In England she was declared to be a Canadian and a loyal subject of Her British Majesty. The French papers now state she is a French woman, her real name being Lajeunesse, and that she was 'born in the state of Albany, in the city of Canada' [*sic*]. I understand French newspaper writers study geography. The other day one of them announced that the *Amérique* had gone ashore in the 'New York River'. Therefore their somewhat mixed statements respecting the birthplace of this Franco-Anglo-American-Canadian prima donna are not to be wondered at." (121–122)

While Albani did not, like Maud Allan appears to have done, promote this confusion, her changing names—from Lajeunnesse to Albani to Mrs. Gye or Albani Gye—and the identities they signaled or obscured—French/French

Canadian, Italian, American,²¹ English—gave reporters plenty to speculate on. Yet what is most pertinent here is not the competing claims to Albani (which, with the exception of Canadian and French-Canadian claims, appear not to have survived her), but Lady Hooper's characterization of Albani's nationality as "elastic." It is a fitting term for her memoir's strategies of representing her national identity as she seems flexible enough to accommodate not just the needs, but the claims of multiple national spaces. Canada, French Canada, the US, and to a limited degree Britain are recognized as making particular claims to her, but she does not discriminate among them or their claims. All are invited and welcome to call her their own, and she recognizes and appreciates the various roles each has played or, in the case of the French Canadians, failed to play, in supporting her career. However, what is remarkable about this elasticity is the general indifference with which Albani narrates *all* spaces and people: despite their attachment to her and her gratitude for their affection, each place is rendered as though she were a beloved visitor rather than intimate citizen. Unlike Pickford's sentimental attachments to the land of her birth, Albani is markedly detached from both Canada and French Canadians: she is notably proud of the beauty of the landscape and pleased with how her native "countrymen" welcome her (209), but she seems no more fond of French Canadians than other national groups nor more at home in Canada than anywhere else. Thus while she acts as an instrument for others to feel affective ties to their home, it becomes increasingly apparent in the memoir that Albani—born in Canada, raised in both Canada and the US, trained throughout Europe, travelled and performed all over the world, married to an Englishman, and raised a son in a Geneva boarding school—is herself without a "home, sweet home."

Albani, Pickford, and Allan: three women with three very different strategies for articulating the transnational conditions their celebrity had engendered. These women would have undoubtedly heard of each other and perhaps even crossed paths at some point (although there are no records to indicate that they did). What might they have thought of each other's attempts to manage their Canadian roots and the various claims to their national identity? Would they have recognized in each other the elasticity that characterized their own tactics? Today, the discourse of transnationalism offers us a ready means by which to understand the celebrity experience these women sought to express, but the availability of such discourses of identity, as we have seen, still does not preclude individuals and institutions from attempting to claim these women for a particular nation. However, if understood in the context of the celebrity "terrain" wherein multiple participants are continually negotiating and shifting the meaning of the celebrity, these past and present claims made by Canadians, particularly when they exist in conflict with other claims, ultimately work to keep the celebrity's identity in flux. Whereas death typically consolidates a celebrity's image and what it means (and to whom they belonged), the lack of consensus regarding these women's national identities can prevent any one claim from dominating the "negotiated terrain" of their celebrity. In short, Canadian claims to transnational celebrities may create friction, particularly with other nations' claims or the celebrity's system of self-identification, but it is a productive friction that can allow for, rather than close down, the ongoing, dynamic processes of celebrity image-making. For Allan, Pickford, and Albani, who sought in various ways to represent the contested and elastic nature of their identities, those Canadian claims are thus not only to be expected, but can be recuperated, even annexed, into their own histories of the transnational self.

Notes

I am much indebted to Ryan Veenstra for locating the stamp images of Albani and Pickford and to Mary Bowden for securing permission from Canada Post to reproduce them.

1 As Robin Elliot and other critics have pointed out, there is still no evidence confirming that Albani was born in 1847 (110). Some have suggested she may have been born later; however this is the date widely used by Canadian sources.

2 By "nation-state" I refer to geopolitical entities recognized as countries as well as those political states seeking or having achieved sovereignty within these countries such as First Nations and Québécois communities.

3 The first "Canadians in Hollywood" stamp series was issued in 2006 and included Mary Pickford, Lorne Greene, John Candy, and Fay Wray.

4 "Flexible citizenship" is a term frequently used by Ong in her work on transnationality.

5 The National Council of Women of Canada's 1900 publication, *Women of Canada: Their Life and Work*, suggested that "Women who have literature, music, or art for a profession are also unhampered in the exercise of their talents. But the country is too young and too thinly populated to afford an adequate field for the exercise of unusual gifts. In consequence, Canada's most celebrated singer is seldom heard at home; the best books are published first in London and New York. But they are of Canada and for Canada and loved and honoured by Canadians for present worth and future promise" (62). It is likely that the "most celebrated singer" referred to here is Emma Albani, who is given a generous biographical portrait later in the text (233–234).

6 Mount reports that over a million Canadians left for the US in the 1880s and 1890s (6), and while women did not make up a significant portion of the expat community in the US, Mount argues that there was still more opportunity for them to develop writing careers there than in Canada (39).

7   When her husband became too ill to continue his political career, Black campaigned for and won his seat in the House of Commons in 1935. Black was seventy years old and the second woman to be elected to the House of Commons.

8   In the June 1917 issue of *Everywoman's World*, however, Allan and her dancing were extensively reviewed and praised (Winans).

9   By the 1960s, the media coverage of Pickford's visit to Toronto and appearance on CBC's game show *Front Page Challenge* is considerably more subdued. The *Toronto Star*, for example, which had in previous years spilled much ink on most anything related to Pickford, covers this visit with a few small articles by the Women's Editor, Helen Palmer, who presumes that audiences don't know who Pickford is.

10 There is some confusion as to whether Pickford actually did lose her citizenship: some fans and critics maintain she never lost it (Frank, qtd. in Veillette), although the terms of the 1914 British Nationality and Status of Aliens Act suggest that she must have upon marrying Douglas Fairbanks. (It is also possible that Pickford ceased to be a British subject upon her first marriage to Owen Moore if Moore was an American and no longer an Irish national.) Others have argued that Pickford was repatriated upon request in 1978 (Lucas, Patterson).

11 There are many examples from her life to choose from, but, to start, one might look to Arthur Stringer's extensive portrait of Pickford in *Maclean's* magazine in 1918, Pickford's interview with CBC in 1959, and the heritage plaque marking her birthplace on the lawn of Toronto's SickKids Hospital.

12 These claims are troublesome, as Elliot rightly points out, because of the ways in which Albani's image and politics have been cleaned up in order to make her fit for particular political agendas (119). See Elliot's article "Constructions of Identity" for further discussion of the implications of claiming Albani for Quebec.

13 See Lorraine York's *Literary Celebrity in Canada* for a further exploration of how celebrities in Canada have used the "apprenticeship narrative" to buttress the value of their labour and celebrity.

14 Mata Hari was the name used by Dutch-born Margaretha Geertruida Zelle McLeod for her exotic dancing career. Reinventing herself as a Hindu temple dancer from India and often posing in various Eastern costumes (one of which bears an uncanny resemblance to what Allan used for her Dance of Salome), she enjoyed considerable success and celebrity from her first performance in 1906 (Conyers 236–238).

15 In "American Idol: Mary Pickford, World War I, and the Making of a National Icon," Christel Schmidt also details how Pickford's war efforts made her a potent "national symbol" for Americans (146). Pickford's celebrity and films have made her a popular subject of study amongst scholars. See, for example, Gaylyn Studlar's examination of Pickford's child characters in *Precocious Charms: Stars Performing Girlhood in Classical Hollywood Cinema*.

16 In both the 1916 and 1979 articles Pickford does pay tribute to her Canadian roots but claims to feel or be American.

17 Pickford's paternal grandmother's was born in England, her mother was Canadian-born, and two of her three husbands were American-born.

18 Previously, Pickford had published a life story (ghosted by Frances Marion) in *Ladies Home Journal* in 1923 (Ponce de Leon 64). In 1954, an abridged version of *Sunshine and Shadows* was published in *McCall's* magazine as "My Whole Life" and is now available on the Mary Pickford Foundation website.

19 In Allan's *My Life and Dancing*, both the content (which warmly praises the English) and the publishing conditions (written for a London newspaper and issued as a souvenir for London audiences) indicate that Allan was writing for an English audience. Albani's *Forty Years of Song* (also published in England) devotes considerable attention to the refined cultural tastes of the English, and the frequent allusions to her close connection to British royalty, most particularly Queen Victoria, strongly suggest that the text was written for a British audience. The initial, abridged publication of Pickford's narrative in *McCall's* clearly sought an American market, but the book-length version arguably casts a much wider net.

20 Albani suggests that the song became "a national as well as popular song ever since, and is even now to be found in nearly every cottage throughout Canada" (183); however, it is probably more accurate to say that this French song from "Pré aux Clercs" with its rousing lines, "Rendez-moi ma patrie / Ou laissez-moi mourir," was popular amongst French Canadians rather than Canadians in general.

21 Although an Italian name, "Albani" was often mistaken as a stage name adopted in tribute to the role that Albany, New York, played in fostering her career.

3

Terry Fox and Disabled Celebrity

Valerie J. Millar

In 1977, at the age of nineteen years, a young man named Terry Fox was diagnosed with osteosarcoma and underwent the amputation of his right leg. In partnership with the Canadian Cancer Society, he began a run across the country, a "Marathon of Hope," in 1980 to raise money for cancer research. After 143 days and 5,373 kilometres, Terry stopped because his cancer had spread to his lungs ("Facts"). He died just ten months later. He was twenty-three.

Terry Fox holds an honoured place in Canada's recent history. The images and texts of Terry Fox that circulate in Canadian culture render him in mythic proportions, but, if he has become a myth of sorts, it is a myth based on stereotypes of illness, disability, strength, and courage that have been shaped by an ableist culture and a Canadian nationalist narrative. The endurance and unassailability of this myth are troubling to me and, I expect, to some other Canadians who are ill and disabled. It is troubling because Fox's posthumous celebrity consolidates features of disabled experience that are privileged within the economy of disability discourse. Moreover, the perpetuation of Terry Fox's disabled celebrity and all that it signifies confirms, reproduces, and sustains able-bodiedness in the able-bodied/dis-able-bodied binary. The unremarked, normative body needs the disabled body in order to conceal itself. This myth of Terry Fox does not engage with the reality of our lives; therefore, it must be defamiliarized from a critical, disability-centred point of view.

Other Canadians have written interesting, factual, and emotional pieces about Terry Fox. Sally Chivers, in "Ordinary People: Reading the Trans-Canadian Terry Fox," works within a Canadian Studies and disability studies framework to argue, among other things, that while illness has been the main focus of most stories told about Fox, more attention should be directed to the role of his highly visible prosthesis in refiguring current cultural representations of disability. She importantly points out that the "super-crip" narrative has the effect of sidestepping ordinary disabled people (83). Tanis MacDonald's "Terry Fox and the National Imaginary: Reading Eric Walter's *Run*" works within the framework of literary studies and notes the various literary appetites that keep the many texts about Terry Fox circulating, especially among young Canadians. Deborah Harrison, in "The Terry Fox story and the popular media: a case study in ideology and illness," explores the motif of the dying hero who unburdens himself in order to spare others. While valuable to my argument here, none of these works reflects upon the role of ableism in constructing our narratives of Terry Fox or of disability more generally. My approach differs because it frames these narratives within feminist and queer contexts to make strange the underlying ideology of "ableness" or "normalcy" that covertly supports *any* discussion of disability. So I write less about Fox's illness/disability per se from an unremarked, ableist stance as Chivers, MacDonald, Harrison, and others have done, and instead focus on the function of ableist and nationalist ideology in framing disability scripts. For me, the celebrity of Terry Fox presents an opportunity to unpack and recast taken-for-granted meanings of ability and disability within a larger, Canadian socio-political context. In this chapter I look to the socio-political and historical moment circa 1980 that gave birth to Terry Fox the hero and speculate on the complex relations of power behind the creation of Terry Fox the myth. I will explore how the annual Terry Fox Run works to collectivize people, raising money for cancer research while simultaneously reaffirming able-bodied hegemony and reproducing the ideological Canadian nation-state. Finally, I will examine how certain representations of disabled people come to be "naturalized" through repeated print messages and visual images of Terry Fox (and other disabled celebrities) and what these representations say to different audiences. My purpose is to lay bare the web of power relations that created the myth that undergirds the continued production of Fox's posthumous celebrity.

Terry Fox: Hero, Celebrity

It is necessary to make a distinction between hero and celebrity as others before me have done in order to establish my position. In "From Hero to Celebrity: The Human Pseudo-Event," Daniel Boorstin makes a clear distinction between the two, privileging the former and disparaging the latter (74). Like Boorstin, I, too, privilege the hero; however, to discredit celebrity as Boorstin does underrates and obscures celebrity's multifaceted functioning in contemporary culture. To me, Fox is unequivocally a hero. He embodied bravery and determination in the face of life-threatening illness. He undertook a physically demanding event motivated by high ideals. He never lost hope that a "miracle" could happen. His unwavering belief in a cure for cancer and his motivation to help others in the cultural "fight" against cancer endures to this day. Whereas conceptions of "the hero" are dealt with differently by some cultural theorists, I choose, perhaps too simply, to follow the *Oxford Canadian Dictionary*'s definition of a hero as "a person distinguished by courage, noble deeds, outstanding achievements," and, I would add, a person who inspires hope in the populace.

While Boorstin and others saw celebrity as a falling away from the ideal of the hero, more nuanced engagements with celebrity culture, such as those undertaken in P. David Marshall's *Celebrity and Power*, Graeme Turner's *Understanding Celebrity*, and Lorraine York's *Literary Celebrity in Canada*, have worked to establish the value of celebrity and to unpack the ideologically complex workings of this phenomenon. Celebrity is "one of the key places where cultural meanings are negotiated and organized" (Turner 6). Moreover, celebrity "at least holds open the possibility that being celebrated need not always be a negative thing, that it can operate and signify variously within culture, and that audiences, in turn, can act and signify upon it" (York 11).

While Fox's heroism is indisputable to me, the meaning of his posthumously constructed celebrity is a more complicated matter worthy of exploration rather than dismissal. He is famous because his 1980 Marathon of Hope run across Canada was cut short when his cancer returned and he was hospitalized, dying just ten months later. Nonetheless, his run raised millions of dollars in donations for cancer research. He became a symbol of tenacity in the face of adversity and stands as a model figure to other fundraising campaigns that have taken hold since 1980. What is unique about Fox's long-lasting fame is that it appeals to abled and disabled Canadians alike and despite differences in regional outlook, economic circumstances, or political beliefs. His celebrity is everywhere evident in Canadian culture, from the creation of monuments and stamps in his honour, to fourteen schools and fifteen roads given his name, to his induction as the youngest member of the Companion of the Order of Canada, to his legacy in literature. The list of accolades and artefacts bestowed on Fox in his lifetime and posthumously bespeaks the high esteem in which he is held.[1] In the years since Fox's death it seems the icons, or "tools," of disability, most notably the prosthesis and the wheelchair, have been intensified and curated to stand in not only for chronic and/or life-threatening illnesses, but also have come to represent acquired-through-accident disability. I propose that Fox is the founding, key figure in current translations of disease disability on which acquired disability seems to have piggybacked. Canadian disabled celebrities such as Rick Hansen and others, who undertook fundraising or other athletic events after Fox, profited from the cultural worth of the original Fox fame. Fox's posthumous celebrity negotiates the indistinct boundaries and sometimes competing claims between disease disability and acquired disability, between the always contextual nature of being "abled" and being "disabled," and between the various audiences who have a vested political, nationalist, monetary, or ableist interest in replicating a particular kind of disablement.

According to Marshall, unlike the hero, the celebrity is "acted upon by media and constructed into appropriate icons" (16). Many celebrities are not passive, but actively influence the construction of their image and fame; in the case of Terry Fox, the Fox family, in some measure, influences his posthumous celebrity. The media, however, are not the only shapers of celebrity, as Marshall notes: various industries and audiences have expectations, motivations, and desires that might best be met through strategic rendering of a particular kind of image. Thus, celebrity provokes a "condition [that] is itself productive of uneasiness" (York 4). Canadian nationalist interests shape Fox as the ideal citizen. The medical and pharmaceutical industries have an interest in perpetuating the posthumous celebrity of Terry Fox because his brand translates into money for research and manufacturing. Individuals with cancer may look to Fox for inspiration and most likely rely on treatments developed because of donations made in his name. Others, like myself, might trouble over what is concealed behind any "strategic rendering" of Fox's fame. I am discomfited by the use of Fox's celebrity that sustains ambiguous meanings of ability/disability within the disability community while simultaneously privileging nationalist, capitalist, and ableist goals. As one of many Canadians labelled disabled by medical discourse, I acknowledge my perspectives on Terry Fox as a cultural text are marked by ambivalence.

A Symbol of Nation Building and Nationalist Ideology

Nineteen eighty was the year the Marathon of Hope began and Terry Fox came to Canada's and the world's attention. Given the threat to Canadian confederation by the forces for sovereignty in 1980, and given the federal Liberal government's overt agenda to keep Canada unified, Fox's April to September Marathon of Hope cross-country run rapidly acquired a nationalist framework that was, if not explicitly used by the Canadian government, certainly promoted in Canadian media-produced imagery and rhetoric.

The May 1980 Quebec referendum was to determine that province's place in Canada. For pro-separatists, Quebec sovereignty was the only route. The referendum results favoured continued unity. Prime Minister

Pierre Trudeau was an ardent nationalist who made it his political and personal mission to maintain a unified Canada. As supporters of Trudeau's nationalist-federalist agenda both inside and outside of Quebec sighed in relief at the province's decision to remain in Canada, the country turned its attention to Terry Fox "as a symbol of a united country—his run was a reconfirmation of Quebec's decision" (Taft 765). The image of Fox running along the highway with the maple leaf emblazoned on his T-shirt quickly emerged as a symbol of Canadian courage, perseverance, and unity.

Fox's run through Quebec was, however, disappointing for him. In response to a question from a CBC reporter about his success in securing pledges, Fox replied that "Quebec was not very good" whereas pledges in other provinces, including those he had yet to visit, had "really started to pick up" ("Reliving Terry Fox's Marathon of Hope: Day 79"). Fox felt his marathon had not been well publicized in Quebec, "[n]or was he helped by the attitude of motorists and the police" (Scrivener 97). Fox appears to have hit a low point in his run through Quebec when he writes in his journal: "I am tired and weary because people are continually forcing me off the road. I was actually honked off once.... It is so frustrating" ("Terry's Journal Entries and Map"). Quebecers, it seems, were less enthusiastic about his Marathon of Hope than others across the country, but this was not acknowledged in Prime Minister Trudeau's message to the House of Commons upon Fox's death in June 1981:

> It occurs very rarely in the life of a nation that the courageous spirit of one person unites all people in the celebration of his life and in the mourning of his death.... We do not think of him as one who was defeated by misfortune but as one who inspired us with the example of the triumph of the human spirit over adversity. (qtd. in Scrivener 182)

Less than one year after Trudeau's House of Commons address, the 1982 Charter of Rights and Freedoms in Canada was entrenched. The Charter, preceded by the 1980 Judicial Conduct and Disability Act in the United States and followed by the 1990 Americans with Disabilities Act, set the stage for the disability movement in North America to gain momentum in political and public discourses. As well, cancer awareness and narratives were on the rise partly because the stigmatization previously borne by cancer "victims" was largely transferred onto those with AIDS (Sontag 103–104). The myth of Terry Fox began to take shape at a time when our country wanted to believe in its future under the new Charter and to register its own course and narratives. Fox emerged from this moment as an icon of the disability/cancer movement in Canada and as a narrative of a "new," more distanced relationship between Canada and the Commonwealth, but the promise he seemed to offer of a heroic figure untouched by or distinct from the colonizing, nation-building effort collapsed into a celebrity mythos that only served to affirm the primacy of dominant, nationalist, able-bodied narratives.

The attempts to create a modern Canadian nation-state that began in the nineteenth century under Confederation required that values and assumptions be called upon to fix boundaries and establish who does, and does not, belong. The Enlightenment subject of the Confederation era and the first half of the twentieth century was autonomous, industrious, productive, self-directed, and a good citizen, one able to work hard for the common good. This subject presupposes a masculine, white, heterosexual, *normal* body. The national interest creates templates for bodies it needs and privileges a set of concealed and unexamined background assumptions of the ideal citizen.

However, the disabled body can also validate national expectations and norms, as the reworking of Fox's disability into superhuman ability demonstrates. Historically, the disabled body is often feminized or racialized (Davis 45); thus it "becomes a repository for social anxieties about such troubling concerns as vulnerability, control, and identity" (Thomson 6). Therefore, the hyper-masculine, hetero-normative, unmarked (white) body plays a strategic role in creating a new, Western democratic nation-state and reproducing its narrative of strength, power, and identity (Erevelles 123), important ideals for a vast country eager to attract capital and Western European immigrants to help build a prosperous economy and cohesive social order. The disabled body, though, has the potential to disrupt expectations and norms of national identity (Hall, "Reimagining Disability" 8) by becoming "a kind of repository for the anxiety that arises from mediation between old [colonized] and new [decolonized] cultural norms" (LaCom 162). Disabled bodies must be regulated, literally and symbolically, because they are "understood to have the potential to undermine the project of nationalism" (LaCom 162). However, Fox becomes the "norm" of the abnormal, disabled body. He is inside disability because he is marked by his prosthetic leg, yet he is outside disability because he is a high-performance athlete on a scale that is unattainable for most able-bodied people. He is celebrated for his tenacity, his athleticism, his unmarked norms (whiteness, heterosexuality), and, of course, for his capacity to raise millions of dollars for cancer research (Scrivener 96–97). Fox is the effect of a homogeneous national narrative that valorizes the ability to overcome adversity and to be economically successful. He is the ideal Enlightenment subject because his disability, turned into ability, upholds the able-bodied narrative of self-determination, progress, and "an ontological sameness upon which the notion of democratic equality is predicated" (Thomson 64).

The quest, or journey, motif of Terry Fox's 1980 Marathon of Hope parallels the cultural progress narrative. An assimilationist politic runs through both. The progress narrative incorporates the belief in scientific advancement and the model of medical mastery that imposes a normalizing imperative and discourse through "the cure." Scientific advancement's desire to assimilate the disabled body—the ungovernable, potentially disruptive, unbounded body—is accomplished, in Fox's case, by a technologically intricate prosthetic leg that transforms his inability into ability. Fox's ability, in turn, permits him to undertake a cross-country run to raise money for research to find a cure for cancer, thus aligning his personal quest with the medical mastery imperative. Fox's personal and selfless deed is then transformed into a metaphor for national unity in the cultural consciousness, undergirded by political motivation, I would argue, to support an assimilationist drive to integrate the potentially recalcitrant Quebec pro-separatist supporters (the ungovernable, potentially disruptive, unbounded, *political body*) into mainstream Canadian culture—that is, the predominantly Anglophone values held throughout the rest of Canada—in order to fit a unified national narrative. If Fox could bring his own disordered body under control, political motivation would ensure he was held as an example *par excellence* of the need to bring ethnic social disorder under the control of one unifying banner—*Canada*.

The Imperative to Cure and the Terry Fox Run

Fox's celebrity is intertwined with a white, male, heterosexist, and *able-bodied* nationalist ideology and gets full-scale support from the medical/pharmaceutical complex and its imperative to cure. This complex reaps financial rewards through the sustained circulation of Fox's celebrity just as the many people with cancer benefit through the development of new and better drugs to treat it. The discursive regime of medicine organizes the appearance of illness or impairment as a medical matter, and therefore a problem to be cured, and if not cured, then managed through an ever-increasing plethora of pharmaceuticals, again with the goal of achieving assimilation, a sameness to the normal body, or at least a close approximation of it.

Samantha King, in *Pink Ribbons, Inc.,* argues that the "culturally appealing link between breast cancer, femininity and nurturing" (vii) in the United States helped facilitate individuals' and large corporations' willingness to be associated with the cause and invigorated organized giving to charity through the development and purchase of consumer-oriented products in support of finding a cure for breast cancer. She correctly claims the boundaries of the state and the corporate world are thus blurred "as each elaborates the interests of the other, often at dispersed sites through-out the social body and through practices that misleadingly appear to be outside the realm of government or consumer capitalism" (xi). Similarly, a culturally appealing link between limb cancer (or loss of limb function through accident), masculinity, and athleticism might be made, as the cel-ebration of Canada's (mostly male) disabled athletes suggests. Whereas King focuses on state and corporate motivations behind the development and selling of varied consumer-oriented products in support of breast cancer research, I use the intersection of "celebrity" and "disability" in Canada to illuminate the hidden operations behind our consumption of the Fox name and image—a brand that has consistently rebuffed corporate endorsement as it paradoxically enables corporate growth in areas related to cancer research and its many spinoffs.

Fox made it clear from the outset that he was running to raise money to find a cure for cancer. He provided a strategic moment for that complex to join in the discourse of cancer, propped up by political motivation and with its anchor point in the public desire to conquer cancer. The Terry Fox Foun-dation, faithful to Fox's wishes, supports "**cure-oriented, biomedical** cancer research around the globe" ("Terry Fox Foundation Research," emphasis in original). Effective April 1, 2013, the Terry Fox Research Institute (TFRI, previously established in 2007) partnered with Canadian Institutes of Health Research (CIHR) to establish the New Frontiers Program Project Grants to provide funding for groups of researchers working together, as well as the New Investigator Grants to assist those beginning a career in cancer research ("Research Investment Portfolio"). The Terry Fox Research Institute now directs its funds to shape research undertaken by national agencies that rely on academic researchers. (And academic research has a tendency to shape itself to where the funds exist to support it.) The TFRI's focus on funding "**cure-oriented, biomedical** research" rather than access to or payment for cancer treatments sidesteps issues of inequality based on location, socio-economic status, race, gender, and sexual orientation. It ignores the role of prevention (King xxx). Other arms of the CIHR do, though, conduct research in areas of societal, cultural, and environmental influences on the health of populations ("Canadian Institutes of Health Research Act").

The public's donations are critical to sustaining this fundraising/research machinery and thus Terry Fox and his image must be protected. Fox's deification arises from brand management through media reporting, and the Fox family endorses only those images and narratives that are com-plimentary to the memory of their son and brother. The Canadian media also participate in this deification of sorts, most notably every September to nurture interest in the annual Terry Fox Run. Even Margaret Atwood in her dystopic novel *The Year of the Flood* weighs in on this phenomenon with "Saint Terry Fox" who "showed what the human body can do in the way of locomotion without fossil fuels" as he "raced against Mortality, and in the end outran his own Death, and lives on in Memory" (403).

In order to be useful, profitable, and ideologically persuasive, this "saintly" image of Fox's must be clear and present in our consciousness as often as possible through accolades bestowed, cultural artefacts, media representations, books and TV shows, and, of course, through the yearly appeal to participate in the Terry Fox Run. The Terry Fox image is thus *put to work* in ways that raise questions not just about the labour of the disabled, but the hidden labour of disabled celebrity. Just as the medical/pharmaceutical complex is based on capitalist demands for increasing profits, so too is an individual's productivity measured in terms of dollars earned. It is, therefore, incumbent on individuals to take their physicians' advice and take whatever pharmaceutical is required to make them feel better and be more productive; otherwise, they are labelled non-compliant. The labour power of many disabled people is of little value in the competitive marketplace. Disabled people are a liability to the state, unless their value is determined on a scale other than that offered in dominant economic and cultural systems (Erevelles 127). Terry Fox's labour power in 1980 became measured by the dollars he raised for cancer research, and his celebrity extends to the present day partly because its economic and cultural value perpetuates medical research, medical equipment manufacturing, and pharmaceuticals production, which, in turn, drive employment and consumer purchasing.

What Fox's celebrity veils is the assumption that ill and disabled people aspire to normalcy. I do not want to suggest that people should not avail themselves of every opportunity to regain health. Certainly, I would be the first to line up if a cure were offered for my disease because of my desire to feel well and my fetishization of bodily integrity and intellectual productivity within capitalistic schemata, all of which shape my ambivalent identification with Fox's celebrity. Perhaps all of us must recognize our complicity in effecting what amounts to "compulsory able-bodiedness," which in a sense "produces the disease or disability in the first place" (McRuer 2). However, such a perspective fails to address the physical pain of debilitating illness and disability. It does not offer relief from implacable illness. Terry Fox understood pain and suffering and pushed through it, literally, until he could no longer. His Marathon of Hope was the *de novo* event that set in motion the annual Terry Fox Run.

The measure of the economic and cultural power of Fox's posthumous celebrity today might be gauged in the effects of the annual Terry Fox Run.

This event works to collectivize people, disabled and able-bodied, to gain recognition for those who have cancer, to pay tribute to those who have died from cancer, and to raise money for cancer research. It takes place every September in all provinces of Canada and in other countries worldwide at varying times of the year. Over two million people participate each year and funds are raised through pledges made to The Terry Fox Foundation. The Foundation, in turn, partners with research initiatives supporting close to $20 million in discovery-based research each year in Canada ("Mission Statement and History"). Of every dollar raised, eighty-four cents goes directly to cancer research in Fox's name ("Foundation Policies & Guidelines").

Participants in the annual Run are consumers of Fox's name and image—his brand has become synonymous with cancer research. They pledge money to The Terry Fox Foundation in, perhaps, an unconscious effort to purchase a forestalment of their own encounter with the dreaded cancer. Participants support medical research and pharmaceutical production, hence building the Canadian economy while simultaneously staving off fears of the abject Other within themselves (Kristeva 2–3) and reaffirming standards of normativity. The ill/disabled body's ability to haunt the normal body operates not only in the Terry Fox Run, but also more generally in Telethons and other fundraising and awareness campaigns that come to us through the media, evoking pity and/or fear and thus eliciting contributions to the cause.

Disability, like heteronormativity and celebrity, is a socially created, culturally perpetuated, and reiterative phenomenon. All three have in common their reliance, to varying degrees, on the production of staged events to keep their cultural worth in circulation. The Terry Fox Run is a spectacle, not unlike many celebrity events, in the sense that it is advertised, watched, participated in, and commented on across Canada and elsewhere in the world. The advertisements leading up to the Run invariably show images of Fox running. Media coverage of the Run reflects, sustains, and produces representations of disability. Just as repetitions are required to maintain heterosexual hegemony (McRuer 9), normative hegemony, too, requires reiterative acts. In everyday life these operations go largely unnoticed; however, in the conventions of spectacle the objectified impaired/disabled body (like the celebrity body), is made to appear as the representation that has been created. The physical difference of the body from the "norm" is emphasized and disability becomes *the* identity marker—the *core* identity—effectively obliterating all other subject positions of the individual.

In the Foucauldian sense, the disciplining panoptic gaze is turned on all who participate in the Terry Fox Run, and knowing they are in the field of visibility, they take up their subject position as either ill/disabled or non-disabled, unconsciously policing themselves to meet the standards of disabledness or normalcy. Participation in the annual Terry Fox Run is a reiterative, ritualistic, voluntary performance that nonetheless perpetuates medicine's ideological practices grounded in the normal/abnormal binary, but this performance is not, in and of itself, constitutive of the abnormal or normal subject. The voluntary act of choosing to participate in the Run is a self-reflexive act within the larger context of iterability, a process of ritualized performance (Butler, *Bodies That Matter* 95). We might, therefore, think of the Terry Fox Run not as a single, annual performance voluntarily undertaken by an individual but one of many cultural performances that are imbricated in hegemonic notions of normal and abnormal, abled and disabled, that enable our always-already subject position under the constraints that such subjection entails. Additionally, the Run traverses the space between the normal/abnormal body and citizenship. It disciplines "proper" citizens. Because Fox is inextricably linked to the Canadian nation-state, the Run is also a cultural performance of nationalism voluntarily undertaken, not unlike the ideal citizenship we see publicly practised yearly at Canada Day celebrations. Hence the Terry Fox Run melds philanthropic practice with the single concerns of cancer and citizenship while marginalizing the social, economic, and social complications of these two issues. As King rightly notes in *Pink Ribbons, Inc.,* because fundraising events and state-sponsored celebrations get their legitimacy from good-intentioned citizens, "they [event sponsors and organizers] are particularly resistant to critique or dissent" (124).

Ableism in Operation: The Overcoming Narrative and Disabled Celebrity

Narratives of overcoming disability are a familiar strategy in an able-bodied culture; they signal disability as a lack. These narratives are supported by scientific medical technologies and knowledge that offer a cure, a return to the fantasy of the normal, which is a veiled form of control. The more a disabled person can be seen to be normal, or least trying to be, the less likely that person will be stigmatized. That is the reward. The narrative of overcoming is believed by abled and disabled alike to be the best position one can have in relation to disability. Unfortunately, it does not reflect understandings of embodied experience. Therefore, I have come to representations of Terry Fox, and disability more generally, with a commitment to locate (but not fix) those meanings within social, political, and economic structures, processes, and relations (McRuer 210), and to allow for the possibility (desirability?) that in the spirit of critique, we can open up "a critical gap between disabled figures as fashioned corporeal others whose bodies carry social meaning and actual people with atypical bodies in real-world social relations" (Thomson 15). If I feel some unease with the way in which disability and celebrity intersect in the current historical moment, then perhaps others do as well.

Foucault's analysis of the disciplinary function of medicine shows how the embodied subject comes to be labelled and interpreted through the medical gaze and the power invested in it such that medical space can traverse and penetrate social space (31). Medicine, over time, has taken on an educative role to promote health, mainly for the benefit of the state (34). Health and physical ability are "not absolutes nor pre-given qualities of the human body, but function both as norms and as practices of regulation and control that produce the bodies they govern" (Shildrick and Price 433). Despite the ever-present possibility of any person becoming disabled at any time, most people do not see disability as a common fate but rather as an unfortunate and extraordinary circumstance. According to Tanya Titchkosky, maintaining current conceptions of disability tend to take precedence over knowledge of actual rates and kinds of disabilities: "Overcoming narratives, then, are part of how our consciousness of disability is governed" (181). The structure of the overcoming narrative invokes the "lone individual acting over and against disability imagined as a non-social condition" (184). The disability is turned into ability through the intervention of medical knowledge and technologies (Fox's prosthesis) and those benefiting are positioned between disability and ability in which "able-ist 'can do' values shine forth as if they are merely normal and even natural" (184). Against the figure of the normative Canadian self of Enlightenment ideals operates the impaired, disabled body as the stigmatized other "whose social role is to symbolically free the privileged, idealized figure of the [Canadian] self from the vagaries and vulnerabilities of embodiment" (Thomson 7).

Terry Fox undertook his Marathon of Hope to raise money for cancer research. He literally and wilfully took on the position of stigmatized other so that those with cancer in the future might be spared. He claimed: "Somewhere the hurting must stop...and I was determined to take myself to the limit for this cause..." (qtd. in Scrivener 63). Those were the words of a 1980 hero. Today, his constructed celebrity symbolically circulates to lend a shape and narrative to Canadian cultural values and sense of nationalism. His celebrity has currency because it valorizes the narrative of overcoming, which, in turn, confirms, reproduces, and sustains the ideal normal and normative Canadian, i.e., the *able-bodied*, young, white, male, heterosexual, middle-class person. When the Canadian Broadcasting Corporation (CBC) launched the 2004 television series *The Greatest Canadian*, for example, Terry Fox was celebrated and championed by CBC radio host Sook-Yin Lee in demonstrably ableist discourses.[2] As Julie Rak has also noted, Lee's argument rested mainly on the fact that "Fox himself rejected the trappings of celebrity when he refused corporate endorsements" (62–63), suggesting that true greatness eschews celebrity. However, Rak seems a bit uneasy, and rightly so, that Lee's supporting argument "does not fully embrace the contradictions and irony of celebrity discourse" (63). Rather, according to Rak, Lee's argument zeros in on the presentation of Fox's "merit and ordinariness as dialectical" and therefore these "traits become the values of the Canadian national imaginary" (63).

I, too, feel uneasy with Lee's depiction of Fox's traits because these are framed within an ableist interpretation, or at least an interpretation pitched to an ableist audience, that negates the very real difficulties and pain faced by ill and disabled people—they are anything *but* ordinary compared to the able-bodied, as much as they might or might not aspire to be. On the other hand, "ordinary" disabled people within the economy of disability discourse itself are masked by the "extraordinary" appeal of the Fox narrative of overcoming (Chivers 83). From a critical, disability-centred perspective, we might admire Fox's idealism and good old-fashioned "pluck" and want to be like him, yet we despise him for showing us what we cannot be. *There is no middle ground* for those of us who simply want to "be" in our disability without expectation or judgment imposed upon us by ableism's binary that insists we be either an athletic overachiever or an underachieving, passive, pathetic, pitiable person.

I ask that readers think beyond the celebrity of Terry Fox to consider other famous disabled Canadians—Rick Hansen,[3] Colette Bourgonje,[4] and others with acquired disability—to consider how the trajectory of their lives differs from those disabled by disease. The narratives of overcoming constituted in everyday radio and television news stories tend to organize around healthy, previously "whole" persons who have become disabled through accident. Like Fox, their disability commonly involves impairment of one or more limbs, perhaps because of spinal cord injury, perhaps for some other reason. Unlike Fox, however, they appear not to have a long-standing, debilitating, or life-threatening disease. Those with acquired-by-accident disabilities often live long and prosperous lives; those with serious underlying diseases, like Fox, often do not.

Moreover, the public presentation of individuals with an acquired disability frequently adheres to the signs and symbols of youth and vigour. Acquired disability distances itself from disease disability through the social production and circulation of staged events intended to visually reify the positive, the hopeful, the "one must overcome" refrain that becomes subtly internalized to mean *all* can overcome if they put their minds to it. Think, for example, of the wheelchair bungee jumping trend kick-started by the well-publicized September 2009 bungee jump by Rick Hansen and Rick Mercer at Whistler.[5] It is such activities that keep in circulation the "supercripple" image of disability that scholar Tobin Siebers likens to masquerade because "it serves a larger ideology requiring the exaggeration of disability, although here it is for the benefit of the able-bodied audience, not the disabled heroes themselves" (13). According to Sieber, the able body is the baseline in the definition of the human; therefore, human interest stories, such as those on wheelchair bungee jumping, that focus on a disabled body must "give an account of their protagonist's metamorphosis from nonhuman to human being" (13).

So how do the disabled, themselves, feel about Terry Fox's celebrity and disabled celebrity more generally? Earlier in this chapter I stated that my subject position as a disabled person living in Canada was such that I approached Terry Fox as a cultural text marked by ambivalence. I keep troubling over the cultural meaning of his celebrity and why I am fascinated by it, recognizing my implication in its perpetuation by the very act of writing this piece, yet wanting to dislodge the underlying ableist ideology to reframe the myth of the man and his continuing celebrity from a critical, disability-centred perspective grounded in the humanities. The "invisibility" of my disability marginalizes me within disability communities yet subjects me to the disbelieving gaze of able-bodied communities. However, in my claiming "disabled" as an identity marker, to quote Judith Butler on the subject of gender, "I would like to have it permanently unclear what precisely that sign signifies" ("Imitation and Gender Insubordination" 1707–1708). I provisionally assume that essentialist, marginalized subject position in order to resist the hierarchy of knowledges that have historically disqualified descriptions of disabled experience as statements of knowledge (Allen 103). In fact, the words "normal" and "abled" are floating signifiers with multiple meanings on which are superimposed totalizing master discourses that are motivated by a desire to return to the "normal," to the "origin," to the "authentic." Such a desire is doomed to fail, though, according to Judith Butler, because, like gender, "normal" "*is a kind of imitation for which there is no original*; in fact, it is a kind of imitation that produces the very notion of the original as an *effect* and consequence of the imitation itself" ("Imitation and Gender Insubordination" 1713, emphasis in original). Furthermore, "impairment," thought by many following the social model of disability to be reducible to a biomedical abnormality of the individual that becomes a disability through social arrangements, can instead be seen differently, as "no less a social construction than a credit rating or an income-tax bracket" (Allen 94–95). Critical disability theorist Shelley Tremain claims that "the materiality of the body cannot be dissociated from the historically contingent practices that bring it into being.... Indeed, it seems politically naïve to suggest that the term 'impairment' is value-neutral, that is, 'merely descriptive', as if there could ever be a description which was not also a *prescription* for the formulation of that to which it is claimed innocently to refer" (34, emphasis in original). Tremain's interpretation of impairment acknowledges corporeality and locates it within one of many disciplines of knowledge and discursive practices that have been brought to bear on the body over time. But even so, it does not take *fully* into account bodily pain and suffering. Pain is not socially constructed.

Therefore, I come to the myth of Terry Fox and Canadian disabled celebrity as one situated at a particular relational and historical juncture. I do believe that Terry Fox, the young man, was a hero given my understanding of how "hero" has been defined over time. We need our heroes; we need the hope they give us. His words inspire most Canadians, myself included: "I'm not a dreamer, and I'm not saying this will initiate any kind of definitive answer or cure to cancer, but I believe in miracles. I have to" ("Quotes from Terry"). However, I am troubled by the constructed celebrity attached to his name and image that has the effect of validating the disabilities of some but increasing the "otherness" of many more disabled people because they cannot meet the ideal of physical activity required (Wendell 64). Moreover, persons with many variations of illness and impairment are made invisible by the hyper-visibility of the white, male, middle-class, heterosexual athlete. From my situatedness, I do not see myself in that representation and I would argue many other ill and disabled Canadians do not either.

Notes

1 See "Facts" on The Terry Fox Foundation website for a list of the many accolades bestowed on Terry Fox during his lifetime and posthumously. See also Tanis MacDonald's "Terry Fox and the National Imaginary: Reading Eric Walter's Run" for a discussion of Fox's legacy in literature.

2 Fox placed second in the contest behind Saskatchewan Premier and "Father of Medicare" Tommy Douglas. All of the top ten Canadians were white, able-bodied men, with the exception of visible minority David Suzuki and disabled Terry Fox.

3 Rick Hansen is a Canadian Paralympian and activist for people with spinal cord injuries. He is best known for his 1985 Man in Motion Tour in which he covered 40,000 km in his wheelchair through thirty-four countries on four

continents. He raised $26 million for spinal cord research and like Terry Fox, was hailed as an international hero ("Man in Motion Tour").

4 Colette Bourgonje is one of the few Canadian athletes to win multiple medals in both Paralympic Summer and Winter Games. She competes in both wheelchair racing and cross-country sit-skiing ("Colette Bourgonje").

5 A March 2012 video of Christine Rougoor, an ambassador for the Rick Hansen Foundation, bungee jumping while strapped to her wheelchair has, for example, gone viral ("Paraplegic bungee jumps off B.C. gorge in wheelchair").

Canadian Political Celebrity: From Trudeau to Trudeau

Jennifer Bell

When Pierre Elliott Trudeau burst onto the Canadian political landscape, he brought an energy that revived and refreshed the country and electorate, inspiring both worship and vilification. From his candidacy for Liberal Party leader in 1968, to his multiple re-elections as prime minister, the media lavished attention on him, as did electrified and adoring crowds. He projected a cultural image that could turn the electorate into an audience, and voters into fans. While television had already begun to change the way politicians performed on the public stage in North America, Trudeau was the first Canadian politician to capitalize on its power. Trudeau matured as a leader as the country itself came of age, developing a relationship with the public through the increasingly relevant medium of television. He capitalized on the cultural festivities of the late 1960s in which Canadians were waving a new flag, revelling in the country's centenary, and celebrating Expo 67. Trudeau benefited electorally from his ability to represent and project this changing socio-political culture, and he constructed a public image and political celebrity status within this frame of reference.

This chapter interrogates how political celebrity operates and has evolved in a distinctly Canadian context. Media and public consideration of the politician as a celebrity is not a recent development; nor is the fact that attention is often lavished on politicians themselves, rather than on their policies. Changing modes of communication only increase this phenomenon, and political performances must continually adapt to such changing cultural expectations. This evolution has operated in conjunction with a shift from a traditional commodity-focused model of politics, where politicians function as consumer goods, to a show-business model, where politicians function as cultural goods (Street, "Celebrity" 92). In this model, aesthetics, image construction, and presentation are even more crucial to political success, as politicians build relationships with the public through traditional and new media. While successful impression management is not synonymous with political celebrity, it is certainly a key element of its development in popular culture.

As such, political celebrity does not exist in isolation; it operates and evolves within cultural and historical periods. This chapter considers Pierre Trudeau's growth as a celebrity figure beginning in the late 1960s and compares it to his son Justin Trudeau's ascent to the public spotlight fifty years later. Pierre Trudeau engaged with cultural constructions of celebrity through changing political conditions within Canada, the rise of television and its affective function, and the use of symbolic imagery and performance. In Justin Trudeau, as leader of the Liberal Party of Canada (LPC) and the twenty-third prime minister of Canada, we see the emergence of a public figure through the strategic manipulation of digital communications and witness how he must both embrace and resist his familial political inheritance and ascribed celebrity status while attempting to create his own achievements and brand.

Political Celebrity—Venal, Vapid, and Vainglorious?

To begin, it is crucial to both clarify and muddy the notion of political celebrity, and to consider how it operates within the broader context of celebrity, as well as within Canadian political and popular culture. John Street identifies two general classifications of political celebrity: the elected politician who uses celebrity or the techniques of popular culture for political gain, and the celebrity who speaks out on political issues and attempts to influence government or elections based on his or her fame ("Do Celebrity Politics" 346), to which I refer as celebrity activism or celebrity endorsement. This chapter is concerned with the first category, broad as it is. Marsh, 't Hart, and Tindall further parse this first category into the "politician celebrity," an officeholder whose public behaviour, private life, or association with celebrities transports his own public persona from beyond the traditional political sphere into the celebrity sphere, and the "politician who uses others' celebrity," an office-holder who uses specific celebrities and others' fame to endorse his own candidature, party, or policies (327). These narrower categories, however, often overlap, as do the distinctions between public performance, ambition, and lifestyle choices. Many politicians, such as both Trudeaus, occupy both of these categories.[1]

Of course, the constitution and production of celebrity are not uniform across cultural domains or industries (Turner 17). Political celebrities are sometimes considered outside the realm of celebrity because of their perceived legitimacy within the public sphere. Daniel Boorstin's famous definition that a celebrity is a person who is "known for his well-known-ness" (*The Image* 57) would then not necessarily apply to a politician, who has earned his or her public status very self-consciously, even though Boorstin acknowledges that politicians have become increasingly engaged in constructing and projecting images of themselves to the public (*The Image* 249). David Meyer and Joshua Gamson also dissociate traditional celebrity status from formal, institutional power, claiming that celebrities possess autonomy from state institutions, and derive any influence they may have from attention. In contrast, they suggest that other elites command public attention because of their power to influence (184). Politicians, for example, derive their status explicitly from these institutions, even if they cultivate their notoriety and encourage the dissemination of their constructed image. Graeme Turner also separates the notoriety of public officials from that of celebrities. He writes that the contemporary celebrity usually emerges from the industries of sport and entertainment, and suggests that their private lives will eventually garner greater public interest than their professional lives. He contrasts them specifically with public officials, by claiming that their fame "does not necessarily depend on the position or achievements that gave them their prominence in the first instance" (Turner 3). Echoing Boorstin, he writes, "the modern celebrity may claim no special achievements other than the attraction of public attention" (Turner 3). Again, Turner attributes the public interest in public officials to their position alone, rather than the cultural value they hold because of their position.

Underlying these descriptions of celebrity is an assumption that contemporary culture is both inauthentic and vacuous (Turner 6). As such, it is ironic that elected officials are distinguished from these characterizations, as inauthenticity is usually a quality associated with politicians. Far from being heralded for their accomplishments, in Canada, politicians are often treated with disdain and distrust by the media and public for being "venal, vapid, and vainglorious" (A. Cohen 203). The political celebrity thus hangs perilously between two, often negative, cultural stereotypes: that of the celebrity, and that of the politician. A contributing factor to this perceived inauthenticity, for the political celebrity, is the notion that celebrity is not an inherent quality, or a property of specific individuals, but rather a calculated process based on deliberate performance, public relations objectives, and media decisions. Politicians, their staff, strategists, the media, and increasingly public relations and publicity industries (Turner 10) are all involved in the production of constructing the politician's public image and promoting it to the electorate. This process appears remarkably similar to the construction of the celebrity for public consumption. As Chris Rojek states, "No celebrity now acquires public recognition without the assistance of cultural intermediaries who operate to stage-manage celebrity presence in the eyes of the public" (10).[2] These processes can appear contrived and untrustworthy, leading to negative stereotypes. As a result, one of the factors in a politician's success is the ability for his or her performance to address political realities in ways that appear to be sincere and believable (Drake and Higgins 390), and not part of a contrived production.

This model of successful political performance and communication has been long recognized, but has evolved with changing technology and cultural practices. Joseph Schumpeter, in 1943, established a connection between the world of commodities and the world of politics, proposing that political communication was a branch of commercial marketing. For Schumpeter, a politician achieved power by selling the public a desirable product (Street, "Celebrity Politician" 87). This model remains influential, but seventy years later, in an age of visual and instantaneous communications, the added element of aesthetics is crucial to making this product. While the art of public relations—the calculated presentation of politicians and their policies—is now the accepted practice for gaining desired media and public attention, it is nonetheless often treated as suspect by a probing media. Journalists attempt to unpeel the layers of political performance they perceive as inauthentic, to expose an unadulterated, uncontrived public figure whose story may have more resonance with the public than campaign talking points. The attention laid on the politicians themselves, rather than their policies, lends itself to the politics of personality, and in turn helps create and promote the condition of celebrity.

The media's attempt to expose and unmask public figures is also of commercial advantage to the news industry in a competitive market increasingly dominated by entertainment-hungry and personality-driven consumers. Journalists and news organizations thus often frame politics in a more personal manner in order to attract and retain the public's interest. Political leaders and parties respond in kind, focusing on their public image and consciously manipulating lifestyle symbols to construct an ideal, responsive public (Taras, *Power* 48). This reciprocal relationship between politicians and the media promotes and encourages a focus on aesthetics and celebrity within politics. When politicians are presented as performers, and appear to be more concerned with their public image than with their constituents, it can feed public cynicism and scepticism, in turn justifying these preconceived stereotypes. Street suggests that political communication is a branch of show business rather than commercial marketing, where "the currency is celebrity and fame, and the products are stars and performances." He maintains that politicians are still commodities, but they belong to the field of cultural goods rather than consumer goods ("Celebrity Politician" 86, 92).

In Canada, this is exemplified through electoral politics and campaigns traditionally being reported as horse races. The media generally pit the leaders of the contending parties against each other, thereby creating digestible and familiar narratives for the public. Coverage of campaigns and Parliament focuses on leaders, strategy, tactics, public opinion polling, as well as personality and conflict (Waddell, "Berry'd" 121), all of which places the public figure, rather than the policy, at centre stage. For decades now, during federal elections, the leader's tour across the country has been the focus of each party's national campaign, and therefore that of the press (Taras and Waddell 77). Parties provide the media with pre-assembled and carefully scripted crowds, rallies, photo opportunities, and spectators available for comment. In other words, they are building up the politician as celebrity, encouraging him or her to adopt this role. This prominence of leadership in media coverage encourages a strategic focus on the leader as individual (Drake and Higgins 376–377), which in turn lends itself to celebrity politics.

Canada: The Times They Are a-Changin Have Changed

In Canada, politics in the nineteenth and the first half of the twentieth century generally operated behind a veil of propriety and respectability (D. Marshall 243). While a persuasive performance had always been necessary to achieve political success, and a mild suspicion had certainly accompanied those who sought life in the public sphere, in Canada, the media most often covered politicians with a respect befitting the office. In this environment, public recognition was directed toward the position and the politician's civic actions, rather than the individual (Inglis 4). By the 1960s, however, both politically and culturally, Canada was changing. Journalistic practices and literary conventions were being restructured, the rise of television was changing mass media, and far-reaching social reforms were being introduced, all of which helped set the stage for the rise of political celebrity in the form of Pierre Trudeau. A more open and tolerant attitude was emerging in Canada about what could be "discussed, written, and printed" (D. Marshall 243), which included both political reporting and life writing. Politicians were no longer being held in reverence: where political biographies had once been restrained, authors were now willing to expose previously private details, and not afraid to be penetrating and incisive (D. Marshall 243).[3] This coincided with a boom in memoir, where cabinet ministers were revealing information and personal details once considered inappropriate for public consumption.[4] No longer were politicians inaccessible; the political and societal barriers that were being eroded meant that "The social dimension of the human experience was also critical to understanding what it meant to be Canadian. The personal was now political" (D. Marshall 246).

The backdrop to this trend was Trudeau himself. As Prime Minister Lester Pearson's justice minister in the mid- to late 1960s, Trudeau introduced legislation that would reform divorce laws, and proposed amendments to the Criminal Code which would entrench more liberalized notions of family life and sexuality in Canada. Social consequences of these reforms included the fact that traditionally private affairs were becoming more open in the public sphere, and gradually less regulated. Trudeau represented that debate and progress (D. Marshall 245). Trudeau also firmly promoted a Canadian federalism that included Quebec, and eschewed his home province's separatist leanings, which heightened his profile. Celebrated Canadian communications theorist Marshall McLuhan, who maintained an active correspondence with Trudeau throughout his time as prime minister, argued that Canada had never possessed an identity and that Trudeau's image was shaped by this cultural gap (McLuhan, "Story" BR 36), giving Trudeau an opportunity to serve as a "unifying image" during the campaign (McLuhan, Letters 356). Furthermore, Canada was celebrating its centenary, and Expo 67 brought the country together in a celebration of achievement and hope. For some, the figure of Trudeau, and the reforms he championed, "reflected the spirit of a country that wanted to change" (English, *Citizen* 471). As Peter C. Newman wrote, "in pre-Expo Canada it would have been almost impossible to imagine [Trudeau] as a serious contender. Now we don't have to go on muttering hopefully, 'the times they are achangin.' The times have changed" (quoted in English, *Citizen* 471). Trudeau was a sophisticated, intellectual nonconformist who possessed the ability to inject new life into old institutions, and a great deal of the public responded with enthusiasm. Trudeau himself was aware of the influence of this cultural climate on his success. As he wrote in *Memoirs*, "I had to believe, too, that the phenomenon was part of the spirit of the times. We had just come out of the Centennial celebrations; the year before had seen the remarkable success of Expo 67. The mood of the country was still one of festivity, and I happened to be there to profit from it" (P. Trudeau 100). While previous politicians in Canada had gained popularity and renown, this erosion of the boundaries between the public and private spheres, and these cultural changes, helped Trudeau create a different, more visceral relationship with the public as well as a notion of political celebrity new to Canada.

Cool Face + Cool Medium = Hot Press

The changing nature of political communication, in the form of television, was critical to Trudeau's emergence as a political celebrity in Canada. Television had contributed to his rise as a public figure prior to his political career, and while he professed initial discomfort and wariness with the medium, he quickly mastered his presentation, developing a warm and symbiotic relationship with the camera (English, *Citizen* 256). Television had made visual image management crucial, as political strategists had witnessed very clearly with the success of John F. Kennedy in the United States. As John English, Trudeau's official biographer, wrote, "The choice of Trudeau as Liberal leader and then as prime minister arose from the transformation of politics caused by television" (*Just Watch Me* 34). Trudeau's personal magnetism and affinity with the camera made television an ideal medium for him to engage with Canadians and cultivate fame. As McLuhan wrote to Trudeau in 1969, "You are the only political image of our time able to use the T.V. medium without being forced to become a tribal buffoon or cartoon" (Letters 363). An astounding seventeen million Canadians watched the Liberal convention in which Trudeau was elected leader, and almost as many watched the leaders' debate of the 1968 election (English, *Just Watch Me* 18–19).[5] McLuhan identified Trudeau as possessing "'cool' TV power" (Letters 354) and suggested to Trudeau in their extensive correspondence that he "came into his own with TV" ("Story" BR 36). For McLuhan, "cool" media, like television, was that which required more active participation from the audience for them to determine meaning. For Trudeau, this meant he was able to construct his own audience, and he shared McLuhan's intuition that the new media had transformed not only politics, but also what a politician represented to the electorate (English, *Just Watch Me* 18).

Trudeau effectively used television to cultivate an enigmatic image of himself, as well as to connect to viewers, carefully constructing his public image for the camera. As English writes, "the mystical mingled with simple good luck and crafty planning to make Trudeau's television presence so striking. He consciously created an aura of intrigue, adventure, and intellectual brilliance about him" (*Citizen* 258–259). McLuhan wrote to Trudeau telling him that his image was a corporate mask, as it was "inclusive" and did not require "private nuance"—he appeared iconic and sculptural. McLuhan elaborates by saying that "a mask 'puts on' an audience. At a masquerade we are not private persons" (Letters 354). Trudeau acknowledged this public mask in the documentary based on his memoirs, where he discussed the politician's role as consummate performer, and the necessity of donning a mask to be successful in the House of Commons or in speaking to a crowd (*Memoirs*). As we see with Trudeau, creating this esoteric element was crucial in the making of his celebrity, as it increased the public's desire to know and understand him. Fred Inglis identifies a powerful contradiction underlying the phenomenon of celebrity—the incongruity of knowability and distance. He asserts that political leaders are intensely familiar by way of their presence in our homes (through the media), but that they also possess the remoteness of the supernatural, and this may suggest the reason why people both worship and vilify the famous (Inglis 156). Television allowed Trudeau to embody the condition of celebrity as both pervasive and remote, and the prominence he gained through this medium contributed to the worship and vilification he received from the Canadian public.

Television, and the intimacy and proximity it can generate, also enabled Trudeau to build on his relationship with the public through the contagious nature of affect. Because television can amplify and intensify affects, and dramatically increase the rapidity and reach of its communication (Gibbs 1), it helped generate Trudeau's remarkable ascent. Furthermore, as Marusya Bociurkiw argues, "These contagious affects give [viewers] a sense of belonging—if not to the nation then to the virtual community of television watchers and newspaper readers" (108). The images of Trudeau amongst throngs of supporters that were televised to citizens across the country inspired this sense of belonging and connection in viewers—increasing Trudeau's appeal and building his celebrity stature. While it is impossible to identify the exact rationale behind voters' intentions, the Trudeaumania sweeping the country, escalated in part by television, helped explain the Liberals' 1968 election victory, and the healthy 75 per cent voter turnout. These televised images would encourage and propel more citizens to engage in this cultural moment. As Trudeau wrote in his memoirs about the 1968 campaign, "Almost everywhere I went, exceptional enthusiasm was apparent in the crowds that I found around me. People came in droves to rallies where I was speaking...the streets would be lined with masses of people of all ages and all races" (100). In Victoria, he wrote that he had to be "lowered from a helicopter down to a park at the top of a hill that was totally surrounded by thousands of people" (100).

The media scrutiny and public attention continued to increase, even as Trudeau vigorously attempted (with only limited success) to separate his public and private lives. The transition between public figure and celebrity, Graeme Turner postulates, occurs when media interest in politicians' activities transfers from their public role, such as their specific achievements, to the details of their private lives. Often, Turner argues, it is the high profile achieved by politicians' public activities that prompts, or provides the alibi for, this process of "celebritisation." Conversely, however, the celebrity's general claim on public attention can overshadow his or her original achievements (Turner 8). Indeed, the press could be merciless, as Trudeau's former wife Margaret Trudeau wrote in *Consequences*: "I hated the way people felt they owned me, so that they could comment on my actions and beliefs with impunity as rudely and critically as they wished. I felt constantly under observation of the harshest and least forgiving kind" (11–12).[6] This personal scrutiny was often unwelcome, damaging, and was based, in part, on the public's hunger to consume the private lives of celebrity political figures in simultaneous worship and vilification.

The press often disregarded Trudeau's fierce desire for privacy, but it appeared willing to accept the image that Trudeau was cultivating—that of a masculine, athletic, paternal leader. These features lent themselves to media attention as they focus on personality, performance, and image. For example, the media portrayed Trudeau as an attentive father who maintained a warm relationship with his three sons, an image which showed an alluring personal side to the prime minister, but also reinforced paternalism in a masculine world of politics. Trudeau also encouraged media attention and celebrity status through his athletic ability, a quality, for a politician, again associated with conceptions of leadership and masculinity. He gave the media many opportunities to capture photos of him swimming, surfing, skiing, and canoeing. Trudeau extended his political performance beyond oral and aural communication to his advantage. He excelled at creating meaning through kinetic, gestural, and embodied performance (Drake and Higgins 386), another element of his celebrity performance. As McLuhan informed Trudeau in December of 1968, "Your Grey Cup kick-off was, of course, a media triumph. This is audience participation and image-making at its best" (Letters 359).

Trudeau also encouraged the media and public to view him through the lens of celebrity by affiliating with national and international leaders and other celebrities. While it is customary for a prime minister to meet public figures, by promoting these associations, he increased his own cultural value and status. Rumours and speculations concerning his dating life and romances abounded; he was photographed entertaining various popular music and film stars,[7] as well as sport stars and prominent Canadians. Trudeau's associations with international celebrities lent him additional status and glamour.

But despite the public's growing fascination with Trudeau's private life, his public life still provoked the greatest stir, and the details of his life that often elicited the most commentary were those relating to his position on French-Canadian nationalism and separatism (D. Marshall 248). While he rose to a new level of fame in Canadian politics, his stature still worked in conjunction with his policies, rather than overshadowing them.

One potentially adverse effect of the predominance of the politics of personality and image is that in order to remain media and television friendly, political leaders might abstain from healthy, critical public debate and civic discussion to avoid clashes with the media (Taras, "Past" 7). Furthermore, the prominence of political celebrity in political culture has the potential to detract attention from substantial policy issues and the complexity of serious events. Ironically, some journalists and politicians fear that an emphasis on celebrity undermines the reputation of parliamentarians, which in turn could weaken Canada's democracy. For example, in reference to the national campaign of 1968, Trudeau stated, "I may have been a bit concerned that people were responding less to my ideas than to 'the Trudeau phenomenon,' as the press called it. But I was in the middle of an election campaign, and I could only rejoice that so much interest was being shown by the electorate" (P. Trudeau, *Memoirs* 102). While Trudeau was somewhat wary of this attention, he certainly recognized its strategic and political value.

These changing norms of political culture, communication, and performance can also, however, be very positive. Celebrity politics, according to Mark Wheeler, can be used to engage disaffected members of the electorate in a reconfigured political process.[8] Furthermore, such forms of activity can provide "a basis for those citizens who wish to participate in terms of their own political efficacy to define a wider sense of the common good" (Wheeler 421). The politics of personal style offers popular appeal and emotional identification. It has the potential to cut through the bureaucracy and institutions of government and downplay traditional party allegiances. As such, the celebrity politician can make debates concrete because, as David Marshall claims, people can more readily identify with personalities than with abstract concepts (D. Marshall 236). Citizens, through their captivation with Trudeau, could thus become more engaged with the country and the political process itself.

Even if Trudeau encouraged a reading of himself within the discourses of celebrity, as a politician he and the media were still focused on his policies and his contribution to Canada. He could make a significant impact on Canadian policy, as noted, in part because of his prowess with political communication and his celebrity status. While he was a divisive and controversial political figure for many reasons, his initial celebrity status and popularity (which certainly wavered) helped him gain loyalty and drive his initiatives forward.[9]

Ascribed, Achieved, Attributed or Avoided...Political Celebrity from Pierre to Justin: (Re)Branding the Brand

While Pierre Trudeau represents the pinnacle of political celebrity in Canada to date, the politics of personality are still integral to contemporary political life. Former prime minister Paul Martin, for example, publicly associated with celebrity activist and rock star Bono to increase his own visibility and align himself with the cause of African relief. While more reserved elected officials, such as former prime minister Stephen Harper, might appear as Canadian antitheses to this concept of political celebrity, the role of politician is always a highly constructed performance. Speaking to reporters during a 2007 G8 summit, Harper told them that "meeting celebrities isn't my shtick...that was the shtick of the previous guy" when asked why he wouldn't be meeting with Bono during the Summit ("Harper says"). His goal, at the time, was to create differences between himself and the previous government, and to show that he was more interested in serious issues and public policy. (Years later into his tenure as prime minister, he and the other party leaders did meet with Bono.) Even if Harper's public image was not always considered media-friendly, his image management was still tightly controlled and is designed to project stability and confidence in Canada and its economy. He still used celebrity discourses to perform his leadership role in an environment where aesthetics are important, and all forms of communication are constructed for political advantage or public promotion.

Despite Harper's many years of electoral success based, in part, on this model of public image management, voter turnout across the country was only 61 per cent in the 2011 federal election. Public opinion polls revealed that a majority of Canadians shared a negative opinion of politicians, viewed them with a combination of mistrust and suspicion, and didn't find any of the political parties satisfying (Taras and Waddell 74). While exceptions exist, the fact that many citizens lack confidence in elected officials, are disinclined to join political parties, and have a dwindling attachment to governmental institutions is discouraging for the democratic system (Giasson, Lees-Marshment, and Marland, "Introducing" 19). While Rudyard Griffiths shows that a growing number of Canadians might be involved in other forms of political engagement, such as community networks, local advocacy, internet activism, public demonstrations, or consumer boycotts rather than formal political engagement, he argues that this shift can erode a sense of shared nationalism, civic literacy, and citizenship, and can lead to a "loss of community or sense of connection to a public life of larger meaning" (38–39, 51). Even with the galvanizing power of social media and these non-traditional forms of political engagement, electoral studies show that the number of individuals under the age of thirty who join civic organizations or political parties, volunteer in their communities, donate money to causes, or vote in elections has decreased from previous generations (Taras, "Past" 4).

It is within this cultural and political climate that Justin Trudeau, almost fifty years later, galvanized voters. If the cultural conditions that led to Pierre Trudeau's emergence as a political celebrity reflected a new sense of Canadian nationalism, ironically, the citizens' potential alienation from political activity, in part, encouraged Justin Trudeau's leadership campaign and then general election campaign to return to an unambiguous promotion of the politics of personality. Justin Trudeau's leadership campaign deliberately promoted the candidate, rather than policies or ideology, and consciously used celebrity politics and digital communication to fill the aforementioned social void. Shortly before he won the leadership of the LPC, he remarked that his campaign drew in "lots of Liberals who'd grown disaffected...young people who...didn't think that politics had any room or space or interest for them" as well as newcomers to politics, people from other organizations, and other parts of the [political] spectrum" (Den Tandt, "Justin" 3). This approach was intended to be broad, inclusive, and positive, and he vowed to practise politics differently than his Conservative and New Democratic Party (NDP) opponents (Den Tandt, "Justin" 2). Many of his leadership campaign events were held at university campuses to youthful audiences, a demographic under-represented in the democratic process. As he speculated before he entered the leadership race, youth are "tremendously frustrated because they don't see politics as changing anything. That's where I think a bold message will wake them up" (Geddes 5). His leadership campaign, however, lacked this bold message in terms of a policy platform; he was selling his image and approach as the message.

The speech in which he announced his bid for the leadership of the Liberal Party, for example, was ambiguous, generic, and vacuous. Canadians learned that he "absolutely loves Canada" and that Canada needs a foreign policy "that can bring us hope." While this rhetoric was vague and unsubstantiated, as one journalist noted, "no matter, he said it with apparent conviction" (Weston). This supports the perspective that celebrity politics does not necessarily diminish or undermine political literacy—it is merely a different form of political communication, which possesses the ability to reach different audiences. As Street writes, "political communication cannot be separated from popular culture...it is about capturing the popular imagination, about giving acts and ideas symbolic importance" (*Politics* 38). Political celebrities with an aptitude for media relations might then be in a better position to advance their agenda, as charisma, according to Alex

Marland, is a natural communications talent that cannot be manufactured by image handlers (3). Justin Trudeau took this one step further, in that he purposefully lacked an agenda, and his leadership campaign was intentionally thin on policy. Conviction along with the elusive likeability and inherited celebrity status appeared to be enough for him to achieve political success, as witnessed by his victory in the Liberal leadership campaign. Furthermore, as leader, he did not immediately propose any detailed policy alternatives to the governing Conservative Party of Canada (CPC).

Shortly after Justin Trudeau was elected leader, the CPC released attack ads on both television and the Internet portraying the new leader as shallow and inexperienced. The ads accused Trudeau of lacking the qualifications and judgment required to be prime minister and mocked his experience, in part because of his celebrity stature, and were adorned with tinselly flashy stars, emphasizing his famous last name. They also showed Trudeau undressing in a simulated strip show for a charity event—all to suggest a frivolity, foolishness, and shallowness unbefitting a prime minister. Throughout the 2015 federal campaign, the CPC ads continued to criticize Trudeau's lack of experience or readiness for the position of prime minister. The ads even mocked his coiffed hair, implying that he represented superficiality over substance. Meanwhile, Trudeau claimed that his pre-writ ads were "built on the same positive, hopeful and hard-working tone" that he pursued during his leadership campaign ("Trudeau says"). These ads focused on defining Trudeau on his own terms, as an individual, in an attempt to differentiate himself from what he considered the negativity and cynicism of the CPC. He reinforced this message on his website, where he encouraged Canadians to "be part of the change" with the tagline "Hope and Hard Work," rhetoric which again avoided policy and invoked successful slogans of the late opposition leader Jack Layton and United States President Barack Obama.[10] Trudeau's campaign ads initially very purposefully eschewed the discourse of frivolous celebrity with which the CPC had attempted to brand him. As the campaign progressed, however, and Canadians began responding to the Trudeau brand, he adapted his performance and was able to play up his chosen discourse of celebrity—an inspirational leader of buoyancy and optimism. His campaign ads culminated in an image of throngs of supporters surrounding him—a throwback to the Trudeaumania of his father's generation, and a visual showing that he was embracing his role as celebrity politician and encouraging that reading.

The political environment in which Justin Trudeau built his cultural capital is far more sophisticated in terms of political marketing and technology than that of his father. While national Liberal Party campaigns in the late 1960s and 70s were employing electoral techniques still practised today,[11] the time spent by operatives planning and executing campaigns, as well as resources allocated to writ and pre-writ campaigning, has increased significantly since this time period. Furthermore, the pace has quickened, and instant communication is necessary and expected due to a twenty-four-hour news cycle where events unfold in real time over multiple mediums. Political marketing now includes a range of political communication, such as advertising, public relations, telemarketing, and campaign decisions across various media and digital platforms (Giasson, Lees-Marshment, and Marland, "Introducing" 4). Market research allows political operatives to make informed and responsive decisions about campaign strategy and tailor messages to particular demographics (Marland, Giasson, and Lees-Marshment xii). The successful implementation of these techniques works in conjunction with the promotion of the individual and construction and cultivation of celebrity. Here, we see the importance of Schumpeter's marketing model of politics as a building block to Street's show-business model.

One aspect of political marketing that lends itself to the formation of celebrity in Canada, as well as around the globe, in the twenty-first century is successful branding. The creation of a brand, and relationship to that brand, is important not just for a successful outcome, but in creating an attachment and trusting relationship between voters, the politician, and the party. Ideally, the relationship can "sustain itself over the long term through crises and the ebb and flow of political fortune, while offering a differentiated brand from the competition" (Giasson, Lees-Marshment, and Marland, "Introducing" 10). Justin Trudeau possessed the immediate, advantageous ability to build on his father's brand because he entered the public sphere by occupying what Rojek identifies as "ascribed celebrity," where his status is acquired through blood relation, rather than achieved (17).[12] While Pierre Trudeau was often a polarizing figure, and certainly not universally popular in Canada, he still represents a period in time when the Liberal Party was thriving, and Justin Trudeau's surname alone was enough to provide political operatives with a sense of potential for his electoral success.

Most Canadians were introduced to Justin Trudeau, as a public figure, at his father's funeral in 2000, where he delivered the eulogy. His carefully crafted performance inevitably sparked rumours about his political ambitions. Trudeau's funeral, as Bociurkiw wrote, created "an insatiable desire for images and memories of Trudeau," which in turn produced other desires "for an imaginary historical moment of democracy and justice; for an alterity that predated the hegemony of globalization; for the innocence of the 1960s" (103). This performance indirectly invited Canadians to consider Justin Trudeau within the same discourse of celebrity as his father.

While this reading might burden Justin Trudeau with false opportunism, he admitted in an interview two years later that he was well aware of the power of his eulogy: "Yes, it was theatrical. It was as bad as [the movie] *Armageddon*, punching all those buttons. But that's what it needed to do. It wasn't designed to please journalists" (Gatehouse, "Profile"). Whether this statement is idealistically naive, supercilious, or both, it implies that Justin Trudeau felt that he and his messages did not require media approval and that he could cultivate a relationship with the public independently from them, based on his ascribed celebrity. Returning to the eulogy, his skilled and emotional oratory reminded many viewers of his father and the era that he represented, intentional or not (Bociurkiw 112).

Despite Justin Trudeau's association with his father's brand, he remains a line extension of it, which means by definition that he is somewhat different from the parent brand (Marland 9). As Trudeau stated when running for leader, "My father's values and vision of this country obviously form everything I have as values and ideals. But this is not the ghost of my father running.... This is me" (Gatehouse "Justin"). Justin Trudeau's success relied on being able to capitalize on the positive aspects of his ascribed celebrity and brand extension, but also to foster and achieve an independent image for the public to embrace, rather than allowing the CPC to define him through attack ads.

Justin Trudeau's candidacy as a young, affable individual with ascribed celebrity status was also crucial for the rebranding of the Liberal Party. Since 2005, when the Liberals lost power in Parliament, their political fortunes had spiralled downward. In the 2011 federal election, they were reduced to third-party status for the first time in Canadian history. In order to remain relevant and a credible option for Canadians, the party required a breath of life. Personality politics had been extremely effective for Jack Layton and the NDP in the 2011 federal election, and this NDP surge was part of the reason Liberal support had collapsed. Justin Trudeau's presence in the Liberal leadership race in 2012 was crucial to re-energizing the Liberal Party and Liberal brand. While the two previous unsuccessful Liberal leaders, Stéphane Dion and Michael Ignatieff, were formidable intellectuals, they did not inspire mass adulation in Canada. Justin Trudeau, meanwhile, with his ascribed celebrity status, possessed the ability to change the image of the LPC and differentiate it from the governing CPC.

Follow, Tweet, Like... Vote?

As leader of a third party constantly trying to improve its electoral appeal, Justin Trudeau was required to reach out to Canadians and to market himself in a contemporary political landscape. He, like his father, used the communications media of his historical moment to his advantage. All Canadian political parties have become increasingly tech-savvy—they have heightened the quality and quantity of their digital communications, and their on line presence has become more integrated with overall marketing and election strategies (Small, "Friends" 193). Justin Trudeau's leadership campaign, for example, relied on gaining supporters on digital platforms such as Twitter and Facebook to create momentum and publicity within this social media landscape. His use of digital communications was inextricably tied to his engagement strategies and how he created relationships with voters. The final weekend before the LPC's leadership vote, Trudeau was the clear front-runner in the race. At that point, he had collected over 198,000 Twitter followers, more than the other five candidates combined, as well as receiving more than 75,000 likes for his Facebook page (Sagan).[13]

Putting these numbers in perspective, 198,000 Twitter followers only represents a very small percentage of eligible voters, and one can appreciate why Tamara Small maintained in 2012 that Canadian parties had not embraced e-democracy.[14] While the Internet can be an important tool in campaigning and building celebrity, to date, it has not transformed Canadian democratic processes (Small, "e-ttack" 171). Small argued that the Internet is still being used to perform and supplement traditional and off-line campaign activities, rather than create new possibilities. For example, the attack ads previously mentioned might be a clever marketing tool but they are still unidirectional. The 2011 federal election was promoted as Canada's first "social media campaign," but these grand expectations fell flat. While parties and candidates adopted new technology in the campaign, they used it for conventional purposes—to broadcast their messages rather than to engage in debate and dialogue with voters (Waddell, "Final Thoughts" 370). Furthermore, despite all of the public conversations about engaging young people and social media, only a very small percentage of younger Canadians used social media to follow the election, and voter turnout among this demographic was modest, changing little from 2008 (Taras and Waddell 75, 82).[15] In the 2015 campaign, early analysis indicates that the use of social media had increased. Twitter reported that there were over 770,000 election-related tweets on election day, with over 150,000 tweets sent directly to @justintrudeau (R. King). Concerted initiatives by Elections Canada as well as less formalized efforts by other groups to engage youth voters had also increased. This paralleled and complimented Justin Trudeau's strategy. His attention to social media and the youth demographic kept his name in the public sphere, and he used it as a means to promote himself. Voter turnout increased to 69 per cent. Political marketing, branding, and social media do not necessarily create a celebrity in politics, but they can influence the performance and contribute to the process.

On October 19, 2015, Justin Trudeau and his LPC swept to power with the largest ever increase of seats in Canadian history. The CPC had set expectations low for Trudeau, categorizing him as a celebrity politician not capable of the demands of the role of prime minister. At the beginning of the campaign, when the writ was dropped in August, this was still a perceived reality—polls indicated that the Liberals would not have won a general election. The polls, however, gradually shifted over an extremely long campaign. While there are multiple reasons for this, Canadians were receptive to Trudeau's star power and his approach to politics, as insubstantial as the CPC might perceive it. Since being elected prime minister, Trudeau has embraced the spotlight, the performance, and the role of popular and political celebrity, both in Canada and internationally. He has been dubbed "Prime Minister Selfie" because of the inordinate amount of photographs he takes with the public, with voters, and with people attracted to his celebrity status. He was named the Canadian Press Newsmaker of the Year for 2015. Before doing one-on-one interviews with any Canadian news agencies, he had international features in the magazines *VOGUE* and *New York*. Trudeau is actively cultivating a personal relationship, through his celebrity status, between the politician and the public. When asked about his ubiquity, and whether his "charm offensive" was part of an overall strategy, he responded that "It's not about image, it's about substance" (Maloney). However, of course, it is very much about image, and this star power had, in part, increased political engagement and the Liberal Party's fortunes in the general election. Critics, however, would justifiably question this substance to which Trudeau refers, and how it might detract from how policy decisions are made.

Celebrity has changed and evolved in Canada since Pierre Trudeau's leadership. All politicians perform their roles in the public sphere, assisted by political marketing, communications strategy, and impression management. But while political celebrity may be an advantage, voter behaviour, of course, encompasses many more considerations (Marland 3). As Pierre Trudeau wrote in his memoirs, in recollecting the height of Trudeaumania, "The real question, of course was whether all those people had come to hear me, personally, or were they simply there to see this newcomer, this neo-politician who had made such a splash as the head of the party in power?" (P. Trudeau 100). Ultimately, it was probably a combination of both. Political celebrity, where individuals create and embody national history, affects Canada's democratic processes and parliamentary system: it can downplay traditional party allegiances and minimize the influence of detailed policy platforms. But in this process, politicians invite the public into a historical process and political world that often appears inaccessible, and engaging with political celebrity can be a form of engaging in active citizenship. Pierre Trudeau achieved his celebrity status by embodying cultural conditions and consciously developing his stature. His policies, however, remained integral to his performance and his brand. Over a generation later, Justin Trudeau entered the public spotlight on the basis of this ascribed celebrity status, marketing himself in a new age of digital communications on the intangible qualities of hope, positivity, and charisma. Celebrity status will never be the only reason Canadians elect a prime minister, but all candidates will be employing the frames of celebrity, and it will be the victor of public performance who will be elected to govern.

Notes

1 The three other categories of operators on the "Celebrity-Politics Interface" that Marsh, 't Hart, and Tindall identify are celebrity advocate, celebrity activist/endorser, and celebrity politician (327).

2 While all politicians are entwined with discourses of celebrity by nature of participating in the public performance of politics and seeking public recognition, some politicians actively pursue celebrity status, while others possess features that lend themselves to be characterized as such, for example, a propensity for the dramatic or participation in perceived scandalous activity. The nature of leadership contests and the first-past-the-post electoral system is rooted in the reality that some politicians will be more successful in their performances than others—but successful performance does not equate celebrity, nor the other way around.

3 Two such examples are Peter C. Newman's *Renegade in Power*, about Prime Minister John Diefenbaker, and C.P. Stacey's *A Very Double Life*, about the private world of Prime Minister Mackenzie King.

4 For example, the second female cabinet minister in Canada, Judy LaMarsh, was very candid about her loneliness as a politician and her frustration with her colleagues in her memoir *Bird in a Gilded Cage*.

5 By many accounts, the 1968 debate was flat, stilted, and unremarkable. The politicians were not yet comfortable with the medium and came across as ill at ease (Nesbitt-Larking 301). McLuhan related the awkward nature of the 1968 debate to the disparity between the medium of television and the format and expectation of debate (Letters 352). As he remarked on the 1968 debate, "The witness box cum lectern cum pulpit spaces for the candidates was totally non-TV" (Letters 354). It is interesting to note that there were no televised debates in the federal campaigns of 1972 or 1974.

6 Margaret Trudeau wrote two memoirs, *Beyond Reason* (1979) and *Consequences* (1982), both which focused on her life in the media spotlight because of her relationship with Pierre Trudeau. She also wrote a third, *Changing My Mind*, published in 2010, which focuses on her experiences with mental illness.

7 Such celebrities include John Lennon and Yoko Ono, Elizabeth Taylor, and Barbra Streisand.

8 President Obama's 2008 presidential campaign exemplifies this notion of celebrity-driven politics being used to invigorate and engage an electorate. As Evan Thomas wrote in an analysis of the campaign, "Obama understood that he had become a giant screen upon which Americans projected their hopes and fears, dreams and frustrations. Maybe such a person never really existed, couldn't exist, but people wanted a savior nonetheless" (7).

9 The Canadian public were deeply divided, often based on regionalism, on many of Trudeau's decisions including, for example, to invoke the War Measures Act, to institute mandatory wage and price controls, to develop the Official Languages Act, to introduce the National Energy Program, and to create a Charter of Rights and Freedoms.

10 Some of the closing of words of Jack Layton's letter to Canadians prior to his death in 2010 was that "Hope is better than fear." A poster of Obama, iconic during the 2008 campaign and after, was an image of Obama's face, with the word "HOPE" printed below.

11 The late 1950s and 1960s saw the introduction and growth of American-style campaign techniques in Canada —brought to the electoral landscape by young Liberal Party operatives (Nesbitt-Larking 144).

12 Rojek's models of celebrity also includes celebrity that is achieved through open competition and celebrity that is attributed by the media (Rojek 17).

13 While these were certainly positive numbers, it is difficult to measure their precise effect on outcome and how this digital campaigning translates into actual votes. A large online following, as Sagan outlines, does not necessarily mean an active one. For example, when CBC News filtered the Liberal candidates' Twitter accounts through an online analytical tool, it found that only 45 per cent of Trudeau's followers were considered "good," meaning users who were active on Twitter, rather than fake or inactive accounts. This was a much lower percentage than the other candidates. Furthermore, Twitter followers do not necessarily represent Liberal Party supporters or even eligible voters.

14 Chadwick defines e-democracy as "efforts to broaden political participation by enabling citizens to connect with one another and with their representatives via new information and communication technologies" (Small, "Friends" 206).

15 In the 2011 campaign, Taras and Waddell concluded that social media did not figure as prominently as commentators assumed it would because of the limited number of active social media participants, the narrow range of issues those participants highlighted during the campaign, the lack of impact made on the issues that were discussed, as well as the paucity of uses that were found for social media during the campaign (96). As in past elections, the media's emphasis remained firmly on strategy, tactics, personality, and conflict. Furthermore, journalists and partisans interacted on social media platforms, sharing information and gossip that excluded rather than included the general public (Waddell, "Berry'd" 126).

5

Celebrity and the Cultivation of Indigenous Publics in Canada
Lorraine York

*For a number of years the Hollywood medium
has used the Indian, so now the Indian is using
the Hollywood medium.*

—Shelley Niro

She stands, smiling, looking directly at the camera, over a household table-top rotary fan that has been placed on its back on the ground. She is dressed in a blonde wig and a white halter dress. The fan blows her dress into a bell shape, mimicking the iconic Hollywood image of Marilyn Monroe standing over the subway grate in *The Seven Year Itch* (1955). She holds the shutter release clicker in her hand, and its cable extends into the foreground of the photograph toward the viewer: a witty signal of conscious self-fashioning. The image, entitled "The 500 Year Itch," is of Shelley Niro, the Mohawk filmmaker and visual artist, and it forms part of her 1992 triptych series *This Land Is Mime Land*. In a number of these triptychs, Niro places portraits of herself in popular culture costumes on the left (in one, she dresses as Elvis Presley) and non-costumed, everyday dress portraits of herself on the right. In the middle, she situates photographs of family members, as though to signal the central values of community and collectivity that more individu-alistic conceptions of celebrity overwrite. In thus positioning these images, Niro signals the complexity of contemporary Indigenous subjectivity, and the ways in which images and values from Western popular culture are both oppositional to and partly constitutive of that subjectivity. For example, there is no question that Niro sees the image of idealized white femininity that Monroe embodies as exclusionary; as she has observed, "the beauty she possessed is way beyond anything a lot of people I know could ever attain

Shelley Niro, *The 500 Year Itch*, 1992
Gelatin silver print heightened with
applied colour, mounted on masonite,
frame: 187 × 126 × 7.5 cm; image:
182 × 121.5 cm; object: 73.3465 ×
49.3307 × 1.9685 in.; 186.3 × 125.3
× 5 cm. Gift of Victoria Henry, Ottawa,
2003 National Gallery of Canada,
Ottawa. Photo © National Gallery of
Canada. With permission of the artist.

or even come close to" (Abbott). But she is just as quick to recognize the
way in which Western cultural texts and practices have inflected Indigenous
life in ways that can link as well as sever:

> instead of accepting what people say you should be, I'm questioning why
> can't I be like I am, why can't I like parts of other things in contemporary
> society? Regardless of how Indians are viewed, as being very isolated and
> alienated, we still watch TV, we read the papers, we listen to music. There
> are many other commonalities with the dominant culture that I probably
> wouldn't want to live without and exclude myself from. (Abbott)

Accordingly, in Niro's triptych, the operations of cultural influence are
bidirectional; by inserting herself into one of Hollywood culture's iconic
images, Niro alters it in turn, and reveals its failure to exclude her entirely.
In the costume photograph, for example, Niro retains the pair of round,
dark-rimmed glasses that she wears in her contemporary self-portrait on
the far right of the triptych. The boundaries blur. While acknowledging Hollywood's uses and exclusions of the Indigenous, Niro is equally
"using"—and Indigenizing—"the Hollywood medium."

In this chapter, I take Shelley Niro's artistic engagement with Hollywood celebrity as a model for a way to conceive of the relationship between celebrity and Indigeneity in Canada. As in "The 500 Year Itch," that relationship is multidirectional, involving both Indigenous contact with non-Indigenous celebrity-producing systems and systems of Indigenous production of celebrity, some of which may also operate through the kind of knowing inhabitation of non-Indigenous cultural production systems that Shelley Niro figures in her work. Indigenous celebrity in Canada exists sometimes in a state of opposition to non-Indigenous media cultures, and at other times in a consciously incorporative relationship with them, but, more important, there are also Indigenous media cultures in Canada that are going on their own independent way, busily producing celebrity and publics across a whole range of media, whether recognized by non-Indigenous media or not. In theorizing this variegated Indigenous media landscape in Canada, I turn to Kathleen Buddle's notion of an Indigenous public sphere that "develops alongside but interdependently with the mainstream and both overlaps and conflicts with this arena" (34). Buddle's concept of the Indigenous public sphere allows us to register Indigenous reworkings of mainstream culture while studying the way in which alternative Indigenous publics—and celebrity systems—concurrently take shape. This takes us beyond an oppositional stance that leaves Indigenous culture simply and only ever reacting to non-Indigenous mainstream culture. As I will examine in the second half of this paper, Indigenous creativity in television, music, and digital media reveals both a repurposing of mainstream media practices and the production of alternative celebrity systems and patterns of consumption that operate across these media. I argue that the formation of Indigenous publics in Canada and their enabling of alternative and overlapping celebrity phenomena offer us a means of decentring existing assumptions about the individualistic nature of celebrity (even as individualistic modes of celebrity continue to circulate within those publics). Indeed, Indigenous media publics in Canada hold the potential to reconfigure celebrity as a collectivist achievement.

Given the prevailing view of celebrity in many cultures as the unearned and cynically commodified social visibility of selected individuals, the few existing scholarly considerations of the relationship between celebrity and Indigeneity tend, not surprisingly, to paint that relationship as bluntly oppositional.[1] And while there are examples aplenty of the harmful effects of non-Indigenous celebrity culture on Indigenous subjects, as Thomas King has reminded us in *The Inconvenient Indian* (2012), characterizing this relationship as necessarily oppositional can have harmful effects as well, recasting the Indigenous cultural producer in a non-agential, purely reactive role. One example of this oppositional approach to celebrity and Indigeneity has been the common tendency to figure celebrity itself as synonymous with whiteness and colonization. And while there are historical reasons for doing so, involving degrees of access to mass media, such a move often has the effect of typing those Indigenous subjects who *have* been socially visible celebrities as assimilated victims of imperialism. Daniel Francis, for example, devotes an entire chapter of his influential and valuable book *The Imaginary Indian* (1992; 2011) to "celebrity Indians": those whose main role was to express "aspects of the Imaginary Indian" (155)— i.e., the "image of Native People held by non-Natives" (25). For Francis, "celebrity Indians" such as Pauline Johnson, Grey Owl, and Long Lance were "chosen by Whites" specifically because they "did not challenge the values of mainstream Canadian society" (156). And while Francis raises pressing questions about the cultural manipulation of representatives of minoritized groups, his equation of celebrity Indigenous subjects and the non-Indigenous imaginary has the effect of flattening out the historical complexities of Indigenous subjects who are taken up by non-Indigenous audiences, dismissing them, in effect, as instruments of hegemony. Just the act of lumping Johnson together with Long Lance and Grey Owl arguably delegitimizes her as an Indigenous subject.[2] As critics of Pauline Johnson's performative poetry have amply shown (Gerson and Strong-Boag; Flint), the situation is much more complicated, and Johnson's performances and poems offer instances of both acquiescence and challenge.

A particular drawback in conceiving of celebrity systems as unrelentingly white, then, is its reduction of our ability to theorize non-white celebrity subjects in a way that recognizes the complexity of their positioning. For example, sociologist Michele Byers, in her essay "On the (Im)possibility of Canadian Celebrity" (2012), offers a welcome analysis of race in Canadian celebrity, but she equates celebrity with whiteness in too cursory a fashion. "One of the patterns I saw emerging," she writes, "was that the ideal Canadian celebrity citizen was, at least within a dominant reading, 'white'." To be sure, this argument has the potential to tell us much that is valuable about the ways in which white subjects have historically had much greater access to the institutions and processes of Canadian celebrity production in the mass media (see Lee). But as Byers proceeds to develop this association between whiteness and celebrity, it comes to resemble Francis's suspicion of "celebrity Indians." Citing George Elliott Clarke's essay "White Like Canada" and its energetic critique of Canadian celebrities as model whites—"polite, pacific, respectable...abundantly available for Americans who want to glorify whiteness without alienating African Americans" (qtd. in Byers), Byers takes up the examples of Céline Dion and Drake, showing how each of their star texts overwrites their cultural differences (Dion as Québécoise, Drake as biracial) in the service of this "polite, pacific, respectable" whiteness. Reading Drake in this way, however, is deeply problematic, for it essentially deracinates him:

> Drake... remains true to the hallmarks of Canadian celebrity citizenship as I've already described and as described by Clarke as "polite, pacific, respectable." While not "white" (and I must bracket here the complexity of how multiraciality is read through multiple lenses of identity), Drake does have all the cultural capital necessary for the kind of export Clarke describes. (Byers)

This comes too close, to my mind, to the judging of legitimate and non-legitimate racial identities among racialized subjects.

Byers extends this problematic reading of racialized celebrities to Indigenous stars. Agreeing that popular Canadian television programs such as *Corner Gas* "de-specify their rootedness" in local spaces, in a way that the first Indigenously created dramatic series, *Moccasin Flats*, for instance, does not, Byers rightly concludes that Indigenous performers are often welcomed into the transnational market insofar as they are read as generically "Indian" rather than as tribally specific subjects. But Byers's conclusion hastily equates success, once again, with assimilation: "Where they [Indigenous performers] achieve transnational visibility and success, it is usually through a process of deracination." Again, it seems, one can be a celebrity *or* one can be a legitimately Indigenous subject, but not both.

An awareness of the unquestionable impingements of non-Indigenous media and structures of production on Indigenous communities need not stigmatize Indigenous celebrities as co-opted and deracinated. What we need is a more flexible, multidirectional understanding of the way in which racialized subjects make use of dominant media that does not reduce the fact of that usage to evidence of disempowerment, for such a view denies agency and obscures the significant growth of Indigenous-run systems of production in this country.

As I have suggested, one such model that I propose to bring to the understanding of Indigenous celebrity in Canada is Kathleen Buddle's concept of an Indigenous public sphere that reconfigures and corrects non-Indigenous representations of the "imaginary Indian." Buddle engages with the notion of "syncretisation" or "selective appropriation" to describe this Indigenous public sphere, in which Indigeneity becomes "reformulated...as a partly oppositional, partly incorporative, ideology" (34, 49). Buddle's choice of the term "syncretisation" is a deliberate departure from early post-colonial celebrations of "hybridity" that tended to downplay the very real borders, barriers, and inequities faced by subaltern subjects. Following Arif Dirlik's lead, Buddle argues that one way of avoiding the simplistic celebration of hybridity is to attend "more seriously to the existence of alternative modes of identity formation" (33). Accordingly, Buddle examines practices such as powwows, Indigenous newspapers, and agricultural fairs as opportunities for Indigenous participants to resignify Indigeneity in a manner that recalls Shelley Niro's triptych art, even as they participate in contact zones that are sometimes critiqued as pandering to non-Indigenous desires for "imaginary Indians." Moving from the nineteenth century to the digital age and Indigenous participation in mass media, Buddle maintains that to participate in events that represent Indigenous culture to a broader audience is not necessarily to assimilate oneself to that audience's culture. Writing of the powwow, she argues that

> My research indicates that select subcultures of Aboriginal peoples in South-
> ern Ontario have historically engaged in culturally transformative prac-
> tices...neither to vacate an Aboriginal alterity, nor to simply oppose whites.
> Nor have I uncovered any data that would support the common assumption
> that the assimilation of the outer powwow form ought to be interpreted as
> some uncritical deference to a perceived "authentic" genre of stereotypical
> Indianness. (34)

Although Buddle nowhere mentions celebrity, her model of syncretic performance holds wide-ranging implications for a study of Indigenous celebrity. In comparison to the model of the deracinated, assimilated Indigenous celebrity, Buddle offers us a picture of Indigenous actors in a public sphere who "have strategically engaged with the foreign, bending it to local bidding. They have also refined and reframed white scripted versions of Aboriginality by performing their own preferred variations on the theme" (57).

Even so, it seems fair to ask: does the syncretic model advanced by Buddle, as applied to Indigenous celebrity, have its limits and dangers too? It certainly does. For instance, Buddle is cautious in extending her analysis of the strategic use by Indigenous subjects of non-Indigenous imaginings of the "Indian" to the profitability of those reimaginings; she briefly notes that Haudenosaunee dancers touring Europe and the United States in the mid-nineteenth century "were marketing Indigeneity abroad and turning a profit" (48). There is, of course, nothing wrong with this: such profits constitute fair recompense for artistic labour, and Buddle notes it but emphasizes much more strongly overall in her analysis the political and pedagogical reasons for Indigenous artists to share their work in non-Indigenous markets. However, Maureen Trudelle Schwartz, in her book *Fighting Colonialism with Hegemonic Culture: Native American Appropria-*

tion of Indian Stereotypes, places an inordinate emphasis on the Indigenous redeployment of stereotypes "to empower themselves; by selling product and other means" (4). Chapters include "Marketing Health and Tradition" and "Marketing Spirituality and Environmental Values." There is a risk here of post-colonial resistance degenerating into fighting commodification with commodification, and Schwartz tends not to examine this risk, nor the very real possibilities of reinscribing capitalist values that are widely held to be inimical to Indigenous philosophies of collectivist social organization and relations.

Buddle's work might usefully be brought into conversation with that of Graham Huggan, who *does* explicitly consider the role of celebrity in the production of what he calls "the postcolonial exotic." In his chapter devoted to celebrity, he examines not a minoritized writer, though, but—somewhat oddly, given the book's concentration on post-colonial writing—Margaret Atwood. He argues that Atwood's works speak from a privileged position, whereby any subversive content is "negotiated from the safety of the middle-class family, the middle-class educational system, the middle-class home" (217). Elsewhere in his study, though, Huggan acknowledges the possibility for literary reputation to operate differently for post-colonial writers (though here, he abandons the term "celebrity"): "Postcolonial cultural production is profoundly affected, but not totally governed, by commodification" (26). It is a perception that could readily inform the creation of the sorts of alternative publics that exist both in contact with and independent of (Buddle would say "interdependently" of) the commodifying forces of non-Indigenous culture. Indeed, it would have been salutary to see how Huggan's chapter on celebrity might have played out if he had considered a post-colonial writer or an Indigenous writer rather than Margaret Atwood. Would celebrity itself approach the condition of the "partly oppositional, partly incorporative" Indigenous cultural production that Kathleen Buddle perceives? Instead, it seems telling that the chapter on celebrity in a study of post-colonial exoticism should focus on a white author; celebrity seems necessarily to attach itself to the settler/invader.

A more recent collection of essays entitled *Celebrity Colonialism* (2009) reminds us that celebrities are to be found both amongst the representatives of imperial power and among the populations historically subject to that power, and both positions call out for further study. This volume, edited by Robert Clarke, maintains that "Fame has long been a significant commodity in the cultural and political economies of English colonial regimes" (2), and "they continue to perform diverse, at times ambivalent, functions in the postcolonial world" (1). Essays include studies of celebrity colonizers—

European celebrity activists organizing on behalf of Africa, for instance, or celebrity adopters of children from the Global South—but also studies of Indigenous celebrities like the Australian actor David Gulpilil of the Yolngu Nation of Arnhem Land. Examining colonizing and post-colonial celebrities together usefully reminds us that celebrity phenomena potentially attach themselves to any of the parties in post-colonial relations of power.[3]

What is needed is for these valuable post-colonial critiques of commodification and deradicalization to develop a more flexible theoretical understanding of the workings of celebrity. Here the growing field of celebrity studies can productively play a role in conversation with these post-colonial understandings of the commodification of exoticism. Precisely because a number of key texts in the field of celebrity (Richard Dyer, P. David Marshall) have complicated earlier theories of celebrity as top-down manufacture (Frankfurt School thinkers Leo Lowenthal and Herbert Marcuse), post-colonial study could benefit from adopting a theoretical stance on celebrity that at least admits to the possibility that celebrity subjectivities may not always or entirely function as instruments of hegemonic will. Such a theory would allow, for instance, for the operations of Indigenous agency across media even in the presence of historical relations of colonization and settler/invader violence.

In the second half of this chapter, I propose to do exactly that: to show how Indigenous contact with celebrity in various mass media in Canada can effect the sort of "partly oppositional, partly incorporative" (Buddle 49) syncretism that works toward an ultimate horizon of promoting greater, rather than less, Indigenous control over the means of production. Especially in a time of proliferating media platforms and specialized audiences, these various, multidirectional contacts, combined with growing control over production, may forge a wide variety of Indigenous public spheres across these media platforms. But these Indigenous publics are invisible to a gaze that sees only oppositional, imperialist/subaltern exchanges and contacts.

Indigenous labour and skill in performing arts, in particular, have often remained invisible to this sort of gaze, though it readily discerns the whole range of hurtful stereotypes of Indigenous people that many critics have pointed out, most recently Thomas King in *The Inconvenient Indian*. Kathleen Buddle works hard to place these performances in a less damaging light; she notes, for example, that the roles that Indigenous actors "assumed on radio, screen and television generally bore no resemblance to their realities and therefore required considerable skill" (51). King, on the other hand, emphasizes the downside of this argument: that typically mainstream audiences would mistakenly see an overlap between what they imagined Indigenous subjectivities were, and the roles that Indigenous actors played on camera. Therefore, he argues, Indigenous actors were often not given credit for their acting labour; they were assumed, instead, to be simply representing themselves: "there is a troubling assumption that an Indian playing an Indian is an infinitely easier acting job than, say, an Italian actor playing a mobster or an Irish actor playing a cop" (48). Taken together, Buddle's and King's positions represent the two sides of the debate about Indigenous/non-Indigenous contact in the zone of celebrity.

Although King approaches, at moments, Buddle's position, that constructive cultural work came out of the unquestionably exploitative representations of Indigenous subjects on film, he is not willing to sustain this as his final position. In discussing the Indigenous actor Harry Smith/Jay Silverheels, who portrayed Tonto in the Lone Ranger television program (1949–1957), King first argues that Tonto was, essentially, one of Francis's "imaginary Indians" or Clarke's "polite, pacific, respectable" model minority celebrities: "Tonto was North America's Indian. Trustworthy, loyal, helpful, friendly, courteous, kind, obedient, cheerful, thrifty, brave, clean and reverent" (42). But King is not able to leave his case at that; he discerns additional moments where Silverheels's Tonto does the kind of cultural work that Kathleen Buddle celebrates:

> Silverheels has been criticized for playing a Stepin Fetchit role in the *Lone Ranger* series, but this is a small and mean complaint. Silverheels was an actor, and Tonto was a job, and a very good job at that. And it was the first time that you had a White and an Indian on almost equal footing. Sure, the Ranger called the shots, but Tonto rode as well, fought as well, shot as well as the Ranger, and he had skills that the Ranger did not. (43)

Even so, King reminds us, "*The Lone Ranger* was not about rewriting history" (43). For King, the kinds of interventions that Buddle draws attention to are not sufficient to overwrite the more deleterious effects of the white-dominated medium. And so, at the end of his chapter on Indigenous Hollywood, King replays this same conflict between an acknowledgement of intervention and a mourning of its limits. He offers us a list of Indigenous filmmakers who have produced and are continuing to produce representations of Indigenous life and values, but he laments that their work does not reach a broad audience, partly because they predominantly work in documentary (50–51). Although King is right that Indigenous film and television producers need more access to mainstream media outlets, he may also be underestimating the capacity of the documentary film genre to act as a stepping stone to that access, as well as the increasing visibility of the genre in Canada (with major documentary film festivals such as

Hot Docs and dedicated channels such as CBC's Documentary Channel). King is right that the audiences for these venues remain relatively small, but there are compelling reasons to go beyond unfavourable comparisons with "mainstream" cultural production and distribution. Such comparisons, in their reifying of oppositional, centre/margin ways of thinking, see Indigenous production only in relation to a mainstream that is positioned as uniquely visible and productive of celebrity. As a consequence, multitudes of public spheres escape the critical gaze. For example, Angela Aleiss, in her 2005 book *Making the White Man's Indian: Native Americans and Hollywood Movies*, declares that "Indians have no 'superstars'" (165), and while Aleiss makes this point in order to support Indigenous lobbying for fairer hiring and labour practices in Hollywood, her declaration, and the Hollywood-centric scope of her study, have the unfortunate effect of hiding Indigenous cultural producers and fans from public visibility, and rendering their venues of intervention seemingly less important.

In the case of Canadian media, such an identification of legitimate celebrity with American cultural industries would be particularly unfortunate, for Canada has what, in fact, the United States does not: APTN (Aboriginal People's Television Network), which, as King briefly mentions, is the "only Aboriginal television network in North America" (50). APTN, founded in 1999, was an outgrowth of the earlier TVNC (Television Northern Canada; 1992), a network that carried an impressive amount of Indigenous-sourced programming—more than any other Indigenous network anywhere at that time (Roth, "First" 22). But with the CRTC approval of APTN seven years later, Indigenous programming took its place as a mandatory offering on basic cable and satellite (Roth, "First" 26). This meant that TVNC basically won their argument, in the CRTC hearings, that APTN would not constitute "specialty" programming but, instead, "special status" programming: as fundamental to the country's broadcast mandate as CBC or Radio-Canada (Roth, "First" 25). The story of APTN, which I have cursorily sketched here, and which other scholars have detailed more fully (Roth, David, Bredin), offers us an opportunity to see "partly oppositional, partly incorporative ideology" (Buddle 49) at work.

Although my brief capsule history of APTN's founding sounds celebratory (as it should be), a more comprehensive history of the network shows just how much negotiation there has been between the objectives of Indigenous cultural producers and the contemporary Canadian mediascape that sometimes encourages and sometimes hampers those objectives. First of all, any history of TVNC's victory in winning a place for the new network on the mandatory cable listings also needs to acknowledge the strong opposition to its inclusion from (almost all of the) cable companies and other broadcasters. Their argument was that it was specialty programming, and that subscribers should not have it forced upon them (at a cost of only fifteen cents per subscriber). They also complained about start-up costs (Roth, "First" 26). The industry argument, then, not surprisingly privileged profit over cultural mandate. And in so doing, they said that Indigenous people in Canada were not central to the cultural life of the nation; they were a "specialty" but not "special."

Even now, sixteen years after they gained their licence from the CRTC, APTN continues to work with structural disadvantages, such as their location in the upper numerical reaches of the analogue channel lineup outside the Arctic (in my listings, for example, it occupies Channel 70). As Lorna Roth explains, viewers' channel and current programming listings often end around Channel 50, so this makes it difficult to attract new viewers to the higher end of the analogue scale ('First" 29). For some years, APTN has lobbied the CRTC to move the network down the analogue scale, but they have so far declined to do so.

As this story perfectly encapsulates, APTN is a paradigmatic example of the challenges of inserting new, Indigenously sourced cultural materials into non-Indigenous celebrity-producing systems. And APTN has proved to be adept at speaking to multiple constituencies. As Marian Bredin points out, it is "a hybrid non-profit public network with a specialty-television funding model" because it relies less on advertising revenue and non-Canadian content than the big private networks do (carrying more than 80 per cent Indigenous and Canadian content), but it also has a public service mandate (75). It offers several languages of transmission: currently, 28 per cent of its programming is in Indigenous languages, 16 per cent in French, and 56 per cent in English ("What We're Looking For"). In this way, APTN speaks both to Indigenous language groups, to non-Indigenous francophone and anglophone audiences, and to Indigenous francophone and anglophone audiences. And while the majority of English-language programming can also be read as a bid for numerically dominant "mainstream" English viewers, its English-language offerings also have the effect of subverting and correcting non-Indigenous misunderstandings of Indigenous life.

Still, mainstream exposure isn't necessarily the primary objective of Indigenous broadcasters—or of Indigenous producers working in any of the media platforms I discuss in this paper. Lorna Roth observes that although Indigenous "leaders have had to speak 'media language' ... to talk in sound bytes" and "use the rules of techno-rational discourse," this is only a means to an end: "Of top priority are basic community and regional broadcasting services" (*Something* 183). By carrying those community and local programs to an international audience, she concludes, APTN manages to be "both local and global" (*Something* 216). I read this mutual enfolding of the local and global as a sign of APTN's reconfiguring of standard industry categories, and its creation of alternate platforms for celebrity production in Canada.

It is crucial to recognize, as well, that APTN's operations directly support exactly what Thomas King calls for: an increase in Indigenous cultural producers in the media. Writing in 2012, Marian Bredin argues that APTN "has triggered an important cultural and economic diversification in the domestic television industry in the form of emerging Aboriginal-owned film and television production companies" (74). At the same time, many of the programs APTN has developed are legible as mainstream genres such as home and living, arts and crafts, and reality television; one episode of a popular lifestyle program, *The Creative Native*, for example, was marvellously entitled "Cree Eye for the White Guy" (Bredin 87). Bredin's conclusion chimes in perfectly with Buddle's concept of strategic syncretism: "These types of programs inflect Aboriginal cultural knowledge within the formats and conventions of popular television genres" (87). And they set the preconditions for the further emergence of Indigenous celebrities across various media platforms who will continue this act of cultural inflection.

One example of a mobile, cross-platform Indigenous celebrity who engages multiple publics is the Haida artist, producer, and television personality Tamara Rain Bull. She began her career as a visual artist, and opened the first Indigenously owned art gallery in Toronto, Pow Wow, in 1990 and, later, Cedar Root Gallery in Vancouver. Her work in film, notably her first short film, "The Hunt," brought her into contact with a major source of support for Indigenous public spheres in Canada: Indigenous film festivals such as Dreamspeakers in Edmonton. Extending her work in visual culture into television, Bull, under the name Tamara Bell, became the host and producer of *The Creative Native* on APTN from 2002 to 2007. The show featured the work of Indigenous visual artists in multiple media—traditional arts, crafts, fashion, and design. In 2006, Bull became an executive producer and the host of *First Talk with Tamara Bull*, the first Indigenous talk show. *First Talk* is a perfect example of a format that both reflects the influences of mainstream talk shows and provides content of specific interest to Indigenous communities. The show, in turn, reaches out to other media platforms; one of its recurring segments is "Best of YouTube." And another segment, "On the Spot," documents Indigenous interviewers asking non-Indigenous men and women on the street about their (lack of) knowledge of Indigenous history and customs, in a way that is reminiscent of Rick Mercer's *Talking to Americans*. Bull has moved further into production, as screenwriter for Cedar Root, an Indigenous production company that produces, among other projects, *First Talk*. And Bull has continued to work in visual arts, as a jewellery maker whose creations are held by thirty museums and galleries, as well as a filmmaker who in recent years mainly works in digital formats. She has a well-maintained website, whose page devoted to "speaking engagements" shows that she is in high demand as a speaker for Indigenous and non-Indigenous events. Tamara Rain Bull's criss-crossing, multimedia celebrity activates and addresses many publics in the bidirectional, mutually inflecting way that I see as typical of Indigenous media cultures in Canada.

In music, a similar case can be made for Indigenous values inflecting and altering the industry, even as Indigenous producers work within one of the most conformist of the cultural industries. Because the industry is currently dominated by three corporations (Universal, Sony, Warner), the pressure to conform to standard business models is intense. Not surprisingly, Indigenous music-making is handled largely by independents (Scales 82). However independent those producers may be, though, they still enter the contact zone with mainstream musical celebrity in various ways. Indeed, according to Christopher Scales, their existence is partly owing to the early 1990s increase of mainstream interest in Indigenous music that brought a number of Indigenous musicians to the big labels. This increase in mainstream celebrity kick-started the founding of a number of institutions dedicated to the promotion of Indigenous music: radio stations, Indigenous music awards like the "Cammies" (Canadian Aboriginal Music Awards) and "Nammies" (Native American Music Awards; 84–85). Such developments, in turn, gave independent producers venues for their music (as did, for that matter, APTN).

The industry awards are a prime venue for the creation and promotion of celebrity, but the history of Indigenous music awards, like that of APTN, is a story of working within and inflecting non-Indigenous industries. First of all came the Indigenous music awards sponsored by the mainstream awards shows; in 1994, the first Juno category for Indigenous music (first called "Best Music of Aboriginal Canada Recording," later changed to "Aboriginal Album of the Year"; Scales 84–85). (This was six years before the first Grammy for "Best Native American Music Album" was awarded.) But as David Young points out in his study of "Ethno-Racial Minorities and the Juno Awards," the "Cammies" were formed largely as a protest against the Junos' lack of support for Indigenous music-making. Although, as I have mentioned, the Junos were quicker than the Grammys to recognize Indigenous music in the form of an award category, the process of gaining this small recognition was as difficult as TVNC's lobbying of the CRTC for the inclusion of APTN on basic cable and satellite. Previously, Indigenous musicians were lumped into a category called "Best World Beat Recording" (formerly the "Reggae/Calypso" category). Thanks to the activism of the Haudenosaunee radio producer Elaine Bomberry, and the appearance of no less than Buffy Sainte-Marie[4] before CARAS (the Canadian Academy of Recording Arts and Sciences), the new Juno category was finally approved. However, structural problems remain; the Indigenous album award is often not awarded during the televised portion of the awards program. Also, at present, several Indigenous musicians question the need for a separate category, even as they recognize the historical need for its founding in 1992. This debate intensified in 2014 when, for the first time, an Indigenous group won outside the category: the electronic powwow band A Tribe Called Red won in the category "Breakthrough Group of the Year." Still, as the producer Kim Wheeler reflected, the "Aboriginal Album of the Year" category continues to serve a purpose in view of the independent production of Indigenous music:

> I think it's important because the majority of our artists are not signed to a major label, or any label for that matter. Winning or even being nominated for the Juno in the Aboriginal Album of the Year is a big opportunity for exposure in an industry where recognition doesn't come easily for independent artists who don't have a big marketing machine behind them. (Sterritt)

At present, with Indigenous musicians breaking into other categories, retaining the separate category makes sense as a way of signalling the persistence of independent Indigenous production even as artists join, and thereby alter, the mainstream categories. It also signals and recognizes the multiple paths of circulation within public spheres for Indigenous musicians and their fans, some of which carry no allegiance—or resistance—to mainstream systems of production. "Partly oppositional, partly incorporative," and, I would add, partly neither.

For that matter, in the music industry, when Indigenous musicians do garner mainstream celebrity, there is more than incorporation at work. One particularly striking example of Indigenous musicians reconfiguring the content of existing stereotypes is their resistance to harmful stereotypes that a non-Indigenous audience can bring to Indigenous performance. The most recent well-publicized example of this counter-pedagogy is the statement issued via Twitter by A Tribe Called Red in June of 2013, in response to the fairly common situation of non-Indigenous fans showing up to concerts wearing headdresses and face paint: "Non-natives that come to our shows, we need to talk. Please stop wearing headdresses and war-paint. It's insulting" (Friesen). Mainstream celebrity or not, A Tribe

Called Red was willing to risk alienating some fans in order to mark the limits of their incorporation into the white imaginary. This is a problem that, decades ago, Buffy Sainte-Marie faced as well; her first internationally successful album, *It's My Way!* was scheduled to be distributed in the UK, and the British arm of her record label Vanguard tinted the album cover red, and engaged in other culturally insulting promotional exercises that stereotyped Sainte-Marie's Indigeneity. The central office of the label supported Sainte-Marie's protests and insisted that the British house use the same cover art as the US album in future. As her biographer Blair Stonechild observes, Sainte-Marie "thought that pumping up her Native American image with stereotypes in an attempt to sell records was unfair to Indigenous peoples, unnecessary, and unfairly downgraded her worth as a serious and versatile artist" (99). In Sainte-Marie's case, the offensive album cover was already in distribution; she had little ability, at that point, to engage in the sort of counter-pedagogy that A Tribe Called Red has been able to do through their celebrity use of social media.

As my mention of social media suggests, so many of the operations of the media I have already discussed—film, television, music—have been fundamentally altered by the coming of the digital age, and here, too, we can espy the operations of Indigenous celebrity as a zone of multidirectional contact with non-Indigenous culture. Introducing their collection of essays entitled *Indigenous Screen Cultures in Canada*, Marian Bredin and Sigurjon Baldur Hafsteinsson observe that "Indigenous people are using new media tools to occupy new cultural territory" in a way that recalls their "earlier adaptations of European technology" (11). The most prominent examples are Digital Drum, an online space for young Indigenous people to upload original content: blogs, photos, videos, and audio tracks. Cyber-PowWow (cyberpowwow.net), founded in 1996, is a website and series of chat rooms featuring the artworks of Indigenous artists in Canada. Every two years, when new materials were added to the site, people would log on at the same time, or if they did not have access, go to a gathering space, where they could log on together, creating a social event and celebration. As Jason Lewis and Tricia Skawennati Gragnito explain, "The site's main goals have been to overcome stereotypes about Aboriginal people, to help shape the World Wide Web; and to generate critical discourse—both in person and online—about First Nations art, technology and community." The primary audience for both of these sites is Indigenous people, and they answer an urgent need for online spaces that are supportive, safe, and celebratory, though these objectives exist within the framework of an online world in which others may enter. In that respect, these sites are paradigmatic of the types of celebrity interventions and contacts that I see characterizing Indigenous media cultures in Canada. Participating artists recognize that they are creating within a medium that has also allowed for the broad distribution of discriminatory and harmful representations of Indigenous people. For that and other reasons, Lewis and Gragnito are under no impression that cyberspace is a free space; indeed, they connect that very idea with notions of the empty *terra nullius* that have enabled and accompanied imperialism. Faced with a space that is not free, like the broadcasters, musicians, film producers, and actors I have discussed so far, contributors to CyberPowWow and Digital Drum intervene to revise, to teach, and to occupy.

As this reading of online Indigenous creativity reveals, Indigenous celebrities are working across many media, and part of their address to multiple public spheres operates through this medium-crossing. As I have shown in the case of Tamara Rain Bull, her current focus on digital media exists alongside many other tendrils of her work in multiple media, and the same can be said of the musical celebrities DJ NDN, DJ Shub, and Bear Witness of A Tribe Called Red, not only because of their use of interactive social media to intervene in fandom practices, but also because their performances are themselves so intensively multimedia in nature. Their music is a mixture of traditional powwow and electronic club music, and the digital images projected during many of their performances often "repurpose and digitize" (in their own words; "Traditional and Modern") harmful representations of Indigenous people. Their performances also often incorporate dancers: yet another creative medium—one with deep traditional resonances. They are also intensely conscious of their photographic representations; they have commented that their many smiling publicity photos are deliberately light-hearted so as to break "the stereotype of the stoic Indian" ("Traditional and Modern"). And their first, self-titled album was made available for free download online. From the beginning, operating across multiple media and addressing multiple publics have been at the heart of what A Tribe Called Red do. In so doing, they enact a cultural practise that fully responds to Shelley Niro's call for a recognition of the multiple, overlapping paths of consumption and production among Indigenous and non-Indigenous producers and consumers.

Even so brief and necessarily incomplete an account of Indigenous media activity in Canada as I have offered in this paper leads irresistibly to a crucial question, which I will pose in conclusion. Can the meanings associated with Western celebrity, and particularly its close ties to individualism, ever be made to serve the interests of Indigenous communities for whom collectivity is a primary value? As P. David Marshall has observed, "celebrities are the production locale for an elaborate discourse on the individual and individuality" (*Celebrity and Power* 4) In fact, celebrity is, for Marshall, a means of distinguishing between individual and collective: "The celebrity is centrally involved in the social construction of division between the individual and the collective, and works discursively in this area" (*Celebrity and Power* 25). How can so deeply embedded an ethos of individualism ever find common ground with Indigenous philosophies of the fundamental importance of relationality? All of the interruptions of and interventions into media that I have outlined in this paper tend, ultimately, toward that goal of redefining the nature of accomplishment. When Kathleen Buddle describes the way in which the powwow would eventually "emerge as a powerful vehicle for articulating an inter-tribal discourse on 'being Indian'," she is talking about exactly this reframing of the individual/group dynamic: "the institution occupied an opposi- tional position to the Euro-North American aesthetic of individualism and its attendant fantasy of individual (usually male) achievement" (52). When Marian Bredin describes the decision of APTN's series *Moccasin Flats* not only to cast high-visibility celebrities like Gordon Tootoosis, Tan- too Cardinal, and Andrea Menard but also to derive "much of the cast and crew" from the everyday ranks of "Aboriginal youth from North Central" and to "derive" the storylines from "their experiences," she is describing a reconfiguring of the celebrity field to encompass and value community. And when some Indigenous music is not recorded because it is sacred, this choice, too, upsets the industry mantra of commodification and distribu- tion for personal rather than communal gain. Like Shelley Niro, breaking down and reconfiguring the Indigenous self as a dynamic collision of com- munity, individual, and settler culture, Indigenous production in Canada offers the possibility of reimagining celebrity as collective achievement.

Notes

1 As in my other analyses of celebrity, mainly in the literary industries, I under- stand celebrity to be various in its ideological tendencies. Celebrity is not to be automatically associated with false cultural value or the degeneration of some pristine, idealized past in which social visibility was legitimized by agreed- upon standards of valued cultural labour. Certainly, one can find examples of celebrity that is not based on accomplishments that one might value, but this does not mean that celebrity is, ipso facto, empty of cultural value (see Dyer).

2 In making this distinction between Johnson, on the one hand, and Grey Owl and Long Lance, on the other, I am mindful of the recent, thoughtful readings of Grey Owl, for instance, by Albert Braz, who argues that dismissing figures like Grey Owl and Long Lance as "racial imposter[s]" (53) has the unfortunate effect of ignoring processes by which non-Indigenous subjects may become indigenized through their choice to join an Indigenous community—a controversial and

necessary discussion to be sure. Nevertheless, I would argue that even while one recognizes the complex situations of Long Lance and Grey Owl, placing Johnson, as a Metis subject, in the same category as those two men, as Francis does, erases her Indigenous subjectivity and associates it with imposture.

3 An exception to the tendency to associate celebrity with whiteness is Timothy Brennan's trenchant essay "Cosmopolitans and Celebrities," wherein he examines post-colonial literary celebrities such as V.S. Naipaul, Mario Vargas Llosa, and Bharati Mukherjee. In so doing, though, he returns to the paradigm of celebrity as instrument of deracination that appears in the works of Francis and Byers. He observes, rightly, that such figures tend to be critical of forms of decolonizing nationalisms in their countries of origin, and that they are celebrated in the Global North for precisely this reason (292). I agree that this dynamic is often at work, but it need not be. One of the dangers of extending and generalizing from this argument about politically conservative post-colonial celebrities is the delegitimization and deracination that I have pointed to so far in this essay.

4 Buffy Sainte-Marie is a Cree (Piapot Cree First Nation, Saskatchewan) singer, songwriter, visual artist, and social activist whose songs have won Oscar, Juno, and Golden Globe Awards. She is particularly known for her 1960s protest songs. Her most recent album is *Power in the Blood* (2015).

6

Lament for a Hockey Nation, Don Cherry, and the Apparatus of Canadian Celebrity

Julie Rak

> *Only in Canada could there be such a freak as k.d. lang receiving this award....*
> *I want to tell you my friends and my countrymen that it is OK to be you. It is OK*
> *to let your freak flags fly and embrace the quirkmeister that's inside of all of us.*
>
> —k.d. lang, 2013 Juno Awards speech

Although k.d. lang did not mention him at the 2013 Juno Awards ceremony, like lang, Don Cherry is one of Canada's more unusual celebrities. As the star of the Canadian Broadcasting Corporation (CBC) Television's segment *Coach's Corner*, a vignette shown on *Hockey Night in Canada* every Saturday night since 1981, Cherry has created a reputation for himself as a patriotic English Canadian with right-wing conservative values who advocates openly (and loudly) for a return to an old-time "Canadian" style of physical play and its attendant values of masculine toughness and loyalty. With host Ron MacLean playing straight man to his nearly incomprehensible and often politically incorrect rants about the state of the game and his beliefs about its politics (Dallaire and Denis 2000), Cherry almost always sports the triple-breasted custom-made suits (with high collars and mismatched ties) that he has worn for decades, sometimes topped by a fedora or other eye-catching hat. As he points at the single camera and shouts at or interrupts Ron MacLean with educational asides to "the kids" at home, he is almost a cartoonish figure, lang's "quirkmeister," an anomaly in the mostly earnest corporate environment of sports broadcasting, where commentators are expected to enhance, not eclipse, the star qualities of the

Don Cherry in a typical pose for _Hockey Night in Canada_. CBC photo, used with permission.

athletes. This formula has proven to be a winner in Canada, where Cherry is something of a working-class hero. In 2004, Cherry was the only media figure who was a top-ten finalist for CBC Television's _Greatest Canadians_ miniseries, competing with the likes of John A. Macdonald, David Suzuki, and Tommy Douglas for the honour of being voted the most important Canadian in history. But at the same time, calls for firing Cherry or at least for not renewing his CBC contract have become common as Cherry ages and as his perspective on hockey is increasingly seen as outdated (Sutcliffe). Who is Don Cherry? Is he a buffoon, a national hero, a gay camp icon, or a right-wing mouthpiece? What can his success as a television personality tell us about Canadian celebrity and the cultural industries that create and maintain it? In P. David Marshall's terms, what does his celebrity _signify_ within the apparatus of a national media industry (x)?

It is important to investigate these questions because Cherry's rise to stardom and his enduring appeal show how discourses of celebrity in Canada are created and maintained. My intention is not to create a "Canadian" idea of what celebrity is, an enterprise which Lorraine York has rightly said is fruitless (168). But the existence and popularity of Don Cherry do offer an opportunity to think about the cultural and economic conditions that create a celebrity like him, and how those differ from the apparatus that supports celebrity in different places. Cherry is arguably the biggest celebrity in Canada who did not move to the American entertainment industries in order to become famous. He began as and remains a television personality on the CBC who—other than brief appearances during the National Hockey League (NHL) playoffs on NBC in 2007 and ESPN in 2012—is primarily known to Canadians. Cherry's unique style of delivery probably would make him an obscure figure in sportscasting anywhere else. But this is not the case in Canada, where Cherry remains the most recognizable figure in hockey, perhaps even more than many star hockey players. Although its ratings were beginning to slide before the latest NHL lockout (Dowbiggin 2011), *Coach's Corner* was the most-watched segment anywhere on Canadian television (Cowan).

Attempts have been made to explain why Cherry's rather bizarre performances are so popular. For example, Tim Elcome thinks that Cherry is so watchable because he is "a polarizing figure" in the world of Canadian televised sport, a commentator who embodies either what Canadians think is most important about the idea of citizenship, or who embodies the kind of xenophobia and love of violence that most Canadians do not associate with national values of tolerance and respect for difference. Other commentators have observed that Cherry is a key symbol of the game that most often is associated with Canadian ideas about masculinity and nationalism (Gruneau and Whitson 2–3). These analyses make sense in terms of what Don Cherry *says* on *Coach's Corner*, particularly when his remarks are controversial, but they do not explain how Don Cherry *appears* as he does, and they do not address his hockey conservatism, which I understand as a Red Tory conservatism in the tradition of George Grant's *Lament for a Nation,* a melancholic account of Canadian sovereignty as already lost to Americanization. Both of these aspects of Don Cherry's persona are essential to understanding how Cherry's celebrity works. Cherry's talk functions as the node of an intimate public for hockey where affect and passion matter more than an analysis of the contemporary game and how it works as a business. Cherry's campy image is in many ways the embodiment of celebrity as effect created and maintained at the meeting place between two of Canada's most prominent cultural industries: semi-public television production and the business of professional hockey. And it is awkward. Cherry's costumes and his talk are in conflict because they present different ideas about masculinity. They are analogous to Cherry's understanding of himself as a "regular guy" in conflict with the establishment in the sports and television industries, an establishment which nevertheless he continues to represent. Understanding *why* this image is awkward, and necessarily so, will add to our understanding of what Canadian celebrity is, and how it operates differently from other discourses of celebrity.

The Apparatus of Canadian Celebrity

Before I look at Cherry as an embodiment of fan desires about hockey, it is necessary for me to be more specific about the apparatus in Canada that made and maintains Cherry's celebrity status. As P. David Marshall points out in *Celebrity and Power*, celebrities do not exist apart from the apparatus that creates them. They have no meaning in themselves apart from the system of representation that puts them into circulation and makes them a focus of audience desire and revulsion (56–57). That system, according to Graeme Turner, is economic. Celebrities are commodities within a structure made up of entertainment industries that includes the work of publicists, managers, agents, and others who create a celebrity that, like any other commodity, becomes part of a familiar brand in order to generate revenue (34–35). Joshua Gamson identifies television as a major aspect of this kind of celebrity apparatus in North America because of its popularity and reach, and because as a medium it can quickly create familiarity with a repeated image without having to provide much content about it ("Assembly Line" 13). Like the film and music industries, television creates and maintains celebrity discourses as a way to generate revenue, increase audiences, and create customer loyalty. And along with new media technologies such as online methods of distribution, television is one of the most important means by which sports becomes mass entertainment. As Lorraine York has pointed out in the context of literary celebrity, the representation of celebrity in Canada includes citizenship as a major node in its symbolic economy because of proximity to American literary markets (5). But in the case of Don Cherry, there is a different economy of celebrity at work, partly because Don Cherry as a media figure was never a Canadian export. In Canada, the convergence of the professional sport industries and the unique character of semi-public television broadcasting are responsible for creating a viewing environment that made and still makes Don Cherry possible.

As I have discussed elsewhere, the celebrity apparatus in Canada is less developed than in the United States, partly because its media industries—which are what creates celebrity apart from political celebrity—are not as developed as the for-profit film, television, and music industries produced in the United States (Rak, "Insecure" 4). With the exception of the francophone population of Quebec, which has its own entertainment and cultural industries and its own star system, Canadians generally like to consume American film and television media. This is one of the reasons why Canadian cultural industries—which include publishing, television, and radio and film production as well as theatre and dance—receive government assistance. Since the publication of the findings of the Massey-Lévesque Commission of 1951, it has been assumed that without government support, Canadian cultural industries would not survive the influx of print and media productions from the United States (Beaty and Sullivan 10–11; Szeman 85–86). The result of this belief includes the structure of the CBC, a semi-public broadcaster which is supposed to have a nationalist mandate. As a non-profit broadcaster, the CBC has to think of its audience as a public, not as a market (Tinic 7). However, the CBC is also expected to compete with the budgets and programming choices of for-profit networks and specialist cable channels. These networks and channels are protected by the CRTC rules that allow them to run American programming with Canadian advertisements (Beaty and Sullivan 40–44). The CBC is therefore supposed to be broadly nationalist, representative of the Canadian population, and competitive in a difficult regulatory climate all at the same time. It is also supposed to be watchable, but as I say above, English-speaking Canadians prefer American programming, sometimes distributed by Canadian networks, and do not often watch CBC Television, even when it broadcasts American or British shows (Stursberg 2–4).

In the case of sporting events, CBC Television is not able to meet these conflicting expectations of its mandate very often. In recent years, the network has lost coverage of the Canadian Football league to the specialty sports channel TSN and the French twenty-four-hour sports channel RDS in a bidding war (Stursberg 133). It also lost broadcast rights for the 2010 and 2012 Olympic Games to a partnership formed by Bell Media and Rogers Communications, although it regained broadcast rights for 2014 and 2016 (CBC Sports). But the CBC continues to dominate in one area of sports reporting: its coverage of NHL hockey and its flagship program, *Hockey Night in Canada*, which has been in production since 1952. According to former CBC executive Richard Stursberg, *Hockey Night in Canada* is the only Canadian television show on the CBC that generates revenue (148). If it ever gets cancelled or is sold to another network, Stursberg warns, Canadians will see the CBC as not populist and will not support it. And the network itself will go broke (318–319). Therefore, until very recently, there has been a compelling financial reason to keep Don Cherry's five-minute weekly appearance on *Hockey Night in Canada* because he is a recognizable part of the brand. Like other celebrities, the familiarity of Don Cherry's image helps his network to make money. Stursberg's warning is about to become reality. In November 2013, Rogers Sportsnet purchased the majority of hockey media rights in Canada from the CBC, and has gained control of *Hockey Night in Canada* in the process. Beginning with the 2014–2015 hockey season, CBC will retain its Saturday night timeslot and will get to show *Hockey Night in Canada* for four years, but the CBC will generate no income from the program and will not have creative control either. Cherry himself said at the time that he would like to be "left alone" by Rogers and continue to appear on *Hockey Night in Canada* (Gordon). Although Rogers spokespeople have been supportive of Cherry, others observed that perhaps, at last, Cherry's time as a commentator is finished as Rogers looks to refresh its brand (Loriggio). Maybe, just maybe, it was time for Cherry to retire at last.

But Cherry's shelf life had not yet expired. As Rogers President Keith Pelley said in an interview with the *Toronto Star* during the takeover, "We haven't even had this discussion [about what to do with Cherry and MacLean]. Don is an iconic Canadian. He's made such a big difference in the way in which we experience our Saturday nights" (Rush). Pelley's discussion of Don Cherry refers to his Canadianness, and to his unique position in the history of Canadian sports television. Pelley does not mention that Cherry could be a financial boon to Rogers Sportsnet, but as in the case of most discussions of Cherry's role on television, it is implied. And in fact, Rogers did recognize Cherry's value (and not MacLean's): in March 2014 Rogers announced that Cherry would stay with Ron MacLean in *Coach's Corner*. George Stroumboulopoulos, a CBC Television personality, would replace MacLean as the host of *Hockey Night in Canada* (FitzGerald). It is telling that MacLean is the presenter who will be demoted, not Cherry, because Cherry's image is so iconic and because he is seen as the more lucrative property. And so, Cherry's original position as the iconoclastic face of a semi-public network will survive within the a private network structure.

Another reason why Cherry has appeared on the CBC for so long is cultural. Cherry's performance of patriotism and his trenchant belief that hockey is a Canadian game unite and reconcile the CBC's conflicting responsibilities. When he points at the camera and complains that francophone Canadian and European players wear visors because they are not tough, supports Canadian-born players, or becomes sentimental about the Canadian troops' time in Afghanistan, Cherry carries on a tradition of sentimentality and patriotism about Canadian hockey, and especially about the NHL, which works to naturalize the game of hockey as a game of Canadian dominance and about Canadian values, and it naturalizes the NHL as the pinnacle of professional hockey. Don Cherry therefore represents the CBC as populist and nationalist at the same time, while he supports the structure of corporatized hockey as it is understood today.

Relief from the Political, the CBC, and Hockey Nationalism

Cherry's performances also serve to connect the social position of hockey as a national discourse in Canada with the television industry, but without referring to the business of hockey as what actually brings them together. The close connection between the NHL, national media, and corporate funding has been in place since 1933, when Foster Hewitt's radio program, Imperial Oil's *Hockey Night in Canada,* first aired on CBC. Hewitt's play-by-play broadcasting turned the game from a regional activity to a national event for spectators because radio broadcasts aired coast to coast (CBC Sports). When *Hockey Night in Canada* became a television program in 1952, hockey was well on its way to being seen as Canada's national game because of this level and type of coverage. A generation of Canadians who were not from Ontario or Quebec learned to root for the Toronto Maple Leafs or the Montreal Canadiens as they played the American teams the New York Rangers, the Detroit Redwings, the Chicago Blackhawks, or the Boston Bruins. According to David Gruneau and Richard Whitson, "since 1952 it has become almost impossible to talk about the economics of the NHL without also talking about television" (105) because it was the medium of national (and nationalist) television that created the market for this sport as a central part of Canadian entertainment. By 1960, eighty per cent of Canadian homes had a television, and *Hockey Night in Canada* became the most popular show in Canada just a few years later. Therefore, *Hockey Night in Canada*'s discourse of NHL hockey as the sentimental product of a nation sustained by small communities playing pond hockey for the love of the game masks the growth of the NHL into a business that required the CBC to make hockey seem national and patriotic in order to build audiences, and then expand its markets (Gruneau and Whitson 105–106).

Although the owners of the NHL "Original Six" teams were slow at first to realize how television could help the league to generate major profits, as was the case for other sports leagues such as the National Football League or even for the sport of golf, by the late 1980s—when superstar Wayne Gretzky was traded from the small-market Edmonton Oilers to the large-market Los Angeles Kings—NHL executives realized that the success of hockey on regional cable networks in the United States could be a blueprint for expansion plans. The addition of NHL teams to places far from the regional homes of the sport like California, Florida, and Arizona was in fact driven by changing television viewing habits. These were the states with the most cable television viewers (Amirante 196–97; Gruneau and Whitson 231).

Hockey Night in Canada regularly represents hockey as a naturalized and organic national culture in Canada that it merely records and celebrates. But in fact it is the medium of television, and in Canada the dominance of the *Hockey Night in Canada* program, which created this idea of the game as a national pastime. Cherry regularly represents CBC Television as his opponent and an impediment to a true appreciation of hockey's strategy and politics because of what he sees as its desire for political correctness (*Grapes* 211). Therefore, Don Cherry's image does two things: it works to disguise the central role semi-public television has played in the creation of hockey as a national mythos for Canada, and it elides the existence of NHL hockey as an American-controlled business. Meanwhile, Cherry continues to articulate a type of nationalism which works to fulfill the original mandate of the CBC.

Cherry occupies this double position at the CBC because his hiring coincided with major changes in the NHL, most of which he opposes. As an outspoken former coach for an Original Six team (the Boston Bruins) and as a former player in the NHL and the minors, Cherry's celebrity and his ongoing popularity partly stem from Richard Dyer's idea that stars embody values under threat ("Stars" 83). The threat in this case was to the pervasive idea in Canada that hockey is not a business, but something that men play for the love of the game. Without the threat of big business as the reason why professional hockey works as it does, the relations between the game of hockey and Canadian identity can remain naturalized. As I have mentioned, during the 1980s and 1990s expansions, the NHL went from being a league with teams made up of Canadians and Americans from the eastern regions of the United States and Canada to a league with franchises in most of the regions in both countries. Don Cherry became part of the *Hockey Night in Canada* program in 1980 and became part of *Coach's Corner* in 1981. This was during a period of NHL expansion that saw the NHL absorb several franchises from its last serious rival, the World Hockey Association (WHA). The expansion also included another change: in 1981, thirty-two European players were drafted, double the number of the previous year and more than five times the number two years previously ("Hockey in Europe"). By the end of the 1980s, European players and their style of play, which emphasized skill and speed over fighting and strength, were a major fixture in the NHL (Gruneau and Whitson 182–183). Growth brought other changes to the economy of hockey: the 1994 lockout of players when collective bargaining failed resulted in the moving of teams in small-market cities such as Winnipeg, Minnesota, Hartford, and Quebec City to the American south. As Gruneau and Whitson point out, at the time of the 1994 lockout, the movement of NHL teams could have represented the end of the fantasy that players, and teams, exist in small markets because of the traditions of the game, and that the game itself has not become part of a global entertainment industry:

> They [small market fans] will be disabused, though, of any illusions they might have harboured that their team "belonged" to them. Teams move in search of larger markets and greater profitability, and they trade actively on the discourse of community in their new location... in professional sport the word "franchise" is increasingly revealed as having the same meaning as in the travel or fast-food industries. (233)

At the same time, the myth that Canadian players were the toughest or the best was also threatened by the influx of European players and players from the former Soviet Union. As a conservative pundit in the world of hockey who actively opposes the influx of European players and says that violence is part of the values of hockey itself, Don Cherry as a figure works to stabilize fears about hockey as an international business and about possible changes to the game. As Richard Dyer says about film stars, the "charismatic appeal [of stars] is effective especially when the social order is uncertain, unstable and ambiguous and when the charismatic figure... offers a value, order or stability to counterpoise this" (Dyer, "Stars" 83). Cherry's "old-school" hockey values offer that promise of order and stability for hockey. In his memoir *Hockey Stories and Stuff,* Cherry sees that promise as a social prom-ise for Canada as well, a time (in his mind) when white working-class men were central to Canada's success. He understands that success as lost and forgotten, and himself as the living link to that time, as when he proudly calls himself a redneck:

> Rednecks are the people who came over first to Canada and built Can-ada... they were workin' on construction and in the fields, labouring ten hours a day, bent over so much that the back of their necks got red. So to call me a redneck, I'm proud of it because that means a person who works ten hours a day in the sun. Works! You know what that is? Some people in Canada have forgotten what it means. (Cherry 130–131)

Cherry's identification of himself as working class and with what he understands as lost working-class values is meant to appeal to fans of hockey who understand its values as class, gender, and regionally based (although he says that they are Canadian). As Gruneau and Whitson point out, although Cherry has become a caricature, he still speaks to, and in essence for, a wide constituency of hockey fans. These fans are usually "ordinary Canadians," mostly male, and often with an active connection to the Canadian hockey subculture. They simply don't like many of the changes in 'their' game. They don't like the moves to curtail fighting, and most of them don't like the campaigns waged by reformers to change the character of minor hockey. Underneath these specific charges, they also resent the fact that Canadian hockey seems to be transforming to conform to standards and agendas that come from "somewhere else." This offends their sense of proprietorship of the game; they *feel* their hockey deeply, and they feel "it's not our game anymore." (Gruneau and Whitson 280–281)

This lament for Hockey Nation, as it were, is melancholic. It refuses to understand change as positive. It does not mention the NHL or its business model as the reason for these changes. It is also about a certain idea of the social that cannot be recovered, although it can be invoked. Cherry constructs himself as the messenger of lost working-class values in hockey and in Canadian society, which is why he talks so much in *Coach's Corner* about what the next generation should know about loyalty, teamwork, and masculine toughness. When Cherry became a finalist during the CBC's Greatest Canadian contest, he understood this in a similar way as an endorsement of working-class values and nationalism: "'I think the people, the working-man people, made a statement here, that you don't have to be a college graduate to be a good Canadian'" ("I'm Good"). Therefore, much of Cherry's celebrity appeal comes from the character of this lament. Don Cherry exists as a Canadian celebrity who could not be exported to the United States because the apparatus that supports him requires him to perform a melancholic nationalist narrative. The performance sometimes irritates GLBT activists, francophone Canadians, and many others. As Richard Stursberg says of the calls for Cherry's firing during the European/francophone Canadian visor controversy: "of course, dumping Don Cherry was inconceivable. Cherry, the icon of English Canadian hockey, could no more be dumped than Peter Mansbridge or Rick Mercer. He *was* the CBC" (Stursberg 104). Cherry embodies the very institution that he purports to dismiss, and with it, he embodies not hockey as a sport, but the mediation of it through television. As a celebrity figure he *is* a network's nationalist values and commitment to populism and that is, in P. David Marshall's terms, his semiotic meaning.

The Importance of Being Authentic: Canadian Celebrity

One of the key aspects of Cherry's image that makes his celebrity different from the way celebrity is often understood is the problem of "realness" in celebrity studies. Many scholars of celebrity have observed that the performance of realness—even received ironically—is essential to how celebrity works. This realness, sometimes understood as the private life of the celebrity, must be uncovered or rediscovered for the dialectic of audience fascination and revulsion to operate. The media acts as the revealer of this realness (Gamson, "Assembly" 16–18). Charles Ponce de Leon expresses a similar idea about uncovering of the "real" self as essential to the power of celebrity: "the culture of celebrity...is geared toward the exposure of the 'real selves' that are presumed to lie behind these images" (5). However, the apparatus that supports Canadian celebrity does not require "realness" or "ordinariness" to function in the dialectic in quite this way. What is required is irony about the performance of celebrity so that the celebrity can—as k.d. lang indirectly points out in her speech—be understood as *authentic because the celebrity appears to be independent of the apparatus itself.* In other words, celebrity in Canada that is not created by a foreign celebrity apparatus, such as the Hollywood film or television industries, does not often operate as part of a dialectic of glamour/ordinariness. This creates unlikely celebrities like lang, Rita MacNeil, and Don Cherry himself. As we shall see, Cherry's appearances on Rick Mercer's television program and Bret "The Hitman" Hart's defence of him on *The Greatest Canadian* indicate that Cherry's celebrity operates as a *knowing artifice* that is not meant to be realistic. That is because it is not important who the "real" Don Cherry is. What matters is that Cherry is seen as authentic in other ways. This is the source of Cherry's unwavering belief in his own image, even when it appears to be artificial.

This gesture to authenticity through artificiality makes Cherry's celebrity a node in a specific intimate public sphere of hockey in Canada, a sphere which operates as a performance of sentimentality that Lauren Berlant has called in another context a "relief from the political" (10). In Cherry's case, his performances are often about the politics of the day, but they are not, in fact, political. Rather, they are heavily sentimental and include unpredictable spillovers of affect. Watching these offers relief for Canadian fandom from the fact that hockey as a spectator sport takes place within a framework of American economic dominance. Cherry's patriotism, outrageous behaviour, populism, and unusual outfits *as performances* function as a way to be both ironic about and supportive of American cultural industrial structures, especially for the television industry. In the end, Don Cherry's antics are supposed to forestall the Americanization of Canadian public life and are meant to direct attention away from the fact of American corporate dominance in Canada by appealing to an imagined Canadian dominance of hockey in the past. Don Cherry has not been on

CBC's *Coach's Corner* for decades because he is controversial. He is there to perform hockey as an intimate public in very specific ways, so that fans can still enjoy the spectacle. At the same time, the apparatus that supports Cherry can be strengthened because Cherry makes the CBC matter to hockey fans.

It may seem at first that Don Cherry's wardrobe is at odds with what Cherry says about being authentic and one of the people. Cherry purports to be a working-class hero, but he does not look anything like the part. His clothes—mocked on the blog *Don We Now Our Gay Apparel*—seem, as the blog's title playfully suggests, to be diametrically opposed to his talk of working-class masculine values. What does this presentation mean, and what can we learn from it about the operation of celebrity in Canada? In the early years of *Coach's Corner*, Cherry's presentation of himself as—in his own words in the introduction to Ron MacLean's memoir *Cornered*—a "sharp dresser" (MacLean xiii) provided a direct connection to the suits he wore when he coached the Boston Bruins during the 1970s. In the opener to *Coach's Corner*, a clip plays that shows Cherry as a coach on the bench, where he wears a vest, polka-dot tie, and matching handkerchief. His jacket is a sober black. Other photographs of Cherry show him wearing checked jackets or three-piece suits, which many coaches wore during this era. Cherry's sporting of this suit and others like it, rather than the sports jackets used by other sportscasters, therefore functioned as a visual link to his career as a coach, since his original role on *Coach's Corner* was that of an outsider, an expert commentator who was not a sportscaster.

What is unusual is that Cherry continued to wear the suit pictured in that opening shot decades later, and that after his first years at *Coach's Corner*, he began to wear more flamboyant triple-breasted suits in a dizzying array of colours and patterns (Kubus). The suits have become costumes. At the same time, a gap appeared between Cherry's conventionally masculine tough talk and his outfits. Cherry's talk is connected to what Kristi Allain calls "hockey masculinity," a valorization of toughness, loyalty, independent thinking, respect, honour, courage, and speed. But Cherry's clothing is a hypermasculine performance, where hypermasculinity is understood as an exaggerated performance of "highly developed masculine forms" where there is cultural agreement about what masculinity is, and agreement about whether a performance is excessive (Schroeder 418). This slightly ironic wardrobe performance (Cherry often refers to himself as a good dresser, and to his co-host Ron Maclean as a bad dresser) serves to emphasize his hockey masculinity as that of an independent thinker who remains loyal to the dress codes of benched players (they wear suits to games) and coaches (they wear suits), while its artifice links the performance to dandyism. Much like Oscar Wilde, whose performance of dandyism was not understood as homosexual or even as effeminate in his own time (Thienpont 293–294), Cherry appears as a dandy when he knows that he needs to be public. He exaggerates elements of his costume in a knowing amplification of his former role as a coach, much as Wilde—sometimes in double-breasted or velvet jackets that Cherry's jackets uncannily resemble—deliberately exaggerated the dress of a conventional gentleman in the nineteenth century.

I believe that there are several reasons—beyond personal preference—why Don Cherry continues to wear such costumes on television. First, his adoption of dandyism is meant to align his image not with the CBC network or with the world of professional hosting and sportscasting, but with the players and the fans. This alliance allows him to remain as an expert who is *not* a corporate sellout, and it also allows him to create an affective performance that, like fan behaviour, is meant to be irrational, over-the-top, and sincere in its intent. Cherry is flamboyant enough to pin a rose to the label of every suit he wears on *Coach's Corner*. But as his fans know, the rose is also a mark of sincerity: it is a tribute to Rose, his beloved first wife, who died of cancer in 1997. Second, as my analysis of his appearance on the *Rick Mercer Report* will show, Cherry presents his wardrobe choices as a refusal to be a member of the elite, despite the fact that his suits appear to be custom-made. In other words, Cherry *chooses* to be campy as another way to distance himself from the idea of hockey as part of the sports and entertainment industry, and from the power of the media within that industry. His performance of artificiality is meant to be read as authentic. It is also as melancholic as his talk, despite its campy gaiety. Cherry's constant reminders of what has been lost to Canada and to Canadian hockey in his talk have their visual equivalent in his costumes, in that they reference an earlier time when Cherry was a coach. They also are meant to serve as a "reminder" that the core of hockey is *not* the mediation of the sport through television and other media, but the love for the game shown by players, coaches, and fans. Cherry's constant criticism of general managers such as Brian Burke, the former general manager of the Toronto Maple Leafs, and his diatribes against his own employer mean that his costume is not meant to echo what he considers to be the politically correct and sober business of hockey and the media which supports that business. Therefore, in their deliberately retro styling, Don Cherry's suits function as another lament for what he sees as a simpler time, when bureaucracy did not control hockey and the experience of hockey was unmediated.

Cherry's visual presentation is meant to be seen as another aspect of his authenticity, because it distances him from authority figures and media pundits in its very artificiality. As I have discussed in another context, former professional wrestler Bret "The Hitman" Hart presents the artificiality of Don Cherry as part of his authenticity in his defence of Cherry during the CBC *Greatest Canadian* contest in 2004 ("Don Cherry"). At the beginning of the narrative, a voice-over by Hart says that Cherry embodies Canadian values connected to patriotism, hockey, and honesty: "'He loves Canada. He loves hockey. He's good. He's bad. He's unfiltered and uncensored…he's the heart and soul of this country.'" As Hart speaks these words, a disembodied Don Cherry, pictured as a bouncing head with a cartoon mouth and a puppet body, flits across the screen. Cherry's entire image is reduced to a caricature in a wholesale rejection of heroic discourse. The reason for this becomes apparent when Hart attempts to account for Cherry's celebrity status by exposing the very idea of celebrity as something that is performed, even by honest men like Cherry or himself. Stepping out of a cartoon ring into a ringside set, Hart compares the faint ridiculousness of Cherry's persona as an onscreen dandy with Hart's own, also faintly ridiculous persona as a professional wrestler. Hart says, "I understand Don Cherry. We have a lot in common. He's high collars and fancy suits. I'm pink tights. Let's face it, we're both showmen."

Hart's words stress that celebrity is not real and not to be taken seriously. But at the same time, Hart asks that Cherry's patriotism and blunt speaking be taken seriously because those are the values of "ordinary" Canadians. Brett Hart's defence of Cherry as a showman "like himself" who is willing to be false in order to reveal "the truth" is another expression of dandyism as a strategy. Just as advocate George Stroumboulopoulos argued in *The Greatest Canadian* that Tommy Douglas was a hero unlike American heroes, Hart says that Cherry's working-class values of sincerity, plain talk, and patriotism are authentic, but that Cherry knows that his costumes are not meant to be taken this way. The very artificiality of Cherry's costumes is supposed to remind his viewers that he is winking at the camera, and that he understands his celebrity ironically. In other words, as Cherry says in his 2008 memoir, he appears this way and says controversial things because he has *not* forgotten his roots. In a passage where he contrasts himself with Ron MacLean, who was trained as an announcer and did not come up through the hockey system, Cherry aligns himself with working-class people and not with the CBC:

Hey, I realize I put myself in these positions—quitting school, not learning a trade. I'm not whining or complaining. I'm just telling you how I had to fight. When you're down and out, you do anything to survive. (Cherry, *Hockey Stories* 214)

Other stories also serve to deflate his celebrity persona. Cherry has recounted a story more than once about how, when he first became famous, he was mistaken for the actor who played the Friendly Giant (Cherry, *Grapes* 217; McFarlane 187). This strategy makes fun of celebrity as a discourse and of the idea that Cherry could ever be a "real" celebrity at the same time. Therefore, unlike celebrities who are represented as trapped by their fame, there is no "real" life to Cherry that fans seek to uncover. Rather, the artificiality of Don Cherry's appearance and his hypermasculine performances are understood as a refusal of the discourse of celebrity, even as they are in fact making use of celebrity discourse. As Hart shows, Cherry's cartoonish persona is meant to represent a manipulation of celebrity, which means that he is a free agent not subject to corporatization by the hockey business or by the television industry. *That* is the source of his authenticity.

There is a third reason why Cherry's costumes are important to his celebrity image. Although originally Cherry's wardrobe did not have the flamboyance that it does today, Cherry's current use of loud patterns, unusual suit cuts, and arguably eccentric detailing no longer just echoes times past or distances him from other sportscasters. Cherry's wardrobe—and his choice of headgear during key playoff games—now also deliberately echoes the sometimes outrageous costumes and makeup worn by fans at sporting events. Fan behaviour has been analyzed as carnivalesque performances that have nationalist overtones, as in the case of Scottish football fans known as the "Tartan Army" (Giulianotti). As John Fiske points out, fandom itself is sometimes allied with "official" cultural capital, as at sporting events, but sometimes fan behaviour exceeds the official terms set for it, and it operates in opposition to official discourses (Fiske 42). That is because, according to Lawrence Grossberg, fan activity is the activity of affect: it is about feeling, and not about logic necessarily, and it is closely related to feelings of pleasure and a love of fantasy. Fandom is also connected to difference, in that it marks it out (one can be identified as a hockey fan as opposed to a football fan, or one can be an Edmonton Oilers fan as opposed to being a Calgary Flames fan), but it also has the capacity to suspend types of difference, at least temporarily, because "we redefine our own identity out of the relations among our differences; we reorder their importance, we invest ourselves more in some than in others" (Grossberg 56–58). Therefore, I have many identities, such as Canadian, Edmontonian, academic, white woman, and lesbian, but when I am at an Edmonton Oilers game, I am primarily an Oilers fan and the other parts of my identity matter less, at least temporarily. In the intimate public of hockey, I *feel* connected to other fans, and to the team I am watching and supporting.

This set of temporary identifications and their proximity to affect gives licence to fans to deploy the carnivalesque. When male hockey fans sometimes dress as women or as superheroes, they create carnival identities that temporarily reverse power relations and destabilize their other identities in an endorsement of fantasy. They also show the emotions of love and desire as public feelings, which for normatively masculinized men constitutes another reversal. The costume choices of Don Cherry, who exhibits hockey masculinity but whose costumes show a hypermasculine lack of restraint, are a visual embodiment of these kinds of strategies. Like fan performances, Cherry's performance is seen as real because it is passionate. No one could argue that Cherry does not love the game of hockey or Canada, and he is willing to be carnivalesque as a demonstration of his love. This situation often results in Cherry being interpreted as an inadvertent gay icon because his performances are clearly ironic and sentimental at the same time (he knows that other people see his wardrobe as tacky, but he never agrees). For example, Ron MacLean's story in *Cornered* about Don Cherry's use of stereotypical gay affectation to poke fun at those who would ban fighting resulted in the support of the GLBT community rather than criticism of his performance:

> As a rule, the gay community has always gone to bat for Don, and if I objected to his shenanigans, we got emails and calls from the community telling me to mind my own business. They understood that Don has good command of camp, and what he does is no more offensive than *La Cage aux Folles*. (109)

Whether *La Cage aux Folles* is in fact offensive to members of the GLBT community is an issue that must be left to another paper. What is key here is that MacLean thinks that GLBT people who like Don Cherry's performance understand it to be carnivalesque, because it uses exaggeration and reversal in order to make a point. Since Cherry does not mind looking outrageous and campy anyway, this reversal is seen as acceptable rather than homophobic. The same is not always said of homophobic comments attributed to Cherry; he has apologized for on-air comments about "pansies" at least once and has publically supported gay rights in response to complaints about things he has said on *Hockey Night in Canada* (Stursberg 127).

Don Cherry's appearance on the *Rick Mercer Report* in 2008 is a good example of Cherry's relationship to camp, his ironic use of celebrity status, and his working-class aesthetic. In Mercer's program, all of these elements work together to create Cherry's celebrity persona. As the segment begins, Mercer walks through a large fabric warehouse as he introduces the episode with an invocation of some of the great names of fashion, such as Armani and Dior. Then he says that he has a personal audience with a fashion icon, who turns out to be Cherry, resplendent in a shiny flowered pink suit. Mercer, an out gay man, is dressed in a plain dark jacket and white shirt with no tie. It is clear that of the two of them, Cherry is clearly more flamboyant in this moment than Mercer is, with humorous results. The location is revealed to be not a major design house, but FabricLand, a discount fabric outlet. Cherry says in the sketch that he does in fact get his cloth from there, a reminder of his working-class persona and an endorsement of his sincerity because he does not appear to be joking, although he does know that this could be seen as funny. As Cherry arranges for Mercer to be outfitted in a suit like his own, saying that "I think you'd look lovely in pink," it is clear that Cherry knows he is deploying camp as he has fun at Mercer's expense. The humour here is based on a carnivalesque reversal (Cherry is more *outré* than Mercer, who is the "real" gay man) and on the notion that Cherry believes in his own performance. There is no sense in the sketch that Cherry is mugging for the camera. It is clear in the performance that Cherry really does love the fabric choices he shows to Mercer, even when Mercer laughs helplessly. As Cherry continues to try to talk Mercer into buying patterns in the drapery section, Mercer can only reply, "I'm far more conservative than Don Cherry, as it turns out," a double joke about Cherry's flamboyance and his political conservatism.

Cherry also willingly mocks his celebrity status as he supports it in the segment. Mercer asks Cherry about his memoir *Cherry's Hockey Stories and Stuff*, and Cherry proudly replies that it became an instant Canadian best-seller. Here, Cherry appears to be supporting the trappings of celebrity. Mercer looks skeptical, but then many fans appear at FabricLand, asking Cherry to sign copies of the book. This part of the segment is meant to poke fun at Cherry's celebrity, but Cherry's boast that his book was immediately best-selling is in keeping with his lack of embarrassment about his influence on *Coach's Corner*, where he often says that he is very popular with ordinary Canadians. Here again, Cherry performs authenticity while he remains at a distance from celebrity. He also tells Mercer that he would do *Coach's Corner* for free because he loves it so much, even when Mercer says that he probably should not say that in public. This comment—which is inaccurate, since Cherry is in fact paid more than Ron MacLean, who coordinates much of *Hockey Night in Canada*—is also meant to show his working-class roots, his love of the game, and his lack of belief in his special status.[1] At the end of the segment Mercer appears wearing a jacket that looks like Cherry's, and Cherry says, "I don't know whether to shake your hand or kiss you," as Mercer doubles over with laughter ("Making"). Here, Cherry appears as an authentically camp icon who has the power to make

Mercer appear to be more flamboyant, while he pokes fun at the connection between dandyism and homosexuality. Don Cherry's appearance on the *Rick Mercer Report* is a complex set of performances of his celebrity persona. We learn almost nothing about Cherry's private life (we only find out that he calls beers "pops" because his mother didn't like the word beer) because the emphasis is on Cherry's public persona. We see Cherry not acting as a celebrity at some points because of his unpretentiousness (he chooses his own fabric at a discount outlet). At other times, he fully accepts that he is a celebrity (he autographs his memoir and is proud of its success). We see him distance himself from the corporatized world of television and endorse hockey as a game when he says that he would work for free. And finally, we see him expertly manage the discourse of camp for humorous effect as he jokes with Mercer one moment and seems sincere the next. In the end, just as Don Cherry *is* the CBC in that he represents the institution through his own body, Don Cherry's presentation of himself as a nothing but a performance is meant to be understood as the sign of his authenticity.

Conclusion: The Melancholic Wardrobe
On the April 27, 2013, episode of *Coach's Corner*, Don Cherry once again combined his beliefs about hockey masculinity with a controversial social critique. Wearing a yellow and black checked jacket with a yellow polka-dot tie, a red handkerchief, and a red and white striped shirt, Cherry stated that he had to "get something off my chest." When Cherry was a coach, he allowed Robin Herman, a female sports reporter, into the Boston Bruins locker rooms. At the time he did it to save the young reporter's job, but on April 27 Cherry said that he had changed his mind about women in locker rooms. Saying that "I have seen things, and I have heard things that go on in the dressing room when the women are in there... [they are disgusting]," Cherry recommended that a special interview room be built for female reporters because players cannot behave themselves. Cherry angrily brushed off Ron MacLean's position that the dressing room is a reporter's office, and added that "you would not want your daughter or sister in there, believe me" ("Coach's Corner"). The response to these comments has been negative, as male and female sports reporters rejected Cherry's position (Kelly, "CBC's"; "Women's sports media"; Lafleche).

Cherry's opinion and the response to it show clearly how Don Cherry's appearance and talk represent a lament for hockey nation, and they also indicate what his role on CBC is actually about. First, Cherry's comments should be understood as melancholic and nostalgic. When he allowed Robin Herman into "his" dressing room, he was able to tell his players to behave. Today, Cherry suggests, this is not possible because the days when coaches, players, and fans were more important than business interests are over. Cherry also casts himself as a protector of women when he was a coach, but his present solution leaves current hockey masculinity unchanged, even as he critiques the culture for its lack of classic hockey masculinity values, such as honour. In other words, men need to protect women from other men, because it is not possible to change male behaviour. Finally, Cherry's statements were about affect, not a reasoned argument. He yelled at MacLean when MacLean disagreed with him, and expressed outrage about the way women are treated. All the elements that fuel Cherry's celebrity are present: the outrageous outfit which is louder than his own voice; the evocation of an earlier time when men were more honourable and when he was respected and obeyed as a coach; his belief that he must speak truthfully and bluntly in order to remind people of hockey's values; the fact that the comments are not about hockey, but are about a social issue, in this case, the role of female reporters; the use of emotional intelligence in order to appeal to the intimate public of hockey. Here, too, Cherry's performance as a dandy and his defence of players are placed in opposition to official CBC discourse, here represented by MacLean's disagreement. But as we have seen, Cherry is not actually critiquing the CBC. He upholds the prominence of the media in the business of contemporary hockey by not pointing out why it is that reporters go into locker rooms at all.

It is not easy to look past Cherry's bombast and see how his dandyism, melancholic nationalism, and attempt to "protect" women from hockey players could be linked. The reactions to Cherry in the media included mockery of his outfit for the day and a dismissal of his reasoning as faulty and outdated. But what media commentators missed was that Cherry's outfit, which was garish even for him, was a symbol of his melancholic critique of hockey's (and Canada's) loss of values, which was the real point of his rant about women in locker rooms. Cherry decided to speak as a coach and not to ally himself with the media. On that day, he did not side with the players, but spoke about them as if he were still coaching them. His solution to sexism is to recall the values of chivalry that a team should practice, and not to comment on the pervasiveness of media coverage on which the sports industries depend.

Reporters are in locker rooms at all because sports itself is an entertainment industry that requires the presence of media in order to get the "real" ideas of the stars. Locker room interviews are not a way to get more facts about a game: they are a deliberate invasion of privacy because as stars, hockey players are expected to reproduce their inner thoughts at their moment of greatest vulnerability, for audience titillation and enjoyment.

In an indirect way, Cherry's rant disregarded the role that the media plays in the business of hockey. He preferred to focus on problems that players have with the media. Cathal Kelly, a sports reporter who reacted to Cherry negatively, articulates this position when he says that "some pros resent the presence of women in the media. They also resent the presence of men. Their problem is with reporters as a species, rather than with any particular strand of it" (Kelly).

Therefore, Cherry's position constitutes a turn to nostalgia as a relief from the political. He does not comment on the role of the media, which has made him what he is and which helps to fulfill the mandate of the CBC as a national broadcaster. The media is what has turned players into major stars today, but Cherry does not have anything to say about why stars are treated as commodities. Instead, his words take the form of a lament for hockey nation and its values, and an evocation of his own lost role as a coach. As for that jacket? It is both a cry from the past and a shout for the present because it symbolizes the play of surfaces that makes Don Cherry a celebrity figure. Although he did not talk about Canada that day, Don Cherry's complaint about women in dressing rooms shows much about the Canadian celebrity apparatus that has him on the air, and the values of hockey and nationalism that, despite his protestations, he fully embodies on behalf of the network which supports him, and those fans who still see him as one of their own. Whether Cherry continues this role as a part of the Rogers stable or not, his role has been to create what public and private media broadcasters of hockey in Canada want: a figure who performs national populism and national pleasure as relief from the position of hockey as a multinational corporate business, and a forgetting of the importance of media to the consumption of hockey in Canada.

Note

1 In 2007, Don Cherry made between $800,000 and $1,000,000 per year. Ron MacLean, who had just signed a seven-year contract with *Hockey Night in Canada* in 2007, will make an average of $429,000 each contract year until 2015. In 2012, Cherry's salary was reported to be about $800,000 per year. See "Plenty of Cash" and Dowbiggin 2012 for specifics.

Bon Cop, Bad Cop: A Tale of Two Star Systems

Liz Czach

Released in August 2006, the film *Bon Cop, Bad Cop* (Érik Canuel) has become a landmark in Canadian film history as one the highest-grossing films ever produced in the country.[1] By the time the film won the Golden Reel Award for top box-office film, as well as the Best Picture statuette at the 2007 Genies, it had earned over CAN$12 million.[2] Much of the film's triumph can be seemingly attributed to its claim as Canada's first bilingual feature film, thus appearing to successfully bridge the gap between the two solitudes to capitalize on audiences in Quebec *and* the rest of Canada.[3] Despite *Bon Cop, Bad Cop*'s bilingualism and presumed nationwide appeal, the film actually earned the lion's share of its box office in Quebec.[4] This disparity in box-office draw reaffirms the long-standing split between the struggles of English-Canadian cinema to attract an audience in contrast to the support Quebec viewers frequently demonstrate for domestically produced films. Quebec producers have been effective in making unabashedly commercial films employing familiar genres, populist themes, and local stars that are popular with audiences.[5] *Bon Cop, Bad Cop* follows in this tradition of commercial film production in Quebec and through its use of an established genre, a hockey-related plot, and the casting of "stars," is meant to overtly appeal to a broad audience. An analysis of the careers of the film's two lead actors, Patrick Huard and Colm Feore, will shed light on how Quebec sustains and exploits its domestic star system whereas such a system is underdeveloped in English Canada. It will become evident that Quebec produces *stars* while English Canada, at best, produces well-known or *recognizable actors*, and *Bon Cop, Bad Cop* highlights this asymmetrical star production in Quebec vis-à-vis the rest of Canada. This analysis will draw upon some key ideas put forth in Richard Dyer's groundbreaking works *Stars* (1979/1998) and

Heavenly Bodies: Film Stars and Society (1986/2004), specifically, the manner in which a "star image" is produced and how these star images are then
either matched or mismatched with onscreen characters and roles. I draw
on Dyer's model of star production in conjunction with literary theorist's
Gérard Genette's concept of "transtextuality," to illuminate how the star
images, or what I will argue are more accurately described as the "personas,"
of Colm Feore and Patrick Huard are transtextually produced. Following
this, I will examine how these personas are mapped onto the characters of
Martin Ward and David Bouchard in *Bon Cop, Bad Cop* to demonstrate that
these "personas as characters" are emblematic of the broader mechanisms
and differences of star production in Quebec and English Canada.

   Bon Cop, Bad Cop features two cops, one from Quebec (Patrick Huard)
the other from Ontario (Colm Feore), who are reluctantly thrust together
to work a murder case when a body is discovered straddling the border between the two provinces. Much of the film's humour and appeal
is based on the linguistic and cultural differences, whether perceived or
real, between English Canadians and the Québécois, as epitomized by
Feore's and Huard's characters. *Bon Cop, Bad Cop* is an unapologetically
commercial film employing the popular genre of the mismatched buddy
cop comedy (best exemplified in the profitable *Lethal Weapon* and *Rush
Hour* series), a plot focused on "Canada's national pastime" hockey, and
is directed by Érik Canuel, an unapologetically populist genre film director.[6] But most important to my discussion here is the deliberate casting of
"stars" Patrick Huard and Colm Feore for their potential box-office clout.
I use "stars" tentatively because while Patrick Huard is an indisputable
box-office draw in Quebec, it is arguable whether the same can be said
about Feore. Indeed, one would be hard-pressed to think of a homegrown
English-Canadian actor with the same popularity and fan base as Huard.
It is difficult to imagine an English-Canadian actor who has achieved
stardom primarily in domestic productions and not through his work in
Hollywood, that is, a performer who wasn't being "imported" from Hollywood to lend star power to a Canadian film.[7] In terms of the respective
popularity of Huard and Feore, their casting in *Bon Cop, Bad Cop* pointedly serves to underscore how lopsided the Quebec and English-Canadian
star systems are.

   There is a clear disparity between the box-office draw of Patrick Huard
and Colm Feore. As Pierre Vérroneau has noted, since the 1990s the star
system in Quebec continues "to assert its importance in the industry and it
has become, along with genres, a central element in the construction of the
audience's horizons of expectations" (Vérronneau 104). The same, however, cannot be said for English Canada given its lack of a domestically pro-

duced star system. Consequently, it is unsurprising that English-language media reports on Feore's participation in the production referred to him not as a star, but as "one of English-Canada's best known and respected actors" (Hays 14). This disjuncture between Huard and Feore's popularity can be largely attributed to Quebec's successful production of celebrity and stardom versus English Canada's ongoing struggle to overcome the dominant presence of American popular culture. In Quebec, linguistic and cultural factors also help insulate its popular culture from the rest of Canada and the US so that there exists a culture of stars that are well known within Quebec, but whose celebrity does not cross linguistic or cultural borders. As Leila Basen, a scriptwriter on *Bon Cop, Bad Cop*, explains: "All of my French friends knew exactly who he [Patrick Huard] was, but none of my English-speaking friends did. I had never heard of him. So the gap between us was very apparent" (qtd. in Hays 12). Conversely, when asked to identify English-Canadian "stars," audiences in Quebec as well as the rest of Canada would undoubtedly turn to what Charles Acland has called the "star-system-in-exile," referring to English-Canadian actors who have achieved success in Hollywood such as Mary Pickford, Ryan Gosling, etc. (Acland 191).[8]

Despite the varying success of the Quebec star system versus that of English Canada, the production of stars in either context follows a similar pattern. In the introduction to the 2004 edition of *Heavenly Bodies*, Richard Dyer offers a concise distillation of how stars are produced. Dyer is worth quoting at length for the robust and inclusive account of the mechanisms of star production he offers:

> The star phenomenon consists of everything that is publicly available about stars. A film star's image is not just his or her films, but the promotion of those films and of the star through pin-ups, public appearances, studio hand-outs and so on, as well as interviews, biographies and coverage in the press of the star's doings and "private" life. Further, a star's image is also what people say or write about him or her, as critics or commentators, the way the image is used in other contexts such as advertisements, novels, pop songs, and finally the way the star can become part of the coinage of everyday speech. (Dyer, *Heavenly Bodies* 3)

This expansive description of how the star image is created and circulated can account for how non-mediated (i.e., theatrical performances and stand-up comedy) performances work alongside mediated images, not only in more traditional media of print, television, and film, but also contemporary iterations of celebrity on the Internet and in digital media. In essence what Dyer is describing is a model of star production that suggests strong parallels to literary theorist Gérard Genette's concept of "transtextuality." For Genette, transexuality subsumes four subtypes of textuality including paratextuality, intertextuality, architextuality, and hypotextuality. Genette argues that transtextuality is "all that sets the text in relationship, whether obvious or concealed, with other texts" (Genette 1). Using Genette's transtextuality in tandem with Dyer's model of star-image production creates a framework within which a full spectrum of texts can come into play.

Thinking through the full range of transmedial and transtextual works that inform the construction of a "star image" illuminates some of the limitations of using the term "star." To clarify, the transtextual mechanisms that Dyer describes do not *necessarily* result in the creation of a "star image," and we should be mindful in differentiating between those actor/celebrities that achieve stardom and those that do not. To that end, I distinguish between "stars" and "personas" since an actor can have a clear and identifiable persona, but not necessarily have achieved stardom. Actors and celebrities fall somewhere on the continuum from "somewhat recognizable" to "household name." Thus, I will argue that while both Colm Feore's and Patrick Huard's personas are produced transtextually, that is, across a wide range of performance texts including film, television, radio, audio books, theatre, Internet, interviews, stand-up comedy, and so on, Feore's persona in English Canada is that of a well-known actor, whereas Patrick Huard is an undeniable Quebec star.

The transtextual model of producing personas, while not unique to Canada, is useful for understanding a context where stardom or celebrity is rarely developed through cinematic performances alone.[9] Given English Canada's and Quebec's small feature-film market, few if any actors attain any level of stardom or recognizability solely through film performances or make a living only working in feature films. As actor Sheila McCarthy of *I've Heard the Mermaids Singing* (Patricia Rozema, 1987) and a regular cast member of the CBC Television series *Little Mosque on the Prairie* (2007–2012) noted: "In Canada we get to move around in different mediums. If there's no TV or film happening, maybe there's a play or cabaret I can be considered for" (qtd. in Howley 15). The production of transtextual personas follows a predictable pattern that is similar to the production of cinematic stars although it draws from a larger corpus of texts. Actors make regular appearances in films, television, theatre, Internet, comedy shows, commercials, etc., they become recognizable to audiences through their repeated roles and performances, they develop a fairly consistent and identifiable persona, the media reports on the actor's onscreen appearances as well as his or her offscreen private life, and a fan base follows the actor through these onscreen and offscreen representations. Thinking of image construction transtextually helps illuminate the residual traces that an actor's performance leaves in his or her movement across media in multiple types of texts. "Transtextuality" is productive for thinking through the ways that media texts refer to and recall other media texts, or more specifically here, how one performance recalls and references past performances while anticipating future ones. Using this more expansive transtextual model, a quick overview of Feore's and Huard's careers illustrates not only their movement across different media, but highlights the development of two very different personas: Feore, as a well-regarded classically trained actor associated with high-brow artistic texts; and Huard as a star of less venerated forms of popular culture—stand-up comedy, sitcoms, etc. The social, cultural, and class distinctions of these respective personas dovetail with their onscreen roles in *Bon Cop, Bad Cop* to reflect large differences in star production in Quebec and English-Canada.

Colm Feore
Colm Feore (b. 1958) is one of English Canada's most respected actors. Although American born, Feore has jokingly referred to this as "an accident of birth" and he has lived in Canada for over forty years. His reputation as a serious thespian is largely based on his long association with the Stratford Festival, where he has played leads in innumerable Shakespeare dramas including *Hamlet, Richard III,* and *Macbeth.* This classical theatre experience is one of the dominant transtextual traces that inflect his successive roles and his work across various media texts refers back to this affiliation. He appears regularly in art films that are critically well regarded if not always commercially successful, and in his leading roles in Canadian television and film he is often cast as an elite member of society. In an onstage interview at the Banff Television Festival in 2008, Feore jokingly describes the kinds of roles he has played: "I do dead Canadians. If he's dead and he's Canadian and he's famous I'll be playing him at some point. I joke, but I have played about five or six famous Canadians." Amongst his best-known performances of "famous dead Canadians" are his turns as the idiosyncratic classical pianist Glenn Gould in François Girard's *Thirty-two Short Films about Glenn Gould* (1993) and the former prime minister in the CBC miniseries *Trudeau* (Jerry Ciccoritti, 2002). Feore's roles as these "famous" Canadians—a well-known pianist, on the one hand, and a long-serving politician, on the other—underscore the fact that English Canada produces celebrities primarily in the realms of politics, sports, news reporting, and music.[10] Thus David Suzuki, Peter Mansbridge, Anne Murray, and Don Cherry are more recognizable to mainstream audiences than either Don McKellar or Sarah Gadon.[11] Of importance here is the manner

in which Feore's screen persona is structured by these high-culture associations (Shakespeare's plays and the Stratford Festival) and inflected in his television and film roles representing the cultural, political, and social elite. More recently he had a recurring role on the internationally co-produced "quality television" series *The Borgias* (2011–2013), as Cardinal Giuliano Della Rovere.[12] Additionally, Feore has performed voice work, provided documentary narration for the National Film Board's *The Museum* (Kenton Vaughn, 2009) about architect Daniel Libeskind's expansion of the Royal Ontario Museum, and recorded Timothy Findley's *The Piano Man's Daughter* as an audio book. These various performances, in a wide-ranging set of predominantly highbrow texts, reinforce Feore's screen persona as one affiliated with art cinema, quality television, serious literature, and classical theatre. Despite this significant body of work and hefty filmography, Feore's work in these arguably "unpopular" high-culture texts reaches a limited audience that does not translate into a stardom of a name-brand variety.

The transtextual traces of Colm Feore's career are not limited to his performances in Canada. As an American-Canadian Feore frequently crosses the border and appears regularly in American film and television. At first glance his Canadian "high-art" persona is seemingly at odds with his American one. One of the most striking differences is that in Canada Feore has leading-man status whereas in American productions he is almost exclusively relegated to supporting roles. Furthermore, his portrayal of, as noted above, revered "famous dead Canadians" appears to bear little resemblance to the unscrupulous villains he frequently depicts in his American roles. Despite these apparent differences, I would argue that Feore is regularly cast, both in Canada and the US, in roles that show him occupying powerful positions of authority whether it be as a lawyer, school principal, doctor, aristocrat, cardinal, prime minister, etc. However, in his American roles the limits of this authority are routinely exceeded, often in a maniacal and abusive fashion. For example, in *The Chronicles of Riddick* (David Twohy, 2004) Feore is cast as the powerful and malevolent Lord Marshall set on destroying Riddick (Vin Diesel), the film's hero. Feore similarly appears, although hardly recognizable, as the equally evil King Laufrey, leader of the Frost Giants, in *Thor* (Kenneth Branagh, 2011). If in his Canadian roles Feore plays quasi-benevolent authority figures, and in his American appearances portrays cruel tyrants abusing their power, a third context bridges US and Canadian productions and provides another textual strand worth pursuing—that of Feore's performances in US productions shot in Canada.

In an incisive analysis of *Chicago* (Rob Marshall, 2002), a US film shot in Toronto, Will Straw draws our attention to a courtroom scene in which

Colm Feore and fellow Canadian Sean McCann are cast in supporting roles as, respectively, a prosecuting attorney and presiding judge. Straw contends that each of their roles in *Chicago* "resonates, at least slightly, with longstanding stereotypes about Anglo-Canadian character and its legendary investment in notions of order and propriety" (Straw, "Cross-Border Visualities" 25). To underscore this assessment, Straw notes that both McCann and Feore have played Canadian prime ministers in television miniseries, that is, figures of authority. Elaborating further, Straw argues:

> As is so often the case with U.S. films shot in Canada, the most prominent Canadian actors used in *Chicago* appear as fleeting figures of judicial or bureaucratic authority. The appearance of Feore and McCann in *Chicago*'s courtroom scene exposes the limited exportability of English-Canadian "stardom," but it also repeats a pattern whereby locally-hired performers occupy the roles of passionless enforcers of social or legal discipline. (26)

Straw is indeed correct about the limited exportability of English-Canadian "stardom" and furthermore, his demarcating of "stardom" in quotations suggests a fundamental suspicion of this category's existence. Straw's line of questioning resonates with my own. Elsewhere, I have argued that English Canada has been thus far unsuccessful in developing and sustaining a full-fledged star system (Czach, "Television, Film"). In that article, I suggest revitalizing Richard deCordova's concept of "picture personality" as a productive avenue for rethinking English-Canadian "stardom." DeCordova's model seems to me particularly useful because of the way in which it accounts for actors becoming well known and recognizable but primarily through their textual performances and not for their existence outside of this work. Unlike stars, whose private life is public knowledge, contemporary picture personalities are "known to us through their various screen performances, while their names and the details of their off-screen private lives, the constituents of stardom, continue to remain elusive" (Czach, "Television, Film" 71). Feore is a good example of a contemporary picture personality, that is, an actor well known for his performances and perhaps recognizable to an audience. Media reports on his private life and offscreen behaviors are infrequent. Feore's status as a "star" is thus doubtful and consequently his exportability as a star is equally suspect—whether he is being exported to the US or Quebec. In fact, Feore's role in *Bon Cop, Bad Cop* demonstrates the same propensity for order and propriety that Straw identifies in the supporting roles he plays in American productions shot in Canada. But before turning to how these transtextual traces and his constructed persona resonate with the character of Martin Ward in *Bon Cop, Bad Cop* it is necessary to outline the parameters of Patrick Huard's persona and stardom.

Patrick Huard

Unlike Feore's association with art cinema, theatrical productions of Shake-speare, and other highbrow cultural productions, Patrick Huard's (b. 1969) work in television, film, and stand-up comedy has a decidedly populist inflection. Key to Huard's popularity and populism is his presentation as an ordinary guy, a middle-class or working-class hero, and not a member of a cultural or class elite. Pierre Vérronneau has argued that this "ordinariness" is a fundamental feature of the Quebec star system. He writes:

> Unlike Hollywood stars, whose very status depends on their inaccessibility, Quebec stars are defined by their proximity to the people, by their ordi-nariness. Consequently, ordinary guys and gals like Isabel Richer, Benoît Brière, Patrick Huard, David Boutin, Luc Picard, Roy Dupuis, Jean-Nicholas Verreault and Serge Thériault have become the core of a star system.... (104–105)

Véronneau's attribution of "ordinariness" to Quebec stars, as distinct from the inaccessibility of Hollywood stars, sets up an untenable opposition. As Dyer has explained in *Stars*, one of the foundational underpinnings of the phenomenon of stardom is the ambiguity/contradiction of stars-as-special and stars-as-ordinary that stardom manages to successfully keep in tension (Dyer, *Stars* 43). Quebec stardom, like Hollywood stardom, relies on this paradox of ordinary/extraordinary and Patrick Huard's "ordinari-ness" is kept in balance with his exceptionalness as a charismatic star. Stars, Dyer argues, "may represent what are taken to be people typical of society" (Dyer, *Stars* 43), and Huard's "typicality" has been developed and sus-tained through the transtextual resonances of his various performances from stand-up comedy to popular genre films and a comedy television series that frequently position him as a common everyman.

A quick survey of Huard's career to date reveals the steady growth in his popularity across a number of popular genres and his recurring roles as an ordinary guy. Huard made his feature-film debut in Claude Fournier's gay-themed *J'en Suis!* (1997), a broad comedy of errors aimed squarely at a mainstream popular audience. Huard shares top billing with Roy Dupuis, Quebec's reigning heartthrob at the time, and the two are cast as partners in an architecture firm who pretend to be gay lovers to save their strug-gling company. *J'en Suis!* is a telling first step in Huard's climb toward star-dom, given the manner in which the film positions him as heir apparent to Roy Dupuis's star throne. The film boldly underscores the "beefcake" aspect of each actor, and Huard's status as an object of female and male desire is accentuated in the film and continues to be a key feature of his star persona. While *J'en Suis!* does a candid job of profiling Huard's "talents," the film's middling performance at the box office did not exactly catapult Huard into the limelight. Huard's next film, the first of the wildly popular *Les Boys* series, would be a significant step in his career.

The popularity and success of the *Les Boys* series in Quebec's film history cannot be underestimated. The first *Les Boys* (Louis Saïa, 1997) film made over $6 million domestically (almost exclusively in Quebec) and paved the way for sequels *Les Boys II* (1998), *Les Boys III* (2001)—both of which topped the Canadian box office in the year they were released—and *Les Boys IV* (2005), as well as a television series *Les Boys* (2007–2012). The franchise revolves around the exploits of a team of hockey players made up of a variety of men with different professional and personal backgrounds. The players confront various obstacles that are inevitably resolved with a hockey match in which the hardscrabble group often emerges victorious. The films rely upon the generic conventions of the sports film, predominantly the trope of a gang of underdog characters who manage to unite and overcome their foes. Huard's recurring role as Ti-Guy in the first three films undoubtedly helped establish him as a star, but one that is decidedly belongs to an "ordinary hero" category.

Following the success of *Les Boys,* Huard was cast in a number of feature-film comedies, appearing in supporting roles as an overly emotional biker in *La vie après l'amour* (Gabriel Pelletier, 2000), as a hunky stud in *Comment ma mère accoucha de moi durant sa menopause* (Sébastien Rose, 2003), and then in a starring role as an embittered literary critic in the Christmas-themed romantic comedy *Nez rouge* (Érik Canuel, 2003). In 2003, Huard also appeared in the psychological thriller *Sur le seuil* (Éric Tessier, 2003), which paved the way for a career that would alternate between appearing in dramatic and comedic roles in both film and television. For example, he appeared as a man proclaiming his innocence in the face of a murder conviction in the dramatic miniseries *Au nom de la loi* (2005) as well as the lead in the comedy television series *Taxi-022* (2007–2009) as the frank cab driver, Rogatien Dubois Jr, who comments on the absurdities of modern-day life and expresses exactly what he thinks about his customers. Although Huard's roles have varied, he has largely performed in popular genres such as comedies, romantic comedies, and psychological thrillers. In addition to his work in film and television, Huard has had a very successful stand-up-comedy career and the DVD of his comedy routine *Face à Face* (2004) was one of the best-selling DVDs in Quebec the year it was released. Much of Huard's appeal can be traced back to his many appearances in popular genres and his persona as a typical everyday kind of guy.

In Quebec, Huard is a bona fide star and box-office draw.[13] He is cognizant of Quebec's unique star system and has noted how it functions:

> We have this weird star system in Quebec—weird because it's a small mar-
> ket, but everyone does know the stars here. The actors, the comedians, and
> the directors are getting paid attention. It's because of our television shows
> and newspapers and everything; it's always the local artists who get the big
> part of the coverage. (qtd. in Marchand, "Quebec Fans'")

Whereas Quebec media engages with its own celebrities, personalities, and
stars, English-Canadian entertainment reporting on stars, on shows such
as *eTalk,* focuses primarily on American stars or Canadians successful in
Hollywood. Huard's private life, however, has been under intense public
scrutiny, particularly his well-publicized divorce in 2000 from popular
singer Lynda Lemay, with whom he has a daughter. As Richard deCordova
has pointed out, it is audience interest in the private lives of performers that
shifts actors from being simply picture personalities, actors recognized and
known primarily from their cinematic appearances (deCordova, *Picture
Personalities* 51), to stars, that is, actors whose private lives are of interest
to the public (deCordova, *Picture Personalities* 98). Knowledge about the
private lives of popular Quebec media personalities seeps back into the
roles in which they are cast and informs onscreen performances. In *Bon
Cop, Bad Cop*, Huard's character David Bouchard evokes his off-screen life
as a divorced father of a daughter.

Bon Cop, Bad Cop

Richard Dyer has pointed out that star images are matched or mismatched
with onscreen roles. In brief, Dyer observes that a star's image may work
seamlessly, selectively, or problematically with the creation of a character in
a film depending on how closely the star image and character are in sync in
the meanings they produce (Dyer, *Stars* 126–131). In cases where there is a
slight mismatch between the image and role, the fit is considered selective;
a problematic fit is a complete mismatch; and a perfect fit is when "all the
aspects of a star's image fit with all the traits of a character" (Dyer, *Stars*
129). In *Bon Cop, Bad Cop,* the transtextually produced personas of Colm
Feore and Patrick Huard are matched, in a perfect fit, to their onscreen
characters with Feore's highly cultured stuffed-shirt Anglo police officer
Martin Ward providing a contrast to Huard's sexy, laid-back cop David
Bouchard. In brief, Colm Feore as Martin Ward distinguishes himself as
a member of the Anglo-Canadian elite through his education, tastes, and
dress whereas Patrick Huard as David Bouchard is presented as an unfussy
typical everyman. The cultural, social, class, and linguistic differences of
the actors and their respective roles stand in for the cultural differences in
star production in English Canada and Quebec. *Bon Cop, Bad Cop* serves

Patrick Huard as David Bouchard (left) and Colm Feore as Martin Ward (right) in *Bon Cop, Bad Cop* (2006). Image used by permission of Kevin Tierney/Park Ex Pictures.

as a model text to draw out the differences between English-Canada's pro-duction of well-known, distinguished, and highly regarded actors such as Colm Feore versus Quebec's successful star system that generates popular stars such as Patrick Huard.

As a comedy of cross-cultural misunderstandings, *Bon Cop, Bad Cop*'s humour draws upon stereotypical cultural differences between Martin Ward and David Bouchard. The Anglo Ward (Feore) is an stodgy, over-educated, seemingly humourless, by-the-book cop. Ward, we learn, attended Upper Canada College, speaks Metropolitan French, is a gour-met cook, and dresses with geeky impeccability. This information as well as his dress and disposition unquestionably situate Ward as a member of the elite. Bouchard (Huard), on the other hand, is a chain-smoking, cussing, rough-and-tumble cop who prefers jeans and T-shirts and can't distinguish endive from other vegetables. Bouchard would rather settle matters with his fists and uses a colourful slang-filled Québécois *joual* to express his antipathy toward authority and disregard for social status. When a roadblock delays Bouchard's arrival at the first murder scene of the film, his anger is unleashed in the expletive-filled sentence, "Ostie de câlisse de tabarnak!" When an officer attempts to justify the situation, he addresses Bouchard as "Dave" and Bouchard angrily corrects him: "Pour toi, aujourd'hui," Bouchard barks, "c'est detective Dave!" [14] Even in the throes of his fury, Bouchard is unable and unwilling to pull rank (well, not much rank) on his subordinate. In short, he's a no-nonsense workaday cop who cares little about hierarchy, authority, or appearing well mannered and polite.

The scene in which Ward and Bouchard meet for the first time at the crime scene on the Quebec/Ontario border economically makes evident their cultural, class, and linguistic differences. A low-angle canted shot shows Bouchard pull up in a decrepit old sports car. As he steps out of the car, the film shifts momentarily to slow motion as Bouchard flings a cigarette butt toward the camera; he is dressed in a V-neck T-shirt, unbuttoned plaid shirt, hoodie, jeans, and sneakers. A reverse shot shows Ward with arms folded leaning leisurely against a nondescript black sedan. He is dressed in a three-quarter-length black cloth coat, striped dress shirt, matching tie, pressed pants (he was shown ironing them earlier), and dress shoes. In a few well-composed shots, the premise of two mismatched cops flung together to work a murder case efficiently establishes the linguistic differences between Ward and Bouchard as well as their cultural and class distinctions.

The differences between Feore/Ward as an uptight Anglo-Canadian actor and Huard/Bouchard as a popular and sexy star are accentuated with a number of ongoing jokes in the film. One of the running gags is Bouchard's teasing of Ward's propensity for dressing in turtlenecks, which symbolize Ward's adherence to respectability and decorum. One of the first things Bouchard does upon meeting Ward is to reflect on his dress. "Nice turtleneck," he sarcastically states. "It's really you." Ward returns the disparaging character assessment when he is a passenger in Bouchard's dilapidated car. Bouchard is exercising what he claims is his right to smoke and Ward is desperately trying to open the window when the handle breaks off in his hand. "This car is really you," Ward acerbically comments. This and other similar exchanges of dialogue establish the stereotypical set of differences between the two men. In another scene, Ward and Bouchard meet at the coroner's office to identify the first murder victim. Ward, efficiently flipping through his police notebook, informs Bouchard that the victim was a lawyer, owed three condos, and worked "75 hours a week." To which Ward wryly adds, "which I gather for Montreal is a lot." This observation very pointedly draws a distinction between the supposed hard-working English Canadians and the more leisure-loving Québécois.

The uptightness of Ward, or what Will Straw would call the propensity "for order and propriety" (Straw, "Cross-Border Visualities" 25) in contradistinction to the overtly sexy laidbackness of Bouchard is firmly established. The overwhelming association of Feore with an image of being by-the-book is one of the key transtextual traces that is both subtly and overtly evoked in the film. Ward is a cop who follows rules and procedures and Bouchard's blatant disregard for protocol exasperates him. When Bouchard, driving his unmarked beaten-up sports car, embarks on a high-speed drive, with a detour along a pedestrian pathway, Ward is flabber-gasted by his action. "You can't do that," he protests, "this isn't an official police car. There are no sirens to warn people." Bouchard, however, con-tinues to flaunt his disregard for procedure at every turn. When Bouchard arrives late at a recital in which his daughter is performing he pulls into a parking spot reserved for the disabled. Again, Ward is outraged: "This is a handicap space," he points out. "You can't park here." A few moments later, with Bouchard continuing to ignore Ward's protestations, Ward again lec-tures him: "Rules were made for a reason." By this point in the film, it has become abundantly clear that Bouchard has little concern for the "rules." Eventually this behaviour leads Ward to rebuke Bouchard: "I don't know if you don't respect procedures because you are a lunatic, ignorant, or just because you're French." Indeed, Feore's straightlaced character provides much comic fodder for the film. In a key scene, Bouchard and Ward break into a house without a warrant, much to Ward's consternation, and the house turns out to be a marijuana grow-op, which is then accidentally set on fire. Of course, Bouchard and Ward end up engulfed in the smoke. As *Bon Cop, Bad Cop* co-screenwriter Alex Epstein put it: "Who wouldn't pay money to see Colm Feore stoned? Here was a situation that was waiting to be taken advantage of" (qtd. in Hays 15). Of course, getting Ward/Feore stoned takes a jab at his Anglo-Canadian propriety and order.

Huard's position as star and as sex symbol is underscored perfectly in a scene when Ward and Bouchard conduct an interview with an airport employee as part of their investigation. This interview with the female employee is a telling reminder of Huard's star status in Quebec. The inter-viewee is a slightly dowdy woman sporting a baseball cap and ponytail who is clearly bowled over by the sexy Bouchard. She becomes flustered during the interview and is clearly distracted by Huard/Bouchard's attractiveness and has trouble focusing on the questions she is being asked. When the interview is finished and Bouchard starts to leave, the woman flirtatiously tries to keep him engaged in conversation. She coquettishly inquires about how to get in touch with Bouchard should she remember anything that might be relevant to the investigation and asks for his card. When Bouchard feigns that he is out of cards, she, like a truly star-struck fan, holds up a small pad of paper and pencil, in a gesture that plainly evokes asking Huard/Bouchard for his autograph. Bouchard, however, doesn't fall for the ruse and slowly dictates his number—9-1-1. The joke slowly dawns on the woman and she laughs as her gaze follows Bouchard as he exits the shot.

The denouement of *Bon Cop, Bad Cop* rather unsurprisingly has the two cops working as a team to rescue Bouchard's daughter from the crazed serial killer. More than temporarily setting aside their differences, the conclusion shows Ward warming to Bouchard's way of policing. In the culminating moments of the film, Ward, bloodied and bruised from the confrontation with the killer, dispenses with "propriety and order" to plant a bomb on the psychopathic killer, ensuring his explosive death. The final shot of the film shows Ward and Bouchard walking down a pier away from the camera in slow motion, firmly establishing them as heroes of the film, but doing little to undo their uneven star status.

Conclusion

Media accounts of the *Bon Cop, Bad Cop*'s phenomenal box-office success routinely return to the film's claim as Canada's first bilingual feature, implying that the film appealed to audiences across the nation. But, as I have noted in my introduction, the majority of the film's revenues were generated in Quebec, where audiences flocked to see one of Quebec's homegrown stars, Patrick Huard, light up the screen opposite an English-Canadian actor they were most likely unfamiliar with—Colm Feore. The casting of Huard and Feore was intended to capitalize on their "star" status, but it merely highlights the discrepancy between the success of Quebec's homegrown star system and the questionable existence of domestically produced English-Canadian stardom. An overview of Feore's and Huard's transtextually produced personas across a wide range of texts shows how Huard has been fashioned into an ordinary hero associated with a myriad of popular-culture platforms from stand-up comedy to television sitcoms and genre films. On the other hand, Feore's persona denotes high culture as reflective of his ongoing work in art cinema, quality television, and theatre. The difference continues to be reaffirmed with Huard's onward trajectory toward greater stardom. A much-sought-after actor, he starred in the megahit *Starbuck* (Ken Scott), the highest grossing film in Canada in 2011, but is expanding beyond acting to turn to directing.[15] He has directed two features, both comedies: *Les 3 p'tits cochons*, the highest-grossing film in Canada in 2007, and *Filière 13* (2010), about bumbling cops on a stakeout. Feore, on the other hand, continues to work steadily in Canadian television and film as well as at Stratford, and in supporting roles in the US. He continues to be cast in roles that accentuate his serious persona and theatrical training, including a turn as King Lear at the 2014 Stratford festival—a milestone role for Shakespearean actors. A recurring supporting role in the American-produced television series *Revolution* (2012–2013) once again saw Feore cast in a position of authority as the Assistant Secretary of Defense. Set in a post-apocalyptic world, Feore's character, Randall Flynn, aggressively attempts to gather together, by force and sheer will, scientists to further his own unscrupulous plans. In his continuing role in the television series *The Borgias* (2011–2013) he was likewise cast in a position of power and authority as a cardinal who, after losing the papal election, seeks to oust the current pope. No doubt, Feore's theatrical training and classical repertoire help him bring a particular gravitas to these roles. His work on stage and screen (both small and large) continues to draw critical praise, and he remains one of English Canada's most renowned and revered actors, if not exactly a household name or popular star.

In the opening credits for *Bon Cop, Bad Cop,* the names of Patrick Huard and Colm Feore appear simultaneously side by side, giving both actors equal billing. The advertising campaign in both Quebec and the rest of Canada gives the same prominence to both actors, accurately reflecting the collaborative nature of their input into the film and their corresponding screen time. This equitable approach to their casting and promotion, however, cannot redress the broader mechanisms and differences of star production whereby English Canada, at best, can produce recognized and respected actors, and Quebec successfully generates stars.

Notes

1 There is some debate on whether *Bon Cop, Bad Cop* outperforms Bob Clark's teenage sex romp *Porky's* (1982) taking into consideration such factors as inflation and single-ticket admissions versus box-office totals.

2 According to Box Office Mojo, *Bon Cop, Bad Cop* earned $12,665,721 in Canada. See http://www.boxofficemojo.com/movies/?id=boncopbadcop.htm, accessed January 29, 2014.

3 Bilingual films that precede *Bon Cop, Bad Cop* include Larry Kent's *Fleur Bleue* (1971) and Robin Spry's *Suzanne* (1980).

4 The box office in Quebec was $10,638,568. See http://www.filmsquebec.com/box-office-quebecois-de-lannee-2006/), accessed January 29, 2014.

5 The Golden Reel Award winners for top Canadian box-office shows films from Quebec in the clear majority. While Denys Arcand's auteurist films *Decline of the American Empire* (1987) and *Jesus of Montreal* (1990) were top draws, the remaining films are more firmly rooted in the traditions of popular genres, particularly the comedy, and are decidedly not auteur-driven art-house fare.

6 In defence of genre filmmaking, Canuel has stated: "It is time for genre films to be taken seriously in Quebec, whether it's comedy, romance, fantasy or historical films. For 20 years or more, we have been fed 'autuer films', some are good, but others are morbidly boring. I think it is possible to make meaningful films that are also entertaining" (qtd. in Vérronneau 123, note 2).

7   There is a long tradition of using English-Canadian actors who have achieved success in the United States to provide a "star" presence in a Canadian production while also fulfilling Canadian content regulations. A recent example is the casting of Canadian Joshua Jackson, best known for his work on the American television series *Dawson's Creek*, in *One Week* (Michael McGowan, 2008).

8   Interestingly, a number of Québécois actors who have achieved varying degrees of success in Hollywood's "star-system-in-exile" such as Geneviève Bujold, Karine Vanasse, and Caroline Dhavernas have had successful careers in Quebec before heading south.

9   See Katherine Ann Roberts's discussion of the career of Callum Keith Rennie in this volume.

10   Although Trudeau was bilingual and from Quebec, the miniseries was an English-language production. See Jennifer Bell's chapter on Pierre Trudeau in this volume.

11   See Julie Rak's contribution on Don Cherry in this volume.

12   In her seminal account of the phenomenon of "quality television," Jane Feuer characterizes it as a form of "television which is seen as more literate, more stylistically complex, and more psychologically 'deep' than ordinary television fare" (56). See Feuer, "The MTM Style," in *MTM: Quality Television*, edited by Jane Feuer, Paul Kerr, and Tise Vahimagi, 32-60. London: BFI, 1984. *The Borgias*, an international co-production, that was broadcast on CTV and Bravo in Canada, and Showtime in the US, featured the kind of high production values and narrative complexity associated with "quality television."

13   A quick look over the Golden Reel Award winners for top-grossing Canadian film of the year illustrates Huard's box-office draw. In addition to his appearances in the *Les Boys* series (1999, 2000, 2003) and *Bon Cop, Bad Cop* (2007) he directed *Les 3 p'tits cochons* (2008) and stared in *Starbuck* (2012). From 1999 to 2013, he was involved in one third of the top-grossing films in Canada. See http://en.wikipedia.org/wiki/Golden_Reel_Award_%28Canada%29, accessed July 28, 2013.

14   For an excellent analysis of the French used in *Bon Cop, Bad Cop* and issues in translation, see Hadley.

15   Attesting to the limited exportability of Quebec stars, *Starbuck* was recently remade with the same writer/director Ken Scott for the American market as *Delivery Man* (2013), starring Vince Vaughn.

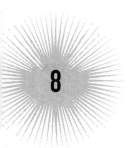

8

Crossover Stars: Canadian Viewing Strategies and the Case of Callum Keith Rennie

Katherine Ann Roberts

Several years ago I found myself teaching Canadian popular culture to a group of undergraduate students at an American university close to the 49th parallel. Despite the university's proximity to Canada, the students' knowledge of all things Canadian was more or less limited to the DIY TV spoof *The Red Green Show* (1991–2002) and Bob and Doug McKenzie's "hoser" comedy *Strange Brew* (1983). As I struggled to find some common ground upon which to begin painting a picture of what I took for granted to be our wondrous bilingual, multicultural, subtle, ironic, nuanced national culture, I realized I was not being taken seriously. Desperate to move away from duck tape, tuques, and Canadian beer in stubby bottles, and inspired by Geoff Pevere and Greig Dymond's quirky pop culture classic *Mondo Canuck: A Canadian Pop Culture Odyssey*, I began to make a random list of famous Canadians in Hollywood, as if this list alone would confer upon us Canadians a much-needed legitimacy. "You see," I seemed to be saying to them, smugly, "we, too, are in the big leagues." I cringe now at the recollection of this moment, which was not particularly effective either from a pedagogical or intellectual perspective. What does it matter if these particular Hollywood stars are Canadian if they are not recognized as such in the United States? What role does stardom play if any in the creation of a national culture? However embarrassing this moment seems to me in retrospect, I realize now that I was tapping into a collective guilty pleasure: rooting for the home team, so to speak, our own "star-system-in-exile," as Charles Acland has termed it (*Screen Traffic* 191), even when the local colours are hidden from view. Canadian media audiences are far from homogeneous, involving multiple points of identification based on region, gender, age, and cultural/linguistic ties. However, I would like to posit from the outset of this chapter that, to a certain degree and undoubtedly not in exactly the same way, Canadians who are engaged in consuming various forms of popular entertainment *know* when Hollywood celebrities, singer-songwriters, and/or television personalities are Canadian, even if this information goes unremarked or is deemed irrelevant by the rest of celebrity marketplace. To follow the careers of these "exile" Canadians is an integral part of Canadian celebrity culture; to investigate this phenomenon is to delve into the very nature of our complex and enduringly ambivalent relationship with the United States.

Given the ubiquity of the Canadians-in-Hollywood phenomenon as demonstrated, for example, by the numerous websites devoted to the top 100 famous Canadians in American movies and television (e.g., Nothern stars.ca), extensive mainstream press coverage of Canadian contenders on American award shows like the Academy Awards and the Grammys, and the simultaneous growth of celebrity studies, the lack of scholarly interest in the star-system-in-exile aspect of Canadian culture is somewhat surprising. Pevere and Dymond's deliberately irreverent and iconoclastic Canadian pop culture "album" was the first text to comment on Canada's contribution to the entertainment export boom. Pevere and Dymond's "'Eh' List" of Hollywood Canucks includes mainly English-Canadian movie-industry pioneers and actors past and present (Mary Pickford, Raymond Burr, Michael J. Fox) with the exception of the Quebec actor Geneviève Bujold.[1] The inclusion of Bujold invites the question of the specificity of Quebec's French-language film and television stars, considerably better known within the smaller, more concentrated Quebec market than their English-language counterparts. I regret that space will preclude me here from addressing this specificity, though I will refer the interested reader to Liz Czach's chapter in this volume on the differences between the Quebec and English-Canadian star systems. I want to focus more closely on those exiled English Canadians whose linguistic and (perceived) cultural sameness with respect to the US has facilitated, paradoxically, both their success and their invisibility south of the border.[2] In *Mondo Canuck,* Pevere and Dymond divide Canadians-in-Hollywood into comic subcategories: "Bland Authority Figures," "Northern Nasties" ("shamelessly hammy villains" [93]), "Support Staff," or "Ice Cream Canucks" (pure and nice as a snowy downfall [93]). While these categories may well seem outdated, subjective, and slightly ridiculous, given how they are organized around notions of cleanliness, politeness, and quiet diplomacy, they have enjoyed a surprisingly stubborn longevity and continue to frame the discourse on

Canadian cultural "niceness" (i.e., politeness, deference, modesty). Two recent discussions of English-Canadian cultural exportability illustrate this point, as they return to notions of sanitization and subservience. In examining celebrities that Canada produces for transnational consumption, Michele Byers argues that our male "exports" (Ryan Reynolds would be a recent example) are safe and sanitized, stripped of obvious markers of "Otherness." They perform a certain kind of "whiteness": "offering something to Americanness that is not already in some sense part of the American/global Hollywood lexicon and yet can be added without taking something away. The Canadians who seem to do this the best are those who are, largely, good (white) citizens." Will Straw's study of popular visuality in Canada highlights how in the courtroom scene in the film *Chicago* (filmed in Toronto), Canadian actors Colm Feore and Sean McCann play "secondary roles embodying stuffy legal authority" that resonate with "longstanding stereotypes about Anglo-Canadian character and its legendary investment in notions of order and propriety" ("Cross-Border Visualities" 25). The "dramatic 'thinness' of these roles," he argues, "contrasts sharply with the psychological complexity and affective expansiveness of the leading roles played by Hollywood stars" (27), and constitutes one of the unacknowledged features of the "intervisuality of English-Canadian audiovisual culture" (28).

While both Byers and Straw make interesting arguments about the "work" done by images of Canadianness, such arguments are by their very nature partial and incomplete. Canadian celebrity exports are not exclusively white (e.g., Sandra Oh, star of ABC's *Grey's Anatomy* [2005–present], Brendan Jay Mclaren of AMC's *The Killing* [2011–2012], and Emmanuelle Chriqui of HBO's *Entourage* [2004–2011]), nor limited to roles of "passionless enforcers of social and legal discipline" (Straw, "Cross-Border Visualities" 26). My point here is that the reiterated discourse of bland affability ends up focusing attention away from Canadian export actors who don't conform to this stereotype. My goal in these pages will be to examine an emerging aspect of English-Canadian televisual culture, precisely English-Canadian actors who have emerged from 1980s/90s Canadian auteur cinema, benefited from the rise in US-based locations industry work within Canada, and who currently continue to appear in *both* Canadian cinema and US film and television. Rather than provide an overview of this exile subset (see Pike 107–143), I want to focus on one of its key figures—Scottish-born, Edmonton-raised Callum Keith Rennie—and offer a close reading of several of his more significant roles on both sides of the border. Rennie's so-called dark, edgy masculinity, aided and abetted by the abundance of villainous roles he plays on US television, coupled with his unorthodox Canadian cinema persona (as a sex maniac in *Last Night* [Don McKellar, 1998], a sadistic pimp in *Suspicious River* [Lynne Stopkewich, 2000], and a serial killer in *Unnatural and Accidental* [Carl Bessai, 2005]) complicates and updates the perennial "Ice Cream Canuck" image of orderly male niceness. More importantly, though, for an analysis of Canadian popular culture and for celebrity studies in general, I will steer away from specifically descriptive aspects of Rennie's career in order to analyze the social function of his level of cross-border "niche" stardom. What can it tell us about the circuitous ways in which Canadians consume and *read* American cultural forms?

Canadian Audiences, US Television, and the Recognition Effect

For scholars in cinema studies, unlike for Pevere and Dymond, the "star-system-in-exile" is no laughing matter, but rather part of the "invisibility" of Canadian cinema. As industry professionals have long lamented, English-Canadian-made movies account for roughly 2–3 per cent of the films shown in Canadian commercial exhibition venues—venues which are otherwise devoted to screening US Hollywood/popular cinema.[3] Judging by the number of both English- and French-language productions funded each year by Telefilm Canada, and the dynamism of Canadian film programs at the key Canadian Film Festivals (TIFF, FIFM, VIFF), Canadian cinema suffers not, as Acland argues, from a lack of films but a lack of audiences (*Screen Traffic* 68). The trope of invisibility traverses Canadian film and television production on many levels. While many Canadian films are not accessible to the public because of a lack of traditional exhibition venue, Canadian producers are increasingly developing audiovisual products (made-for-TV movies and TV series) for a global marketplace where the markers of Canadianness are removed. Canadian places masquerading for "universal" or "anywhere" America in Canadian-based productions destined for the global television market join the large number of US television series, TV movies, and blockbusters that have been filmed in a (disguised) Canada for the past several decades.[4] Yet, as Acland reminds us, these cinematic or televisual forms imported from the US or exported and reimported define our national spectatorship practices. What I find particularly useful (and sobering) in Acland's work is his insistence on recognizing the nature of current Canadian cinema-going practices: Canadian spectators are not "absent" from theatres; they are "present" but consuming US films—not unlike the rest of the world, I would add. Acland's argument for taking a critical look at national spectatorship practices means underlining the "struggles of Canadian audiences who must live and negotiate the existing popular cultural scene" (169). While cinema-going in Canada may indeed produce a feeling of estrangement in the sense that it does not offer an experience of national spectatorship in a conventional sense (Canadians watching narratives about Canadians), this estrangement is simply a "banal fact of global cultural life" (189). What differentiates Canadian spectators from their global counterparts, he continues, is a complex process of recognition in which Canadians acknowledge US popular culture as imported yet find a particular appeal in the recognizably Canadian elements of the import, in this case both Canadian locales *and* Canadian talent: "the U.S. industry plays a role in the measure of accomplishment for Canadian talent. As such, it offers a way for Canadian audiences to view that success, to read a film or a television program as a mark of a Canadian achievement" (190–191). This star-system-in-exile, where Canadian spectators watch local heroes in US film and television, "both links and differentiates Canadian spectatorship from U.S. cinema" (191). The presence of either Canadian stars in US productions or the presence of US stars in Canadian locales produces an "affective element [that] draws the audience into the texts if not for a sense of ownership then a glimpse of recognition" (191). Though Acland's assertions about Canadian spectatorship here are not based on empirical evidence (e.g., audience surveys, interviews, or other data on viewing practices), he deems the "recognizing Canada" thrill to be relatively widespread, enough to be parodied in a skit on the satirical television program *This Hour Has 22 Minutes*.[5] Michele Byers also argues that, though a star's Canadianness may well be irrelevant to people outside Canada, within Canada "the attribution of Canadianness appears to be important for fan identification."[6]

Acland's claim that Canadian audiences have a particular rapport with US culture brings to mind the work of literary scholars William New and Robert Thacker, who have sought to analyze this relationship in Canadian (literary) culture more generally. Rather than seeing US culture as familiar yet "imported," and thus coming from outside—as Acland seems to do—New argues for continental cultural overlap/interpenetration. Canadian culture does not ever absolutely keep itself apart from American culture: "the presence of the American-paradigm-'next-door' is a constant *within Canadian culture*" (*Borderlands* 40). Robert Thacker describes this "embeddedness" as a "bifurcated sensibility," the state of "being *in* America but not *of* it"; in short, the expression of a "contingent duality" (10). Canadian spectatorship practices, though not the purview of New and Thacker, should also be understood within this paradigm of "contingent duality." As Frank Manning has argued in the now classic volume *The Beaver Bites Back? American Popular Culture in Canada*,

> Canadian culture is less the product of its own separate evolution than of its interactive relationship with an American Other. This relationship, as

we have seen, is diffuse, ambiguous and contradictory. It involves imitation and resistance, infatuation and repugnance, collusion and condemnation, submission and subversion, identification and differentiation.... Canadian popular culture "makes sense" only in relation to American alternatives with which it has a counteractive but reversible relationship. (26)

While not going so far as to claim that all Canadian readings or experiences of US culture are by nature subversive, I would argue for an approach to Canadian spectatorship practices that acknowledges their oppositional aspect as part of the deeper psyche/template of Canadian culture. This oppositionality informs, in turn, the study of the star-system-in-exile phenomenon.

Achieving mainstream or Hollywood-level success has been and continues to be the dream of industry professionals (actors, directors) around the world. Yet given the proximity of Canada to the United States, the increasing integration of our media and entertainment industries (newspapers, promotional materials, entertainment shows), the influence of the locations industry (which has provided employment for Canadian actors in secondary roles), the absence of a language barrier between English Canada and the United States, coupled with the relatively small size of our film and television industry, it seems fair to argue that English-Canadian industry professionals experience the pull-to-the-south in a particular way.[7] Some actors can work in "exile" without leaving Canada (in, for example, US-based productions shot in Vancouver) while, conversely, the relatively large community of Canadians living in Los Angeles and the sense of solidarity that has developed among them can mean the pooling of creative energies and financial resources in order to contribute to projects "back home."[8] The discourse that has emerged around these cross-border acting professionals betrays a modest pragmatism and matter-of-factness about the financial need to work in Hollywood that is separate from the search for fame. Actors are quoted as preferring "challenging creative projects" in Canada to more high-profile roles in "formulaic (U.S.) productions" (Monk, "Young Canadian"). Interestingly, this discourse corroborates stereotypical notions of Canadians as quiet and self-effacing, opting for creative fulfillment over power and money.

In his recent monograph, David L. Pike has argued for separating those actors who maintain dual careers on both sides of the border from those Canadians that are solely associated with US productions and seldom if ever identified as Canadian (e.g., Mike Myers, Jim Carrey, Kiefer Sutherland). The former group of crossover professionals (e.g., actors such as Mia Kirshner, Sandra Oh, Molly Parker, Callum Keith Rennie, and actors, writers, and directors such as Don McKellar and Sarah Polley) "retain their local identity while crossing over to establish a solid presence in Hollywood"(107). Building on Pike's categorizations, I want to shift the emphasis in the discussion on crossover stars, like Callum Keith Rennie, away from "identity" (i.e., how actors see themselves or the image created about them by celebrity discourse, neither of which is particularly reliable) to English-Canadian viewing practices and potential cultural reappropriation. Actors like Rennie and Parker might exude a certain Canadianness—more so than Carrey and Sutherland, who no longer work on Canadian projects—but that Canadianness is only visible *within* the nation. By Canadianness I simply mean any physical or attitudinal particularity, however slight (e.g., accent, cultural references, attitude, etc.) that sets actors/performers apart from the American mainstream and makes them "recognizable" to Canadian audiences. I contend that the national origin of this group of actors (Parker, Rennie) is *as* invisible south of the border as their more famous counterparts. In a sense, what we have in this case is the opposite of the kind of visible Canadian celebrity transnationalism studied by Laura Moss in the case of Margaret Atwood, who embodies both a "neatly packaged national identity" and is a "global figure worthy of representing the local for the international community" (23). Here we have the global (Callum Keith Rennie's work on the TV series *Battlestar Galactica* makes him "known" around the world) representing the nation yet "recognizable" solely within the nation, for a particular national subset.[9] This type of circumscribed, paradoxical visible/invisible Canadian celebrity is only enjoyed at "home," a Canadianness not for export but for reimportation and reinterpretation. What I find particularly suggestive in Pike's work is the idea of reading the cross-border careers of these actors—their simultaneous presence in US television and film and Canadian cinema—as one unified oeuvre. What is the correlation, if any, between the roles they play in their US and Canadian work? What sort of persona have they created over the years and what does this have to do, if anything, with their Canadianness? Could what from the outset appears as a *loss*—actors achieving a certain level of mainstream success in US productions that are widely viewed/consumed in Canada while Canadian cinema simultaneously continues to suffer from a lack of popular success—be recuperated as a *gain*? Given our benevolent proximity to the US and the relative exiguity of our own industry should not the work of crossover actors be analyzed as an integral part of the dilemma of Canadian cinema? Canadian star culture also only "makes sense" in relation to the US; and to push this line of argument one step further, given the importance Canadian audiences accord a Canadian actor's US success, to what extent could the star's

American persona have an impact on subsequent Canadian performances, thus increasing the visibility of their Canadian work?

To hypothesize in this manner requires a certain leap of faith. It means presupposing that Canadians *recognize* "their" actors in US productions—which I, like Acland and Byers, believe they do—that Canadians who view US mainstream/cable television are also viewing Canadian cinema and that these same viewers are making connections between roles. What is necessary in order to make these linkages is a redefinition of the role of television in the star-production process. Reviewing the literature on stardom brings to the fore the extent to which these theories have their genesis in the Hollywood studio system and thus must be adapted when applied to different national contexts and brought up to date to coincide with dramatic shifts in the media landscape. One oft-quoted aspect of the definition of stardom that will be pertinent to my analysis here is John Ellis's contention that the star is a "performer in a particular medium whose figure enters into subsidiary forms of circulation, and then *feeds back into future performances*" (emphasis added, 303). The Hollywood star system is based on an offscreen, onscreen duality in which the star is presented as both ordinary and extraordinary, familiar and remote; someone whose private life is of interest to the public. This interest is created and maintained by an interconnected system of photos, news stories, promotion materials, press releases, and entertainment shows that work to create what Liz Czach terms "multiple avenues of exposure" ("Television" 63). In her work on the Canadian star system, Czach has detailed how the low number of feature films produced each year in Canada (compared to Hollywood) coupled with the lack of promotional mechanisms for these features (Canadian-produced entertainment shows focus on Hollywood) and the relatively small amount of public attention devoted to the personal lives of Canadian actors, all work against the development of a star system in English Canada along the lines defined by theorists such as Ellis. Seminal theories about stardom are based upon an understanding of how audience reception operates when they see an actor on film. For Ellis, following Roland Barthes, the star image rests on the photo effect (the presentation of the star in photos) that simultaneously promises cinema and signals its absence, renewing a desire on the part of the spectator to experience the paradoxical presence/absence of the star, incomplete, incoherent, and fleeting (304). Television, Ellis claims, is centrally lacking in the photo effect. It presents itself as an immediate presence, pretends to actuality, to immediacy (313). Lacking the "rarity value" of cinema, television produces not stars but "personalities": "famous for being famous…and only in so far as she or he makes frequent television appearances" (314).

As Czach and others have argued, today's media landscape can no longer be divided into neat categories of the public (going out to the movies) and private (watching television at home). Film is increasingly consumed in the private sphere alongside if not simultaneously with what is termed "quality television," characterized by high production values and complex narrative arcs closely identified with cable networks and other pay-per-view services (see Banet-Weiser, Chris, and Freitas; McCabe and Akass). Films are streamed on the Internet, illegally downloaded or otherwise, and viewed on a variety of apparatuses (even cellphones) in a way that inserts them within the rhythm of the mundane and everyday; conversely, television shows no longer broadcast are released, like films, on DVD (complete with supplementary materials), which gives them a certain prestige or cachet heretofore reserved for cinema. Lastly, recent work by James Bennett and Deborah Jermyn has sought to differentiate the types of personalities produced by television (i.e., the quality television actor who has much in common with the cinema actor) and also chart how certain performances on cable television (e.g., Sarah Jessica Parker on *Sex and the City*) can propel an actor to movie-star-level fame. More important for the context that interests us, i.e., the English-Canadian star system, is the idea that television can be a source, if not a sustaining element, of an actor's possible star status. In "Television, Film and the Canadian Star System," Czach argues that in the Canadian context, the career of Paul Gross "illustrates how film and television roles intersect" (68). She reads Gross's recent appearance as an actor playing a Mountie in the Canadian film *Barney's Version* (Richard J. Lewis 2010) as a making a "tongue-in-cheek intertextual reference to Gross's best known role as the earnest Mountie Benton Fraser on the television series *Due South* (1994–1999)" (68). This reference indicates the degree to which Gross's Mountie character is "identifiable" to audiences. Why, she argues, given this example, "should television performances not feed back into future film performances and vice versa" (69)? Further, given the availability of US-based productions on Canadian sets and screens, and the numerous actors who flourish in our star-system-in-exile, this sort of intertextual reading takes a transnational turn, opening up the possibility that Canadian audiences *read* Canadian actors masquerading as Americans with an added ironic twist.

In the Shadow of Lew(d) Ashby

Examples of Canadian actors masquerading as Americans on American television are common given the large number of successful Canadians professionals in the industry. Yet Callum Keith Rennie's portrayal of flamboyant record producer Lew Ashby, on Season 2 of Showcase's salacious television series *Californication*, provides, in my view, a particularly rich opportunity for exploring an ironic, potentially oppositional, English-Canadian viewing experience. The Season 2 opener of the series, starring David Duchovny as the self-deprecating, sex-addicted Los Angeles writer Hank Moodie, features a party at a Laurel Canyon mansion hosted by Ashby. However, Moodie and Ashby don't meet until the second episode as they find themselves briefly in jail on misdemeanour charges during which Ashby commissions Moodie to write his autobiography. Learning from Ashby that he drinks and womanizes in order to dull the pain he suffers from his failed relationship with a former girlfriend, Jenni Jones, Moodie endeavours, unsuccessfully, to reunite Ashby with Jones. However, Ashby dies of a drug overdose before the reunion can take place. It would be difficult to create a character more obnoxious, sexually rapacious, morally degenerate, and emotionally wounded than the misguided Hank Moodie himself. Yet Rennie's incarnation of the larger-than-life Lew Ashby, by comparison, makes Duchovny's character appear cautious and circumspect. Indeed, Ashby, a ruggedly handsome silver-haired aging party animal and phenomenally wealthy rock impresario (he is driven around by a chauffeur), clad in black jeans, Mötley Crüe T-shirts, and a collarless black leather jacket, engaging lightheartedly in the most outrageous, misogynist sex shenanigans and self-destructive behavior, is at times difficult to watch. Judging by the websites and blogs devoted to the series (e.g., "Californicationwiki"), the *Californication* fan community expressed appreciation for the Ashby character and was disappointed, but not surprised, by his untimely death. Some fans even suggested Ashby had to be "eliminated" as his brash, exaggerated persona was beginning to overshadow the show's lead, David Duchovny (*Californicationwiki*).[10]

Callum Keith Rennie's performance was overwhelmingly well received by viewers.[11] It is unclear, and in my opinion unlikely, that the *Californication* fan community knew or cared that Rennie was Canadian, although one review of the Season 2 DVD qualifies him as "Anglo-Canadian" (Cain). Websites and fan blogs commented on two possible uber-American inspirations for the Ashby character: one real (Lou Adler, legendary Hollywood playboy, producer of Jimmy Hendrix, owner of the Roxy Theatre); the other, literary (Jay Gatsby of the F. Scott Fitzgerald classic *The Great Gatsby*) (Reventon).The latter comparison, as fans have pointed out, is made explicit and sustained throughout Season 2: Ashby refers to Moodie's book as "his Gatsby"; Moodie presses Ashby to explain the Jenni Jones story ("tell me more about your girl…the one that got away, your Daisy Buchanan"); and episode 2 is entitled "The Great Ashby." Further, Moodie finds himself at the Ashby mansion in the opening episode of Season 2 even though he was not invited and does not know the host. And finally, in episode 9, "La Ronde," Moodie describes Ashby to Jenni Jones as someone who "throws these huge parties and these people come and they drink his booze and they act like they're his friends... [and the] guest of honor never shows," which is an obvious reference to Jay Gatsby's lavish parties. Comparing Rennie's Lew Ashby to the Great Gatsby does, of course, lend tremendous gravitas to the role; it is impressive that an English-Canadian supporting actor would successfully incarnate this iconic figure of American literary culture, emblem of the cruelty of the American dream. For Canadian fans, however, I would hazard that there is an added dimension of pleasure and irony in watching Rennie portray a disillusioned rock'n'roll producer who (almost) overshadows David Duchovny. Those Canadian viewers old enough to have money to pay for HBO Canada (which broadcasts *Californication* in Canada)—meaning viewers in their thirties and forties—are also old enough to remember Rennie as Billy Tallent in Bruce McDonald's cult film classic *Hard Core Logo* (1996). If we are going to argue for increasingly transnational responses to US-based globally diffused media, for the interconnection between an actor's film and television performances, for the utility of the crossover concept itself and the importance accorded to Canadian actors when in US productions, then we need to argue that such an intertextual reading—Billy Tallent meets Lew Ashby—is not only plausible but fruitful for repositioning notions of Canadian niceness, as described earlier by Pevere and Dymond and reactualized in more recent scholarly work on Canadian celebrities.

Despite the very large number or US films and television series Rennie has starred in over his twenty-year career, Canadian media, not surprisingly, continue to define and describe him as an award-winning Canadian auteur cinema actor, best known for his role in *Hard Core Logo*; for this reason it is important at this point to offer a brief reminder of the film's context.[12] McDonald's "rockumentary," a road movie/buddy picture, chronicles the reunion of a fictitious punk-rock band, Hard Core Logo, for a benefit concert in Vancouver and a subsequent five-city Western Canadian tour. The conflict of the movie centres around the love/hate relationship between the band's two frontmen: singer Joe Dick (Hugh Dillon), a slovenly, alcoholic, self-destructive bully, "addicted to losing," and guitarist Billy Tallent (Callum Keith Rennie), his aloof boyhood friend, who aspires to leave the band and play for the fictitious "indie" rock band called Jenifur in California. In the film's opening sequence during which each band member is introduced, shots of Joe in the back of a pickup truck are intercut with black and white stills of Billy striding through the International Arrivals Terminal of the Vancouver airport in an obvious reference to him coming back to

Vancouver from elsewhere (in this case, LA). The use of these black-and-white photos of what looks like a confident and glamorous Billy reinforce the distance between him and the rest of the members of the band. As Paul McEwan argues, these photos are an ironic take on glamour and artifice and the artificiality of fame, since they look like they might have been taken by paparazzi, though someone like Billy is not yet famous enough for that (59). When asked in a to-camera interview shortly after the band's show at the Commodore in Vancouver whether he has a steady "gig" playing in California, Billy explains that he is "just waiting for his papers," his "green card," referencing onscreen the dilemma of many talented Canadian performers, biding their time in Canada before finally getting to the green light to head south. Billy's on-again/off-again status with the "indie" group Jenifur changes throughout the film, becoming a leitmotiv for the Canadian–American relationship. At one point in *Hard Core Logo,* Billy receives a telephone call from an agent who informs him that the Jenifur guitarist he was supposed to replace has regained his health: "You should have stayed in LA, man," the agent scolds. This predicament, the need to maintain a physical presence in LA in order to continue to get work, is well known to Canadian artists who attempt to achieve success stateside. (In one recent interview, Rennie mentioned the stress of having only worked a few days in LA in the preceding year. "You have to maintain a presence [in LA] at all times" ["Callum Keith Rennie"].) Journalists and interviewers, including the filmmaker Bruce McDonald, continually barrage Billy with questions about his possible American success, in a sense negating and sidestepping the media attention around Hard Core Logo's reunion tour and staging, as it were, the widespread notion that the only success that counts is success south of the border. Billy's potential departure is treated by the other band members, publicly scornful but secretly jealous, as "selling out," and trading in a more "authentic" punk rock music scene where performers work for the love of the craft, for a superficial world where the trappings of fame take away from the focus on the music. Joe is explicit: "Billy just wants the models and limousines, and I'm happy with hookers and taxicabs," he quips. Watching *Hard Core Logo* now (the film is readily available to stream on the Internet) is at times uncanny in the way that it sets up and warns against the descent of Rennie's Billy Tallent into the vacuous/superficial world of limousines, swimming pools, and movie stars of *Californication*. In McDonald's film, Billy and the band's drummer Pupefitter (Bernie Coulson) share a roadside hotdog while Billy tells of how in LA he is driven in a limo to a rehearsal space shared by the Red Hot Chili Peppers. For those readers not familiar with the LA-based psychedelic/punk band, they achieved their greatest commercial and critical success with a song entitled "Californication" that bemoans the artificial image that Hollywood sells to the world, the title of which was obviously "borrowed" for the HBO television series.

Hard Core Logo is above all a road movie, a genre predicated on the idea of self-discovery. In the end, as Paul McEwan has argued, what Joe and Billy discover about themselves is far from appealing. While Joe realizes that he has no real self beyond his exaggerated stage persona, and Billy seems to be throwing away his real self in "something more akin to a Faustian bargain—he is actively trying to trade it away for money and fame" (74). There is indeed a way in which the Faustian bargain aptly describes Callum Keith Rennie's transformation from the shy, goofy boyfriend in Mina Shum's *Double Happiness* (1994) into an increasingly sinister, sadistic figure, the stock villain for a whole host of television series from *Battlestar Galactica* to the *X-Files* and *24*. All of these roles, taken together, inform what I see as his ultimate performance, as the devilishly handsome, self-destructive, moral degenerate Lew Ashby, constantly laughing at his own pain. Billy Tallent's moving on to "bigger and better things" marks the demise of the band Hard Core Logo and precipitates the death of Joe Dick. Rennie's Lew Ashby completes this narrative turn, becoming an allegory for Rennie's career itself, a commentary on the "price" to be paid for selling out in the US, where fame and money lead only to disappointment and destruction. Underlining the emphasis on disillusionment, falsity, and emptiness, Ashby/Rennie, whose piercing blue eyes are highlighted by the camera, dies of a heroin overdose at the end of Season 2 as Sheryl Crow's cover of The Who's "Behind Blue Eyes" plays in the background. He is the misunderstood "sad man" condemned to "telling only lies."

As mentioned above, *Californication* appears to have a lively fan community, judging in particular by the presence of sites like "Californicationwiki" where fans engage in an active discussion of the series' aims, style, objectives, and the characters' "backstories." The rise in scholarship on post-network television and the convergence of different types of media has been accompanied by new ways of studying television audiences including phenomenon like these fan-based sites. Long considered to be mere passive recipients of formulaic and dismissive content, theorists like Lawrence Grossberg have sought to reconfigure the audience as "constantly making their own cultural environment from the cultural resources that are available to them" (53). New studies in fandom addresses how particular viewers make meaning from television and, with the advent of online streaming, multi-platforming, and brand extensions (i.e., supplementary extradiegetic Internet sites that extend the world of the show), a viewer can, as Kristyn Gorton explains, "unpick, unravel and reveal secret meanings of a text and produce her own online which secures her place within a community and as an expert of a particular text" (35). Studying today's televisuality means taking into consideration these viewing practices, which often involve, for example, watching several episodes of a series at once, returning to specific scenes, and paying attention to the "backstory" of an episode or series. As Henry Jenkins explains: "[t]he result is a television text denser in narrative opportunities for fans than before; it has been designed to accommodate fan-fiction reading; not treat fan-fiction reading as some sort of opposition imposed on the text from the outside" ("*Intensities* interviews Henry Jenkins"). My own examination of the fan site Californicationwiki indeed confirms much of what has been argued by these scholars. More pertinent to my argument here are the various ad hoc websites (collections of photos, clips, and interviews) and "fanvids" (fan videos or montages of brief clips of an actor's work organized around certain themes such as love scenes or action scenes) devoted to Callum Keith Rennie. On these sites and videos, Rennie's Canadian film and US television work are knitted together in one "homespun," "home-edited" fan experience; these "fanvids" juxtapose scenes from Canadian films like *Last Night* and *Curtis's Charm* (John l'Ecuyer 1995) with US television series like *Battlestar Galactica* and *Californication*, etc.[13] There is an eerie placelessness involved in searching these sites as they wilfully mask their creator's personal information thus making it almost impossible to confirm whether the site is emanating from the US or Canada (or elsewhere). Judging from the content, however, such as references to CTV, CBC, the Genie Awards, and the inclusion of recent interviews of Rennie on local Canadian television stations, I would argue that the creators of these "fanvids" are most likely Canadian. It is simply too difficult to get access to the footage from Canadian films that are included in these videos from outside Canada.[14] That such sites and videos exist with their heterogeneous content helps further the argument that it is possible to do a transnational, cross-media, intergeneric reading of a Canadian actor's work.

Callum Keith Rennie's brief appearances in two recent Canadian films, Bruce MacDonald's *Trigger* (2010) and William Phillip's *Gunless* (2010), are also best understood within the paradigm of a crossover reading. Both roles are brief enough and involve so little character development that they could be viewed as cameos, a brief appearance by a "known" person in a work of the performing arts, often unnamed or appearing as him/herself. These roles are common in works in which the actor's presence holds some special significance, such as an actor from the original film in the "remake," which is the case in *Trigger*.[15] Originally planned as a companion piece to *Hard Core Logo* featuring conversation between the original stars

Rennie and Dillon, the plot of *Trigger* was changed to portray two female rock stars, Kat (Molly Parker), now living in LA, and Vic (Tracy Wright), who reunite their band Trigger to play one last time at a benefit concert in Toronto. Backstage they bump into Rennie playing Billy Tallent, clad in a very "Lew Ashbyesque" black T-shirt and collarless leather jacket, and who we learn from the brief dialogue is now a rock and roll talent scout living in Florida. The scene between Billy, Vic, and Kat adds very little to the film on a diegetic level. Its importance lies rather in a complex process of recognition wherein viewers recognize Rennie now as Lew Ashby (with the devious laugh) who used to be Billy Tallent (desperate to market himself to the States). In *Trigger,* Tallent is no longer performing but behind the scenes, further likening him to his notorious California producer/impresario role. Rennie/Tallent also mentions to Vic that he is playing golf in Florida, which reminds the viewer of the much-discussed *Californication* scene in Episode 9 of Season 2 where Ashby, dressed in a kilt (a nod to Rennie's Scottish heritage), and Duchovny's Moodie, hit golf balls out over Laurel Canyon.

In *Gunless*, Rennie's appearance is also "familiar" to certain Canadian audiences in the sense that he is reunited with his *Due South* co-star Paul Gross (Rennie played Chicago detective Stanley Kowalski on the hit TV series). In *Gunless*, Rennie's part as the American bounty hunter, Ben Cutler, who pursues Gross's Montana Kid up into Canada, could also be read as a cameo as the role has almost no meaningful lines of dialogue. Rennie's effectiveness in this film is based, rather, on an ironic process of recognition of him as *both* a Canadian actor, former American partner to Gross the Mountie, *and* a Canadian celebrity actor-in-exile who now specializes in notorious/sadistic villains (*Battlestar Galactica, 24, X-Files*). In short, *Gunless* is either a failed film or a feature-length "in-joke" for Canadian viewers about their "contingent duality" within Canadian popular culture. [16] Gross and Rennie are both wilfully ridiculous as Canadians masquerading as Americans in order to spoof the western genre, riding into this Canadian "community" that refuses to bide by the codes of the Wild West and where duels are delayed due to an absence of functioning firearms. Mountie Benton Fraser of the RCMP (Gross) may have been Canadian TV's most conventional hero. His polite self-restraint was thrown into comic relief in *Due South* in comparison to his more aggressive, "trigger-happy," "American" partner (Rennie). Yet Gross's Mountie performance, as Jody Berland argues, is "simultaneously a stereotypical confirmation of well-behaved citizenship, and an ironic commentary on such stereotypical conventions," part and parcel of a long-standing English-Canadian "preference for play rather than heroic action" (54). [17] In this sense, the comic standoff between

Gross and Rennie at the end of *Gunless* becomes a silly game between two old friends: one, Mr Canada, (Gross), spoofing his former Mountie self; the other, the exiled Canadian (Rennie), wryly counting on his villainous/ degenerate "Americanness" to inform this cameo in a Canadian comedy film wherein this sort of violent persona is traditionally mocked.

Most recently, Rennie won a Gemini for his lead role as a homicide detective with multiple personalities in Showcase's *Shattered* (2010). Filmed in Vancouver, though conceived for export, this ill-fated police procedural epitomizes the dilemma of much contemporary English-Canadian TV drama.[18] The show was no doubt well intentioned, yet the final product was a weak imitation of an American-style police series that underused its stellar Canadian cast (like Camille Sullivan from CBC's *Intelligence* [2006–2007]) and frustrated Canadian audiences by simultaneously evoking and masking Vancouver, thus robbing the audience of the recognition effect, discussed earlier.[19] More to the point, here is the role of Callum Keith Rennie, as the troubled detective Ben Sullivan. Given the chance for the first time to be the "moral compass" in a TV drama, i.e., the chance to "play it straight" as a police officer, Rennie's Sullivan disintegrates. The seemingly straightlaced detective is transformed instantaneously into a degenerate party animal akin to Ashby in *Californication* (replete with excessive drinking and forays with prostitutes) and/or a sadistic/violent psychopath akin to both his US television and Canadian cinema personas. Rennie's "identity" in *Shattered* is never fixed but contradictory, literally schizophrenic, taking the viewer on a roller-coaster ride in and out of American pop culture expectations. While the back and forth between Sullivan's various "characters" made, in my view, for some rather bad television, the Sullivan role could be read on several other levels: for Rennie's fans, for example, as a consolidation of all the actor's previous television and film roles and as a fitting if unwitting illustration of what many literary and cultural critics have characterized as English-Canadian collective ambiguity, marked by disunity, duality, formlessness, and fragmentation (see Kroestch). Rennie's Sullivan contradicts himself into oblivion, each role/ persona a shadow of itself as if to argue that any notion of stable national identity (e.g., Canadianness) is but an impossible fiction.

Far from a sanitized, innocuous, white/nice "Ice Cream Canuck," nor a figure of order and good policing, Callum Keith Rennie's edgy masculinity and cross-border niche celebrity add a different dimension to traditionally exported Canadianness. He allows Canadian audiences to maintain a long-standing ambiguous rapport with American pop culture forms, both appreciated and resisted. In sum, his Canadian fans appreciate his US success, yet take pleasure in an ironic recognition effect that their Canadianness, however difficult to define, marks him (and them) as different, inside US culture yet not contained or completely confined within exaggerated American stereotypes of heroes and villains. Cynthia Sugars has argued that English Canada's precarious cultural existence is compounded by the contradictory fear "that the nation is not identifiably (and singularly) distinctive in any way, and the coinciding sense that there *is* something (however ineffable) distinctive about Canadian culture" (124). In the context of Canadian celebrity culture, particularly crossover stars like Rennie, could not this contradictory "indescribable distinctiveness" identified by Sugars lie not so much in the subject of attention (Rennie himself) but in viewing strategies, in how audiences *read* an actor's origins and, through this reading, *claw back* a little something for themselves in a world dominated by American norms? Crossover stars may well be considered American south of the border, but their real national identity, for those invested in such matters, is never in doubt. More work needs to be done on whether the interest in a crossover actor like Rennie's American commercial work, perhaps more accessible to younger TV-oriented mainstream audiences, could bring new attention to the actor's more low-profile Canadian cinema roles. Focusing on transnational viewing practices in the Canadian-American context, like the readings I offer here, has the merit of helping to make those connections possible.

Notes

1 For an analysis of the transnational career of Bujold, see Czach's "The Transnational Career of Geneviève Bujold."

2 A francophone minority society within North America, Quebec indeed has a small but viable and dynamic star culture wherein local actors and television personalities receive substantial media attention from popular weeklies (e.g., *Lundi, 7 Jours*) and television talk shows (e.g., Radio-Canada's *Tout le monde en parle*) that, in turn, enables audience recognition. For scholarly work on the Quebec star system, see Peter Dickinson and David Pike. In my view, the "distinctness" of how Quebec audiences consume popular culture is somewhat overblown. French-speaking audiences in Quebec are exposed to an inordinate amount of Hollywood films and American television (albeit dubbed in French), to an extent that is almost commensurate with English-Canadian audiences. More research needs to be done on the specificities of Quebec's viewing practices and on how those Quebec actors who achieve success in English-speaking roles either in Canada or the US are received at home.

3 In 2012, films produced in English Canada accounted for 2.5 per cent of the domestic market share. Quebec-made francophone films have traditionally fared better, capturing in recent years between 5 and 10 per cent of the Quebec domestic box office. However, in 2012, Quebec films fell to 4.8 per cent. See Kelly.

4 US-produced "runaway productions" have been a much-discussed feature of
the British Columbia film and TV industry since the 1990s (see Gasher). It is
important to point out the volatility of this capital investment that ebbs and
flows with fluctuating exchange rates and shifting tax incentive programs
in a constant search for new locales that improve the economic bottom line.
Faced in 2012 with an 80 per cent drop in production, members of the BC
Film Industry lobbied the BC government for increased tax credits in order
to attract more productions. See "B.C. film industry seeking ways to survive."
For a rare look at how the Canadian-based locations industry affects the experience of Americanness for American viewers, see Weeks.

5 Acland desribes how this skit involved two Maritimers watching television,
flipping through channels. They happened upon Kevin Spacey appearing at
the 2000 Academy Awards, who tells a brief story about how he forgot his tux-
edo in Halifax where he had been filming *The Shipping News* (Lasse Hallstrom
2001) and had Judi Dench retrieve it for him just in time for the show. The
Maritime characters then screamed gleefully: "He mentioned Nova Scotia, he
mentioned Nova Scotia!"(Acland, *Screen Traffic* 191).

6 Byers's observation here about Canadians and fan identification also appears
to be anecdotal: she cites the particular excitement in Canada and especially
in Halifax around the release of the 2007 film *Juno* (directed by Canadian-
born Jason Reitman) starring Halifax native Ellen Page, who was nominated
for an Academy Award for her performance as a pregnant teenager.

7 For a study of how Canadian comedians experience the pull of the US market,
see Danielle Deveau's work in this volume.

8 Production for Bruce MacDonald's female rock reunion movie *Trigger* went
into high gear once one of the lead actors, Tracy Wright, was diagnosed
with pancreatic cancer. Mobilizing the tight-knit Canadian cinema community, both local (living in Canada) and expat (Molly Parker and Callum
Keith Rennie, who live at least partly in LA), was the driving force behind the
film's lightning production schedule. Rennie is reported to have contributed
$10,000 toward the film's production budget. See Monk's "Coming together
for an actress's swan song."

9 I recognize that for readers of this volume Callum Keith Rennie and Molly
Parker might not be household names; for the Canadian film milieu they are
as close as we get in English Canada to "national" stars.

10 It is worth pointing out that David Duchovny, though an American actor,
evokes Canada for Canadian viewers due to his role as FBI Agent Fox Mul-
der on the iconic science fiction series *The X-Files* (1993–2002), of which
the first six seasons were filmed in Vancouver. The show's successful use
of misty grey forests in fact paved the way for several science fiction series
to use the city as their setting (e.g., *Millennium* [1996–1999] and more
recently *Continuum* [2012]).

11 Californicationwiki lists Lew Ashby as voted the second most favourite supporting actor of the series (now in its sixth season), second only to Moodie's

hapless, dwarfish agent-friend Charlie and despite the fact that Lew Ashby was eliminated at the end of Season 2.

12   In a round of interviews to promote his role on the police procedural *Shattered* (2010), that I will return to later, both George Stroumboulopoulos of CBC TV's *The Hour* and Jian Gomeshi of CBC Radio's Q introduced Rennie as having won a Genie Award for his role as a sex marathoner in Don McKellar's *Last Night* (1998) *but* as best "known" to Canadian audiences for his role in *Hard Core Logo*. The urge to have Canadian audiences "remember" *Hard Core Logo* may well have something to do with the current buzz around the film's co-star Hugh Dillon, then unknown, who is now internationally recognized as one of the stars of CTV's hit police procedural *Flashpoint* (2008–2012) and Season 2 of AMC's *The Killing* (2013).

13   Some of the actor's fan sites include callumkeithrenniefanfusion and The CKR files.

14   In this case I would concur with Michele Byers that it is important to remember that television and video products do not necessarily flow seamlessly across borders. Streaming CBC, for example, is impossible to do (legally) outside of Canada. She argues that "lots of Canadian TV and film doesn't make it up on sites like YouTube at all."

15   *Trigger* is not to be confused with *Hard Core Logo 2* (McDonald 2010), a sequel of sorts that does not feature any of the characters of the original film.

16   *Gunless* was not well received by critics. See Stone.

17   The "playfullness" that permeates CBC's popular detective drama *Republic of Doyle* (2010–) is but one example that illustrates Berland's argument.

18   Thirteen episodes of *Shattered* were broadcast in 2010. The show was not renewed for a second season.

19   *Shattered* featured establishing shots of the city of Vancouver, yet deliberately blurred street names and BC licence plates.

9

What's So Funny about Canadian Expats? The Comedian as Celebrity Export

Danielle J. Deveau

> *...a culture considered one of the funniest in the world; a country without which, it could be argued, there would be no Austin Powers, no Ace Ventura, no "Saturday Night Live," no "SCTV," no "Kids in the Hall."*
>
> —Geoff Pevere

> *What makes Canadians so funny? Would these people all have the same sense of humour if they were, uh, Latvian?*
>
> —Michael J. Fox

There exists a pervasive popular belief that Canadians are funny, and that Canadian comedians have been, and continue to be, highly visible and influential in the US entertainment industries (Marin). Not surprisingly, this belief in the inherent funniness of Canadians is frequently reinforced by popular media and industry insiders, the very people who stand to benefit from such a discourse. It is, in effect, an industry discourse about its own celebrity. Michael J. Fox's question "What makes Canadians so funny?" is not simply a rhetorical one, offered by an industry insider to reinforce the vitality of his own chosen field, but also a discourse disseminated at a much broader, more general level (Fox cited in Clark, "Land of Laughs"). That Canadians are funny, and that Canadian comedians are disproportionately successful in their chosen work, is the dominant and defining mythology of the comedy field in Canada.

The Canadian comedy industry exists within a larger network of Canadian popular culture and cultural industries. While the success and celebrity of Canadian comedians may be a source of national pride, the vitality of Canadian cultural identity and the cultural industries has been a source of concern and frustration amongst policy-makers and cultural nationalists throughout much of the twentieth century. With so much of our popular culture originating in America, the establishment of distinctly Canadian popular cultures has been a source of cultural anxiety, with the media, such as television broadcasting, strictly regulated in order to ensure that some domestic cultural production makes it to air. Other than news and sports, variety comedy is one of the few Canadian television genres that succeed in achieving ratings comparable to imported American prime-time programming (Hoskins, McFadyen, and Finn). This has been particularly beneficial to professional comedians whose style fits with the institutional cultures and brand strategies of broadcasters such as the CBC. For example, performers whose work falls into the news parody genre are most likely to have regular, prime-time comedy roles. However, performers at this level often desire, or face a great deal of pressure, to move on to more lucrative work in the US. This forms a central tension in the Canadian comedy industry, where many domestic opportunities take as their primary referent the nation and national culture, but most career trajectories are oriented toward the US market, where such Canadian comedy content is not relevant and cannot be used to market the performer to US agents, networks, and audiences.

One important way that the field of Canadian comedy is linked to a national sense of self is through its relation to the construction of an emergent Canadian celebrity culture. This celebrity culture is fed by the production of Canadian-born Hollywood stars. In contrast to the stated goal of using broadcasting to construct a culturally distinctive sense of Canadian identity, Canadian media actually succeed in bringing Canadian popular culture into closer contact with the American entertainment market. Work in Canadian radio and television offers performers, writers, and directors a vital training ground and allows them to develop the skills necessary to move into the larger American entertainment industry, which has greater room for career advancement. This natural flow of cultural workers from a small to a large market led John Aylesworth, the Canadian-born creator of American prime-time hit *Hee Haw*, to proclaim the golden rule of Canadian comedy: "In Canada you reach a point where you have nowhere to go but down, to the States, which is up" (Clark, *Stand and Deliver* 60). Canadian performers who succeed in the US gain cultural capital in Canada, and in the case of performers like Jim Carrey and Mike Myers, achieve major celebrity status. Additionally, the widespread consumption of American popular culture, in contrast to the meagre consumption of the Canadian equivalent, means that, ironically, cultural workers have greater access to Canadian audiences through the US entertainment industry than they would have had the performers opted to remain in Canada. This tension between the ability to remain in Canada and the need (and desire) to pursue work in the US is a long-standing one in Canadian entertainment. While opportunities for work in the Canadian comedy industry do exist, comedians, audiences, and intermediaries continue to perpetuate this southward trajectory. As an economy of scale, such a move remains an obvious one.

There is a profound incongruity between the nationalist focus of domestic comedy (think *Rick Mercer Report*) and the need to pursue a global career (in particular to achieve recognition in the US). This can be seen very clearly in the case of stand-up comedians, for whom mid- and late-career opportunities have to date tended to be sparse in Canada. What is of note in the case of stand-up comedy is the extent to which comedians incorporate performances of national ambivalence about their comedy careers into their creative work. In my years watching Canadian comedy for my doctoral dissertation, I found that the relation of the Canadian comedy industry to Hollywood was a comic theme in its own right. These creative discourses about what it means to be a *Canadian* stand-up comedian offer critical insights into the relation of creative work in Canada to the US entertainment industry. Notably, performers both celebrate and deprecate themselves in relation to their Canadianness, as well as promote and express ambivalence about their emergent Hollywood careers and the celebrity that such success can bestow.

Humour offers an indication of the social and cultural setting in which it is formed and can illuminate both dominant norms and critical tensions (Gilbert). In the case of popular parodic news programs, for example, it has been argued that through humour the comedians are able to fill a critical void left by a commercial media, and that this commentary offers a viable articulation of political opposition (Gray, Jones, and Thompson). In discussions praising the politics of humour, the focus is generally on the external interests of the comic text. This is the comedian as cultural anthropologist perspective in which comedians are taken up as expert observers of the world around them, and are able to offer humorous, critical observations about this world, often focusing in on its banal absurdities (Koziski). Given the acceptance of comic texts as critical discourses, it is remarkable that they are seldom taken to tell us something about the more direct social world from which they are derived—that of the professional comedy industry itself. For example, academic studies of popular comedy do not tend to address issues related to comic labour in the creative economy. This is remarkable given the growing focus on creative labour in cultural industries studies (Beck; Deuze; Léger). On the other hand, cultural and media industries studies, focused as they are on production and ownership, have too readily dispensed with critical textual analysis, arguing that the "'textualist paradigm' does not account for external shifts, correspondences, and dissonances in other fields, nor for the historicity and materiality of the fields themselves" (Stabile 406). This chapter takes up the textual analysis of comic material as a production text. That is, I take seriously the jokes that performers tell about their work lives. In particular, I consider the extent to which performers like Shaun Majumder, Debra DiGiovanni, and Nikki Payne exhibit ambivalence in their comic work related to their lives as comedians in Canada and the need to establish US careers in order to gain legitimacy, stability, and celebrity.

Comic Labour and Humour as Explanatory Discourse

As an illustration of some of the tensions that accompany the development of Canadian comedians for the US market, we can consider some of their Canadian comedy performances that engage directly with the challenges of this career trajectory. In particular, the interpretation of labour discourses is a useful point of entry for understanding the field of cultural work. In "Not Seeing the Joke: The Overlooked Role of Humour in Research Involving Television Production," Edward Brennan argues that "humour can provide researchers with a unique access point into the professional cultures of media producers.... Importantly, humour is a central means of performing 'emotional labour' that increasingly precarious media work demands" (819). The relevance of humour to Brennan's study was not initially worked into his research design as a sensitizing concept, but it emerged during his ethnography as an evident and vital tool for the interpretation of occupational culture. Brennan found humour to be a useful tool for the disclosure of serious complaints that could not ordinarily be expressed. He notes that media jobs are highly competitive, increasingly casual, and often have large pools of inexpensive reserve labour due to the increased popularity of media programs in universities and colleges. With so many potential participants in the field, cultural workers are often highly dependent upon "formal and informal networks" for employment (820). Complaints about labour conditions or creative conflicts have the potential to alienate workers from this network, decreasing potential career trajectories. As such, Brennan finds that humour provides an important outlet for frustrations or small rebellions. He suggests that "humour offers a relatively low-risk means of voicing criticism and objection in an environment like television production where a trenchant stance or angry objection is likely to damage one's work, reputation and career prospects" (824–825).

In the case of stand-up comedy, performers' comic utterances about their work lives can be found in not only media interviews that are explicitly about them, their material, and their careers, but also, surprisingly, in the content of their creative material. This is a unique source of data for the study of humour in relation to cultural labour. Comedians discuss the conditions of their work constantly, onstage and offstage, and their comedic material often contains references to the *work* of stand-up comedy. Not infrequently, routines start with "on the plane ride over here," "last night at the hotel," or "the club/town I was working last week" as the comic text revolves around the comedian's real life as a working comic on the road and in strange cities. Their experiences, ambitions, disappointments, frustrations, and achievements are reworked into performance material that offers insight into the preoccupations of the working comedian. In short, stand-up comedy is a unique form of creative work because so much of the comedian's persona and routine revolve around the disclosure of their working conditions.

While attending the Just For Laughs (JFL) comedy festival between 2008 and 2010, I was particularly taken aback by the extent to which the "production" of comedy was brought into the spotlight during club shows. Because performers often have many sets over the course of the festival, they can rehearse at the smaller club venues as part of their preparation for the more important shows that they will play at larger venues later in the week. American comics use these club shows to test their material on Montrealers/Canadians, and many of the comics will work through timing and clean up their sets for the Gala shows, which are recorded for TV. Some comedians are not shy about disclosing the administrative side of the festival to their audience. At a *Comedy Night in Canada* show in 2009, host Steve Patterson reminded the audience that the comics were working on their material for big shows later in the festival, and requested that the audience be supportive. During a *Bubbling with Laughter* set in 2009, Canadian performer Mike Wilmot followed up on an unsuccessful joke with the line, "That went nowhere, so it won't be in the gala." This joke illustrates the repetitive nature of stand-up and reminds audience members of the hierarchy that exists between venues at the festival—the Gala shows are the most prestigious and expensive, and are recorded and broadcast on television as comedy specials. The sharing of insider details also produces humour, as audiences laugh at this disclosure.

Because much of the style of stand-up comedy is conversational (despite being a monologue) and observational, the line between performance and lived experience is blurred. Accordingly, most interviews in the popular press focus as much on the comic's ethnic/national origins, career trajectory, and future projects as they do on the actual material that the comic is promoting. While comedians do have a "stage character," this persona often draws heavily on the actual personality, demeanour, and lived experiences of the comic (Woodrow). I consider some of these comic labour discourses below to provide a clearer picture of how stand-up comedy blurs the lines between personal and professional, often foregrounding "backstage" details like work conditions, career aspirations, and ambivalence about the national context of Canadian cultural production.

Greener Pastures and Comic Discourses on Canadian Celebrity

Comedy is not an industry like any other. Comedy does something else besides produce a saleable product. It also produces discourses that are popularly consumed and is frequently critical or insightful. Most interesting to this project are the instances when the comic discourse is turned in on itself, offering a perspective on the comedian and his or her work life, as well as the larger context in which he or she works. One significant thematic area for Canadian comedy in this regard is the national context of the cultural industries. We listen to the things that comedians say about their (and our) culture. As Karim H. Karim has argued, the ability to perceive and engage in joking is linked to learned competencies of citizenship; all jokes are inside jokes and "their nuances can only be truly appreciated by the in-group familiar with their cultural context.... Humour is an essential part of social bonding, and those who are left out of the circle of laughter also find themselves excluded from the vital occasions for societal participation" (151). This aspect of comedy as an "insider" discourse, shared across a community with common cultural reference points, makes it culturally specific. This is why humour in the national vein is such an obvious genre for television. However, this cultural specificity also makes comedy an unusual candidate for export. Why are the producers of what ought to be a culturally specific performative product so adept at crossing into another cultural context? This is simply the familiar question, put another way, "why have so many Canadian comics, like John Candy, Martin Short, Dan Ackroyd, Jim Carrey, and Mike Myers, to name just a few, been so successful in the U.S. if humour has national boundaries?" (Szuchewycz and Sloniowski 123). This presupposes a relation between the Canadian humorist and Canadian national identity, an explanatory task to which comedy is often put; its utterance can have, after all, critical, subversive, explanatory, and/or political potential.

Comedians and cultural critics alike have suggested that the paradoxical outsider/insider relationship that Canadians have with American popular culture is integral to Canadian comics' ability to "pass" within the dominant US culture. One account of the surprising presence of Canadian humorists south of the border jokingly characterizes these covert foreigners as "ringers" (Carr and Greeves xiv). That Canadian comics can pass so easily as American is not, however, taken as evidence that Canadians and Americans are culturally indistinguishable from one another. The very comedians who work south of the border also frame their comic abilities as proof of their Canadian distinctiveness, suggesting that their comic perspective could be formulated only from the outside looking in. Citing one of Canada's biggest comic exports to date, Kieran Keohane remarks, "Mike Myers identifies a crucial wellspring for Canadian comedy: 'Americans watch T.V. Canadians watch American T.V.' Canadian comics do their best work in the U.S., the object domain outside that really constitutes Canada, that which Canada is Not (Not!)" (148). Not only is Canadian culture overly defined by what it is not—the US—but also, as Keohane's Waynesian double negative reminds us, in most respects Canadians really are indistinguishable from Americans. When boasting about the success of Jim Carrey or Mike Myers, fears of cultural erosion at the hands of American encroachment are replaced with boastful accounts of the Canadian comic as an exported celebrity.

The export of popular Canadian comedians is an entrenched element of the Canadian comedy industry. Today, apart from a limited roster of sketch comics, mainly news parodists, bragging rights do not fall with those who stay, but with those who leave. The role that media companies, such as the national broadcaster CBC, have played in the Canadian comedy industry is an ambivalent one. On the one hand, some of the most popular Canadian television programs have been sketch comedies aired on the CBC such as the *Rick Mercer Report* and *This Hour Has 22 Minutes*. On the other hand, this programming has been limited to satirists, parodists, and relatively mainstream or uncontroversial performers. This has been a source of great frustration for stand-up comics who do not fit the CBC brand, but would nonetheless like to forge a television career in Canada. Where do these performers go if few opportunities exist to build their careers in the Canadian cultural industries? In the late 1990s, as Harland Williams began experiencing modest success in the US market, the comedian expressed frustration at not being given the opportunity to forge a more stable career in Canada:

> I wanted nothing more than to advance my career with my people, so to speak. The CBC had a casting office that was across the street from Yuk Yuk's downtown club. I never heard of anyone from that office calling to tap into the new talent. In the six years I was at Yuk Yuk's no one came to see what was going on. No agents, no one. So I never got invited to the dance. (Williams in Clark, *Stand and Deliver* 244)

Williams felt forced to pursue opportunities for work south of the border, and it was in the US comedy industry that he expected to cultivate a successful career. This trajectory is not unique to comedy. As Jeffrey Simpson finds in his book *Star-Spangled Canadians: Canadians Living the American Dream*, Canadians in a broad range of professional fields opt to pursue their lives south of the border. Comedy does, however, stand out as one of the first fields in which this is established as a dominant norm. As Simpson notes, "Canadians in comedy…long ago learned that North America, not Canada, is their market, a lesson now being learned by Canadians as disparate as computer-software design and computer animation, baking and finance, law and medicine," and the list goes on (312). In the Canadian comedy industry, as well as the entertainment industry more generally, the US remains the "big leagues."

As will be seen in the creative work and career trajectories of the performers whom I consider in this chapter, this expectation continues to shape comedians' attitudes toward their expected career trajectories. I find it intriguing that even while performers succeed in cultivating Canadian careers and express frustration with the linking of success and celebrity with a US-based career, they nonetheless have also worked hard to break into the American comedy field. At times, the assumption that they must pursue work in the United States becomes the butt of their comic material, while at other times they lampoon the inadequacies of the Canadian entertainment industry.

A good example of this phenomenon is Newfoundland native Shaun Majumder, who is a regular at JFL and has been featured in a number of CBC comedy programs including *This Hour Has 22 Minutes* and the reality program *Majumder Manor*, which chronicles his attempts to build an upscale hotel in his native province of Newfoundland. In his career as a sketch and stand-up comic in Canada, Majumder has developed a comic identity dealing with the immigrant experience while displacing his identity as one of Canada's most joked-about minorities—the "Newfie." Son of a born-and-bred Newfoundlander and a South Asian immigrant, Majumder's early comic career frequently played off of the familial and childhood tensions that such a lineage could impose. Majumder is an interesting case study for this analysis because he has been featured regularly and prominently in Canadian media over the past decade or so. He is frequently profiled in interviews and documentaries about Canadian comedy, works on Canadian television, and has regularly crossed into the United States in order to pursue greater opportunities in the American entertainment industry. His comic material is based in personal narrative. Early in his career, his humour tended to focus on his experience growing up in Newfoundland; in more recent years it addresses national themes more markedly, and he regularly mocks Americans, the US entertainment industry, and his own participation within this system. He offers, in short, an ambivalent narrative of comic celebrity, on the one hand living up to the traditional Canadian comedy narrative of the southward-bound performer, and on the other hand mocking this trajectory and the celebrity that he derives from it.

During his 2001 participation in club shows at Montreal's JFL, Majumder started several of his performances with the introduction "I'm from Newfoundland! Do you believe me?" The joke being that an urban audience might not be inclined to accept his being from Newfoundland because he does not look like a comedian whom they might associate with the rural, and primarily white, population. This is the kind of Canadian content that plays well with Canadian audiences—material speaking to regional differences being a particularly fruitful area for comic exploitation (consider, for example, the place-based comedy of programs such as *Corner Gas*, set in Saskatchewan, or *Trailer Park Boys*, set in Nova Scotia). Featured in the documentary *The Next Big Thing*, Majumder is seen struggling to balance the "Canadianness" of his stand-up comedy routine (which proves popular with the Montreal audience) with his need to prove himself to be an internationally bankable comedian. By this time in 2001, he had made some headway in LA and was hoping to break into the American market. Backstage, after one of his shows he confessed to a friend that "I don't want to do all that Newfoundland stuff. Because it's American... this is the festival.... I've got to take it to another level now. That's gonna work in Canada, that's not gonna work down in the States" (*The Next Big Thing*). In this scene, Majumder is suggesting that despite its popularity with the crowd, his Newfoundland material is a poor fit for the festival because he considers JFL to be American. As a cultural intermediary, JFL offers performers an opportunity to be seen by American industry insiders such as talent agents and network executives. Although it is a major Canadian festival, JFL functions, according to Majumder, as a potential link to a US-based career. Several years later in 2005 while hosting a twenty-city JFL tour, Majumder again articulates this link between JFL and the US market: "Internationally [JFL] is a really big thing. It has a reputation around the world as one of the most prestigious comedy festivals. All the big executives down in Los Angeles and New York, they always get up to the festival every summer. They know there's such a big crop of talent at the festival" (Paulson C1). Majumder's adherence to such a standard, even privileged, career trajectory illustrates the extent to which the codes and expectations within the comedy production system are successfully reproduced. In the comedy community, the established hierarchies between gatekeepers are reinforced by such buy-in on the part of comedians.

However, comedians also express their feelings of ambivalence toward this system in their comic performances. Tensions are evident in the way career expectations are mocked by comics for their audiences. In the early 2000s while awaiting his Green Card, Majumder was a regular feature of the Toronto comedy scene (Boshra D7). During a show at the Rivoli in Toronto, featured in *The Next Big Thing*, he openly mocked his own attempts to sell himself in Canada based upon his meagre work experience in LA. Standing in front of a projector screen, Majumder interviews a video version of himself. The two begin to argue when live Majumder asks video Majumder what he has been up to. Video Majumder brings up a couple of failed LA projects (Majumder acquired, then promptly lost, a part working with Ellen DeGeneres) and forces live Majumder to admit that, far from being an LA big shot, his next show is in Ajax, Ontario. Video Majumder finally interjects, "Why don't you get off your high horse, okay, when you're done your show, why don't you go out, get in your car, okay, and drive here to home, where you live with your dad." The camera then pans left and focuses on Majumder's actual father who is sitting reading the newspaper. He looks up and says, "Hi Shaun." Live Majumder responds, "Hey Dad," then berates the video Majumder for embarrassing him during his show before finally demanding that the video feed be cut. The thrust of the comic exchange is one in which video Majumder is publicly critical of live Majumder for trying to sell himself as a successful, celebrity comedian. It engages with the underlying celebrity capital that Canadian comedians obtain from forays, however brief, into the US entertainment market.

While Majumder's official career trajectory conforms to the narrative laid out by major gatekeepers in the field, his experience of this trajectory, as reflected in his creative work, is ambivalent. He was discovered at JFL and he was even given a holding deal (money and an exclusivity contract) with a network in the US, but he is still living with his dad, and working the Ontario comedy club scene, awaiting his big break. His road from obscure Canadian comedian to Hollywood celebrity did not prove to be particularly straightforward. Intent on making the leap into the US, Majumder returned to LA in late 2001 with a Green Card and landed a pilot shoot for a variety comedy show, *Cedric the Entertainer*, which was picked up by Fox. In the fall of 2002 the show was promising to be a prime-time hit (Boshra D7) and Majumder went from being a relatively unknown Canadian comedian to hosting JFL in 2002. While Majumder's role on *Cedric the Entertainer* lasted only one year, he again returned to Canada with new celebrity capital, bestowed upon him as a performer who has been recognized as deserving of a career within the US entertainment system. Majumder's narrative, as featured in *The Next Big Thing*, upholds the assumption that comedians should pursue work in the United States, and that this is essential for acceptance within even the Canadian comedy industry. The documentary ends at the after-party for the filming of *Cedric the Entertainer*: Majumder has made it to Hollywood and, in Clark's estimation, he is "the next big thing."

While the narrative set out in *The Next Big Thing* is a straightforward one, the actual progression of comic careers is seldom so clean-cut. Majumder did not succeed in obtaining enough work to remain in the United States, but rather returned to work in Canada where, due to his mild success in LA, he was rapidly becoming a recognizable Canadian comedian. In 2003, Majumder joined the cast of *This Hour Has 22 Minutes*. In many ways, Canada's sketch comedy tradition serves a similar function as late-night comedy in the US, and comedians who work on Canada's major sketch comedy shows often enjoy a greatly enhanced level of exposure for their material. Indeed, it is in the Canadian sketch comedy tradition that we have the most recognizable examples of performers who did not leave Canada to pursue a career in the US. Comedians like Rick Mercer and most of the various *22 Minutes* and *Air Farce* casts have maintained Canada-based careers. Since this time, Majumder has balanced a dual Canadian/American career: he continues to get work in the US, but he's not too big for the Canadian small screen. He plays JFL regularly and one of his *This Hour Has 22 Minutes* characters, Raj Binder, has made appearances at major sporting and cultural events across the country.

While in his early career, he expressed frustration about his use of explicitly Canadian material in his stand-up, he has continued to address aspects of his Canadian comic identity as themes in his comic performances. During his 2008 Gala performance, he engaged very clearly with national themes:

> I was in the States not long ago...doing stand-up. And I was onstage and I said, "Hey everybody, I'm from Canada." And this woman in the back she's like "Booooo!" Really? For Canada? You're booing? How can you even think about booing Canada. We're your friendly neighbour to the— How dare you boo Canada? We gave you Alan Thicke! Excuse me, you're welcome very much. (Majumder)

As the JFL Galas are broadcast nationally in Canada, and the festival itself acts as a significant meeting point for the Canadian and American comedy industries, jokes about Canada as well as Canada/US relations have tended to be very popular amongst comedians and generally play well with both live and television audiences. Majumder's joke is a fairly typical example of this kind of humour. However, it also engages with the ambivalent discourse of Canadian comic celebrity that I have found laced throughout comic and critical discussions of the industry. This joke presents previous, presumably hypothetical, audience interactions that the comic has had, as well as alluding to other Canadian performers who have ventured into the US entertainment market. It reminds us not only of Majumder's stateside work experience, but also that not all Canadian exports (or is it expats?) achieve the same level of celebrity. Even while Majumder participates in the dominant narrative of the industry and pursues success on the terms set out by the dominant gatekeepers in the field, he also acknowledges the potential pitfalls of a career in the US, and the reality that many Canadian performers don't really make it.

This kind of critical comic discourse can also be found in the creative work of other performers. An episode of *The Debaters* recorded at JFL 2009 provides an effective illustration of this very issue. The debate featured Canadian comedian Debra DiGiovanni arguing that Canadians haven't really made it until they've made it in the US. Conversely, American comedian Judy Gold was tasked with arguing that fame in the US is not necessary. Gold's arguments were generally ones pertaining to artistic quality wherein she remarked that "saying Hollywood is the only standard of fame is like saying ketchup is the only sauce for food." Her point was that achieving recognition in US popular culture does not offer consecration because in her opinion American mass culture is devoid of creative value. DiGiovanni frequently countered with financial arguments, such as how exciting it would be if she and *Debaters* host Steve Patterson could give up their day jobs to pursue professional stand-up full-time. It was, of course, a joke as both DiGiovanni and Patterson have managed to quit their "regular" jobs and entertain for a living. As the ostensibly neutral host of the debate, Patterson also mocks the "vitality" of the Canadian comedy industry:

> We actually have a Canadian Walk of Fame and as a CBC media personality I may actually get my own star etched on that pavement and by process of elimination so might every other Canadian in this room right now. At some point, they just give it to you, so that people can walk all over you, much like they did during your Canadian entertainment career. True story. ("Swine Flu Hysteria and Making It in the USA")

Gold reacted with an appropriately sarcastic expression of admiration. Though Patterson mocks the underwhelming celebrity of the Canadian Walk of Fame and the very notion of a Canadian entertainment *career*, the debate between DiGiovanni and Gold about the merits (or demerits) of succeeding in the US serves well to illustrate that there is something distinctly pleasurable about humour that speaks to norms based on nationally specific cultural knowledge. When responding to the question "Hollywood heartthrob Johnny Depp shuns LA preferring to live where?" DiGiovanni's answer "Winnipeg" receives a significantly bigger laugh than Gold's answer "North Korea." Gold, knowing nothing about this city, is surprised by this response. The idea that an American movie star would choose to live in Winnipeg is funny, and few non-Canadians could really be expected to fully understand why.

The entire framework of the debate is one in which the received narrative of the Canadian comedy industry—that performers must succeed in the US in order to be considered a success in Canada—is called into question. In the vote by audience applause, Gold won the debate. DiGiovanni acknowledged her defeat, congratulated Gold, then proclaimed to the audience: "If there are any American producers or agents listening...I'm a headliner, I do voice work, and I have no gag reflex. Please contact me at iloveamerica@hotmail.com." With this, DiGiovanni illustrates the prevailing paradox of Canadian cultural production: in theory, we can cherish and support our distinct cultural industries in Canada and argue that no talent need ever leave, but in practice such an arrangement would prove financially and culturally inadequate. American acceptance, American cultural goods, American money, and American respect are all so tempting. However, the desire for success in the US is also being framed as dirty and problematic, with DiGiovanni's joke linking success in the US with a willingness to prostitute oneself.[1]

This tension plays out as a compromise between creatively principled work in Canada and the pursuit of wealth through the mass entertainment system in the US. This discourse appears on the surface to be a largely rhetorical one as there is very little indication that the relatively small Canadian production system can actually offer performers more "authentic" creative experiences than those available in the much larger production market in the US. This is a tension that works its way through many of Canada's cultural industries. For example, in 2009, Canadian musician Matthew Good complained that the Junos inappropriately privileged musicians who had garnered international commercial success, at the expense of lesser-known Canadian-based musicians. Comic Nikki Payne, in a guest appearance on *The Hour*, criticized this position, remarking sarcastically:

> What? Show business isn't fair? Canadian entertainers have to succeed in the United States before we're recognized in our own country? Noooooo! Fairy tales! You lie, Matthew Good.

To quote multiple Juno Award winner Anne Murray, "Spread your tiny
wings and" *suck it up, princess*! ("The News with Nikki Payne")

The pursuit of an international career, especially vis-à-vis the US, is the
dominant narrative of cultural work in Canada, and one that, in Payne's
view, hardly merits complaining about. This is the absurdity that Payne's
joke points to. It is neither new, nor unique, and has simply become an
unquestioned part of any entertainer's ideal career trajectory. However, the
deeply entrenched nationalist narratives of the Canadian cultural industries offer artists and audiences conflicting signals in this regard. There is
an inherent contradiction in the explicitly nationalist framing of the Juno
Awards, despite its privileging of performers whose careers, by and large,
take place outside of the country. This is a contradiction that musician
Matthew Good is highly critical of, but that comedian Nikki Payne accepts.

To succeed as a comedian in a complex and rapidly changing market,
Payne's joke suggests, requires a heightened tolerance of contradiction
and ambiguity. As comics enter the field of cultural labour, their working
conditions are generally characterized by unpredictability and low wages.
Performers expect to move up in the field, increasingly engaging in more
lucrative work, potentially with increased control of the conditions of this
work, but the career of a stand-up comedian in Canada is not an easy one.
Life on the road, characterized by late nights and heavy drinking, appeals
to younger performers, but rapidly loses its appeal as comics tire of being
away from family and constantly teetering on the edge of financial ruin
(Stebbins 112–116; Woodrow 26–27). A lack of opportunities for mid- and
late-career comics as well as the constant pressure to "make it" in the US
leave many comedians ambivalent about their Canada-based careers.

The Canadian comedians discussed in this chapter offer hints about
their work lives through comic discourses in their routines. These discourses frequently address issues such as expectations about making it in
the US, a relative lack of financial stability, and frustration with life as a
road warrior. The story of the late-career comic unable to make ends meet,
or who is forced to leave comedy and find other work, is a relatively common one. Following Windsor, Ontario, native Eric Tunney's sudden death
in 2010 the *Globe and Mail* published a story about his life and career titled,
"He could laugh at anything – except not making it big in Hollywood"
(Langan S8). The article discusses the performer's career in which Tunney
almost made it "big" a number of times, but promising projects always
seemed to fall apart just before his big break. Finally, Tunney moved back
to Windsor, took a job as a telemarketer, and did comedy occasionally in
small venues (like church basements) until his death. The journalist con-

cludes, "in spite of being funny, he was depressed. He never got over not making it to the big time" (Langan S8). Some performers do make it, but still fall on hard times late in their careers. Comedian Mike MacDonald was, for a time, one of the most recognizable Canadian stand-up comics on the circuit. At the twenty-fifth anniversary of JFL, he hosted a televised special because he was the only comedian to have performed at the festival every year since its English-language launch. A few years ago, he publicly disclosed a bipolar disorder diagnosis, and became an advocate for those coping with mental illness. Stigma about his bipolar disorder, as well as other ongoing health problems (including a diagnosis of Hepatitis C that led to liver and kidney failure), made it difficult for the performer to book work. Unable to support his family and pay for his growing medical expenses, a crowd sourcing campaign was launched in May 2012 to raise money for MacDonald.[2] In 2013 MacDonald successfully received a liver transplant and has since returned to working as a touring stand-up comic performing with Yuk Yuk's.

With these examples, it is not my intention to offer a romantic reading of the plight of the struggling artist. These scenarios merely point to the challenges that participants in this competitive industry face and the lack of stability and protection for creative workers. Increasingly, an individualist, entrepreneurial model of employment is the norm for many careers and not only a model of work for a small minority of self-employed individuals. The late-career experiences of both Tunney and MacDonald speak to the precariousness of comic labour for performers who never break out of the touring club circuit. For many Canadian comedians, "breaking out" is synonymous with breaking into the US market and forging a stable and lucrative career in LA or New York. For the majority of comedians, however, there are no huge payoffs just around the corner, and living well/ retiring comfortably remains an insurmountable goal for many. Comedy is not "big business" for most club comics, but rather entails a challenging work schedule, often living paycheque to paycheque, in which opportunities can dry up quickly. While the comedians that I have considered seem ambivalent about the southward trajectory of their comedy careers, they must also be well aware that, in order to sustain their careers, a degree of US success is often essential.

While it may be true that Canadian comedians have, in the past, succeeded in the US entertainment industry, the performers considered in this chapter illustrate the extent to which the emphasis on becoming an American comedy celebrity is not simply an illustration of their unique comic ability, but more importantly, of the lack of stable, long-term employment for these performers in Canada. Despite the proliferation of programs that feature Canadian comic talent such as CBC's *This Hour Has 22 Minutes* and Much Music's *Video on Trial*, and more recently CTV's short-lived sitcom *Satisfaction*, Comedy Network's comedian-driven game show *Match Game*, and CBC's *Schitt's Creek* (starring successful Canadian exports Eugene Levy and Catherine O'Hara), there remains a discrepancy between the available opportunities to work in Canadian television comedy and the quantity of talented performers being produced through the comedy club system. That Canadian performers struggle to define their Canadian careers in relation to US entertainment aspirations is not only an indication of the lure of celebrity culture, but also the necessity of breaking into more lucrative markets. The mid-career performers whom I have considered in this chapter all have one foot in each market. Although they have made inroads into the US, none of these performers are household names south of the border. In serious interviews about their work, comedians tend to reinforce the importance of establishing themselves in the US. However, in the case of the comedians whom I have considered, implicit critiques and expressions of ambivalence with the system are manifest through their comic material. While official complaints are seldom waged, humorous critiques are worked into comedy sets, offering audiences a window onto the frustrations, challenges, and contradictory career trajectories of the Canadian stand-up comic. When comedians break with the narrative of official culture, we are forced—through laughter, or discomfort, or having taken offence—to confront the shortcomings of this narrative. This humour does not disrupt, but rather seeks to conserve the conditions that it readily mocks. It represents the reproduction of cultural norms and social codes within the field, rather than offering a salient critique. The gentle mockery of comedy production offered in the acts of performers like DiGiovanni, Payne, and Majumder are distinctly non-transformative. The performers do not offer a project for the alteration of their labour conditions, only a humorous interjection that exploits some of the shortcomings and contradictions inherent in the field of stand-up comedy work in Canada.

It is evident from the discussion above that comedians are at times ambivalent about their Canadian careers. Performers are engaged (or hope to become engaged) in international labour flows that are characteristic of creative work. While a small number of comic performers have been able to "stay home," the dominant narrative for the majority is focused squarely upon breaking into the US market. However, given the often nationalist scope of comedy in Canada, with humour being most effective when performed for those who share cultural codes and are familiar with similar social norms, this desire to infiltrate Hollywood can be an ambivalent one for many performers. Work within Canada tends to be limited and privileges performers who fit nicely within the institutional cultures of broadcasters that are producing Canadian programming as part of a Canadian content mandate. Unfortunately, the support of Canadian popular culture is often geared toward the most obvious examples of "Canadian" content to the exclusion of other narratives and styles. So, while a hotbed of Canadian comic talent toils in the comedy club system, very little innovation is taking place to utilize this talent in creative new ways. As Harland Williams suggests in relation to a lack of interest from the CBC, "I never got invited to the dance" (Clark, *Stand and Deliver* 244).

Notes

1 The broadcast version of the show that is referenced in this chapter does not include the gag-reflex reference made during the live show taping that I observed at JFL 2009.

2 www.gofundme.com/mikemacdonald.

10

Re: Focusing (on) Celebrity: Canada's Major Poetry Prizes

Owen Percy

When the shortlist for the 2011 Governor General's Awards in English-Language Poetry was announced in mid-October of that year, one of contemporary Canadian poetry's more vocal provocateurs, Zachariah Wells, was quick to hit the blogosphere and the usual social media outlets to voice his outrage over its contents. Three of the year's five shortlisted collections were published by BookThug—a relatively small independent press specializing in "innovative" poetry and prose that "extend[s] the tradition of experimental literature" ("About BookThug" n.p.), often by shirking the precepts and presumptions of traditional lyric and narrative convention. Wells's raving criticism of the 2011 shortlist (and of the Canada Council's jury-making practices in general) focused on the facts that (a) juror Steve McCaffery's poetic profile and relative literary celebrity dwarfed those of his two fellow jurors (BC poet and non-fiction writer Joanne Arnott and Nova Scotia-based poet/professor Douglas Burnet Smith), thus rendering him an "éminence *grise*" ("CC Says" par. 4) on the jury itself, and (b) McCaffery's reputation and his general affinity for avant-garde and experimental poetic practice, plus the fact that he had himself recently published with BookThug, unfairly skewered the shortlist in favour of so-called experimental or *avant* poetry. Quoth the raver, "[McCaffery] is a theorist and poetic ideologue dedicated to the promotion of postmodern values in poetry, who would have a number of preformulated arguments at his fingertips, which he would no doubt bring to bear in any discussions with fellow jurors to determine a shortlist. If your average possible juror is *x*, then McCaffery is 5*x*" (Wells, "CC Says" par. 4). McCaffery's visibility and reputation within the world of Canadian poetry certainly dwarf those of his 2011 jury-mates. The problem for Wells, then, is that in his estimation, the other jurors *are* merely *x*—relative non-celebrities whose own poetries tend toward the traditionally lyric and who, Wells fears, were likely to yield to McCaffery's eminence as "a polarising figure who has dedicated his life and work to the promotion of one stream of poetry and the diminishment of all others" ("CC Says" par. 4). In addition to almost certainly overestimating McCaffery's political will and incivility while simultaneously underestimating both Arnott and Burnet Smith, Wells's critique illustrates the fraught relationship between literary prizing and the forces of celebrity that both produce and are a product of the public awarding of such prizes by both private and public institutions.

That said, Wells's criticism of the GGs and what he has elsewhere called its "jurisimprudence" ("I'll Scratch" n.p.) seems well founded given the statistical odds of the shortlist being 60 per cent BookThug when the press submitted only about 6 per cent of the possible contenders. Often a lone gunman in his critical outrage, Wells was quickly supported and affirmed in said outrage by articles in *Quill & Quire* and the *National Post* deriding the GGs' jury-making practice and accusing the system itself of bias and fault. In a response to Mark Sampson's very sensible suggestions on how the GGs might improve their evaluative systems of consecration, a writer with no less prestige and celebrity than Steven Heighton affirmed Wells's suspicions by suggesting that "some jurors have more dominant, forceful personalities than others, or simply possess greater argumentative stamina" (qtd. in Sampson, comment 1). Clearly, Wells had again struck a chord and voiced a concern that many in the literary community might have already tacitly understood but found unfashionable or unreasonable to suggest publically: literary celebrity—even Canadian poetic celebrity—matters when it comes to conceiving of and consecrating Canadian poetry as a field, a family, or a genre. Even when we argue that a jury or an award got it wrong some year, or that history will certainly separate the wheat from the chaff and expose our contemporary predilections as manic fads, the fact remains that we argue. We discuss. We care.

That said, it remains quite impossible to comfortably theorize a jury or to accurately speculate upon the kinds of deliberations, biases, and exertions of power and prestige that *might* inform a committee's ultimate selection of a winner, so to some extent, these critics are appealing to a kind of pastoral ideal that CanLit's historical raft of prize controversies shows has never existed, but that every major literary award promises by virtue of its authority as an arbiter of public taste: a simple, objective, equally collaborative evaluation of a text, unbesmirched by personalities, aesthetic differences, or other extra-textual forces like literary celebrity. The Canada Council responded to these accusations in an underwhelming, predictable press release that assured the public that, although he was the most nationally recognizable juror on the panel, McCaffery was still only a cog in the larger evaluative machine of the carefully built jury as a whole. They insisted that "[t]he Council benefitted from the expertise of all three members of the jury in this selection process" (qtd. in Carter par. 4) and that what they construe as their egalitarian system—one that chooses to ignore or deny the trappings of literary celebrity and power in favour of publicizing its investment in the GGs as an objective evaluative machine—has always been the "Canada Council way." Incidentally, the prize was eventually awarded to Phil Hall's *Killdeer*—indeed a BookThug publication.

It is my contention, though, that for a number of different reasons, the "Canada Council way" invites criticism, controversy, and conversation because of its seeming naïveté and the impossible promise that it makes to its constituents: to satisfyingly recognize, identify, and celebrate the year's best book of poetry on their behalf. Beyond that I wish to suggest that the GGs, precisely because of their proclivity for controversy of this nature, might be seen to function more successfully *as* prizes than the flashier, more lucrative, more celebrity-conscious, and perhaps more prestigious Griffin Poetry Prize—the country's, and the world's, most lucrative annual English-language poetry award. Finally, I'd like to consider the advent of the newish Montreal International Poetry Prize, one primarily funded by poets themselves and that "turn[s] the traditional literary patronage model on its head" ("Funding Model" par. 3) in its structure, its relationship to celebrity and reputational prestige, and its modes of consecration. With an initial purse even bigger than that of the Griffin, this new award poses a challenge to the dominant modes of prizing poetry in Canada because of its overt reimagining of the forces of reputational prestige and literary celebrity that inform and shape other major prizes. Because, simply, if celebrity matters in poetry, then as its most visible public by-product and facilitator, the poetry prize does too.

Although the phenomenon of prizing literature has been a topic of discussion amongst writers, critics, and interested readers literally for centuries, the scholarly theorization of the literary prize is just beginning in North America. Most notably, American critic James English argued in 2005 that "[t]he prize *is* cultural practice in its quintessential contemporary form" (26, his emphasis) and that it acts as a kind of cultural crucible in which different economies, valuations, and exertions of power and politics ultimately, if covertly, come together. Specifically, the literary prize has cast its shadow over the fields of cultural production and consumption in Canada to the extent that critics like Lorraine York, Frank Davey, Stephen Henighan, Kit Dobson, and most recently Gillian Roberts have suggested that the literary economies in Canada are now, to no small degree, prize-driven. Prizes perform a variety of social, political, and cultural functions that ultimately render them, as Roberts puts it in her book *Prizing Literature*, "tool[s] of popularization" (21) for texts and writers that can come to inform literary markets in both textual and extra-textual ways—which can and do alter the way literature is written, promoted, read, contextualized, and eventually even canonized in our contemporary cultural climate.

But we *are* talking about poetry here. Poetry is often still understood to be, as Pierre Bourdieu famously put it, a "disinterested activity *par excellence*" (*Field* 51), and it is one around which prestige still serves as the dominant form of capital and force of exchange. Recent controversies surrounding poetry awards in Canada have opened the field to wider audiences by infusing seemingly popular elements of tabloid-worthy gossip, speculative skullduggery and backstabbery, and sordid voyeurism into field that is often erroneously construed as culturally elitist and civil to the point of unrelatability from the "outside." As a result, prizes and their controversial trappings have begun to rearrange how that prestige, and how its load-bearing forms of capital, are construed and circulated within and beyond the field of restricted production as it has been traditionally understood. Even so, the fact remains that, as Jay Parini wryly puts it in his 2008 manifesto *Why Poetry Matters*, "Poetry *doesn't* matter to most people. That is, most people don't write it, don't read it, and don't have any idea why anybody would spend valuable time doing such a thing" (ix, my emphasis). While there have always been clear triumphs and moments of brilliance in Canadian poetry, it remains no less a truism than it was in 1993 when Frank Davey wrote in the introduction to *Post-National Arguments* that "Canadian poetry is poorly and mostly regionally circulated and read mainly by university-educated readers. . . . Fiction, however, continues to be written for general Canadian audiences, to be widely read, and to be circulated both nationally and regionally" (7). As an example, Heighton is known primarily as a novelist on account of his three Knopf novels *Shadow Boxer* (2000), *Afterlands* (2005), and *Every Lost Country* (2010), sometimes as a short-story writer for his three Knopf and Porcupine's Quill collections, and only occasionally as a poet—the genre in which he first published and established himself—despite his five books of poetry published by Anansi, Quarry, and Oberon. Interestingly, the vast majority of critical thinking on literary prizing and consecration has rooted itself firmly in the realm of fiction, presumably because the genre retains the greatest potential to breach the market economy in a significant way. Roberts's book, like Davey's before it, focuses on prose as the primary marker of prize power, and proffers no consideration of the Griffin Prize or of poetry prizes in general. The fact remains, though, that poetry prizes in Canada are amongst the wealthiest in the Canadian lit-prize economy.

We might still reasonably ask, though, as York does in the first chapter of her 2007 study, *Literary Celebrity in Canada*: "Literary Celebrity?" Really? And, more specifically, Canadian poetry celebrity? Erin Mouré thronged by legions of squealing fans at a book launch? Don McKay swarmed by paparazzi on what his publicist promised him was a remote hiking trail? Leonard Cohen dating fashion models, wearing designer suits and sunglass—uh, nevermind. York herself calls upon John Ellis's definition of a "star" as "a performer in a particular medium whose figure enters into subsidiary forms of circulation, and then feeds back into future performances" (qtd. in York, *Literary Celebrity* 12), and she recognizes that any kind or degree of celebrity "signals the meeting and exchange of the public and private realms" (*Literary Celebrity* 4). And this is why literary prizes, even poetry prizes, must be seen as both the vehicle and the currency of literary celebrity. The awarding of a particularly visible and/or valuable literary prize in effect fosters a degree of literary celebrity for the recipient as being worthy of such recognition in the first place, and the celebrity that results *from* such a recognition affords the winner significant cultural capital as a bona fide, sanctioned exemplar of literary excellence or achievement. That is, a writer might become a relative literary celebrity by winning significant literary awards, and those literary awards render that writer eminently awardable in the future as their excellence and exemplarity have already been publically acknowledged with notable, well, literary awards. This phenomenon hides in plain sight at any and all literary events, readings, and festivals (though not necessarily book launches, which have their own promotional *raison d'être*) in the form of author bios and introductions that consist mainly of litanies of awards won or shortlists populated as markers of the pre-established cultural value of your being there in the first place. Prizes are the primary vehicles of most literary celebrity because they quantify quality in a cultural field where subjectivity normally plays a nearly unquantifiable role. They speak *for* and *on behalf of*, often in an official capacity, and they make relative stars via their consecrations. Those consecrations then remain in a writer's bio and in the popular memory, as a marker of their sustained excellence and importance, and as markers of their seemingly agreed-upon worthiness for future recognitions.

Even though literary celebrity functions in similar, cyclical ways as other kinds of celebrity, poetry and fame still do not seem to cohere unless the practice is tacked onto a recognized writer's accomplishments in other genres (Atwood the writer, inventor, and environmentalist; Ondaatje the scribe of Academy Award–worthy novels; Cohen the rock star—all poets first and last). As a result, we might more usefully think of literary celebrity, and particularly of poetry celebrity, as what Brooke Pratt has called "indie celebrity" (n.p.) or what we might alternately consider "niche" or "localized" celebrity; that is, celebrity localized to a particular cultural, regional, or practical or conceptual realm. The *Canadian Oxford Dictionary* defines "niche" as, among other things, "a specialized but profitable corner of the market" (1049), though in this case we recognize that poetic celebrity is profitable primarily in cultural capital and prestige within a market that we might see as increasingly estranged from the financial. Specifically, and certainly in the case of poetry celebrity in Canada, we can consider figures like the late Al Purdy, McKay, Mouré, Dionne Brand, or even Christian Bök as niche celebrities because they command, exert, and otherwise traffic in prize-driven cultural capital in their Bourdieusian "restricted field of cultural production" (Bourdieu 39). (Wells, despite his personal dislike of McCaffery's work, obviously holds him in a comparable regard even though McCaffery has never won a major award.) In *The Metaphor of Celebrity*, Joel Deshaye points out that, of course, "the scope of public recognition in Canada is narrow" (25), but that celebrity has been among the major cultural forces shaping the field since the middle of the twentieth century. In that vein, although he is gone, Purdy is the closest thing that we in Canada have to a tangible Canadian poetry celebrity, and the closest that we have had (with the notable exception of the reluctantly CanLit Cohen) since Bliss Carman and Sir Charles G.D. Roberts. As Pratt has argued, the case of the star power surrounding The Al Purdy A-frame Trust provides us with an interesting conflation of poetry celebrity and other kinds of celebrity including and beyond the literary; on February 6, 2013, for example, celebrities from the literary, musical, broadcasting, and cinematic fields gathered at Toronto's Koerner Hall for "The Al Purdy Show," a fundraiser for the Trust attended by more than 700 people that raised over $40,000 toward the purchase and restoration of Purdy's A-frame home in Ameliasburgh, Ontario, as a heritage site and writer's retreat. Purdy's poems, and work inspired by them, were read and performed by "Canada's A-list" (Barber, "Why" n.p.)—the likes of Gordon Pinsent, Margaret Atwood, George Bowering, Michael Enright, Gord Downie, and Dave Bidini—all onstage because of their celebrity, and all participating in a historic and public event allowing them to further the breadth or depth of that celebrity and to wield it to particular ends. All this (worthy) celebratory and celebrity mythmaking and more is also on full display in Brian D. Johnson's feature-length documentary film *Al Purdy Was Here*, which premiered at the 2015 Toronto International Film Festival.

* * *

Historically, no awards have held greater sway over the character of CanLit than the Governor General's Literary Awards. The GGs, to quote Ruth Martin, are the face of "a tax-based government program that creates a canon of selected texts through its institution … [it] is a political award; it tells the world that these winners are perceived by the Canadian Government as the best of our literary culture" (102). The GGs are annual awards that consist of a $25,000 stipend, a silver medal, and a special leather-bound edition of the winning work crafted by master bookbinder Pierre Ouvrard. Although they may no longer be the country's most prestigious awards, they remain, as Henighan has noted, Canada's most comprehensive literary prizes (83), and they make consecrations in both English and French in the categories of Fiction, Non-Fiction, Drama, Poetry, Children's Literature, Children's Illustration, and Translation; in this respect, and as Roberts posits, any consideration of the Awards that assumes that they share an equal and straightforward objective with other prizes like the Griffin is somewhat "disingenuous" (29). Rather, because of their national federal mandate, says Roberts, the GGs tend to "invite[] complaints from journalists (and indeed readers) who double as aggrieved citizens and taxpayers" (Roberts 22) when they perceive some incongruity in the system of evaluation and consecration that the Awards promise to perform on behalf of the imagined nation. Most commonly, these complaints—like Wells's—focus on what James English identifies as "judges' dubious aesthetic dispositions, as betrayed by their meager credentials, their risible lack of habitus, or their glaring errors of judgment" (190)—in other words, the fact that the judges on a particular jury have operated under the rubric of their own subjectivities and interpersonal dynamics and not under those of anyone else. The GGs are particularly prone to this kind of criticism because of their adamant insistence on prioritizing what the Council lauds as "representation" on a jury over and above factors like reputation, aesthetic bias, or celebrity. In a personal interview with Joanne Larocque-Poirier, Head of Prizes and Endowments at the Council in 2009, she emphasized that representation—be it regional, ethnic, or gendered—has always been, and remains, a primary concern for the GGs when a jury is assembled (personal interview 5). This policy has been met, as one might imagine (especially when we consider that, officially, the GGs insist that literary excellence is the *only* criteria on which their consecrations are made), with a chorus of criticism, suspicion, and general anxiety about the overall merit of the Awards as markers of that very excellence.

The GGs have had more than their fair share of scandal and controversy since their inception seventy-five years ago, most notably those instances that most scholars of CanLit will list off as a matter of course: Leonard

Cohen's refusal of the 1968 poetry prize; the numerous Québécois and Québécoises who have refused the honour as a political statement; the joint selection of George Bowering and Gwendolyn MacEwen for English-language poetry in 1969 over the heavily favoured Milton Acorn (Mac-Ewen's very visibly ex-husband); and more recently in 2008, when Jacob Scheier was awarded the prize for *More to Keep Us Warm* by a three-person jury containing Pier Giorgio Di Cicco and Di Brandt, both of whom are thanked explicitly for their advice, guidance, and support in the book's acknowledgements. (Brandt, who had a well-documented friendship with Scheier's mother, Libby, is also thanked for her help in the "collaborative translation" from Rilke's German of the book's opening poem and is given perhaps yet another nod in a poem *called* "Di.") So when poets and critics slam the GGs, as Shane Neilson did in an April 2011 essay in *The Winnipeg Review*, for being "awful" because "any award that can be perverted as easily as this one has to be awful" (par. 11), they demonstrate their investment in the promise that cultural awards make (and break) to and on behalf of their constituencies in general, and the promise that the GGs make (and break) specifically: that they can definitively and objectively evaluate a subjective cultural product on behalf of an imagined and coherent nation. The ruse of prize culture, though—its worst-kept secret—is that scandal, which constitutes any deviation from the perceived and objective norms accorded by the award system in question, is in fact a necessary part of that system if the award is to be successful *as an award* and toward the end of popularization that Roberts identifies. As English notes, "scandal is [the award's] lifeblood; far from constituting a critique, indignant commentary about [a] prize is an index of its normal and proper functioning" (208). English goes so far as to suggest that scandal and controversy translate directly into "social capital," which is "often an even more important factor than symbolic capital (and far more important than money)" (194) because it generates both through the sustained interest accrued though media dissemination of said conflict. An award's success, in this respect, can be measured in the amount of ink spilled on its perceived shortcomings and in the amount of conversation that arises out of its seeming debacles.

The GGs then—despite the bland, staunch, and ceremonially conservative processes of award-giving for which they are also regularly criticized (one publisher compares the Giller Prize's black-tie-and-ballgown elegance to the drab grey "dowdy suit [the GGs has] been wearing for decades" [Patrick Crean qtd. in Lahey, "Rewards" par. 23])—have been tremendously successful *as awards* for a very long time. And they remain so even in the face of newer private awards like the Griffin, which engages directly with celebrity and prestige as the very currency of its economy of consecration. After deriding the "relative lack of fanfare with which we hand out our literary prizes," Peter Dickinson has argued that "[t]he glitz and festive theatrics of the Griffin...have been a notable and welcome exception" (specifically, he cites the waving of a dildo in the faces of Margaret Atwood and Anne Michaels by *Kid In the Hall* Scott Thompson at the prize's inaugural gala in 2001) ("Subtitling CanLit: Keywords" 49). Established by philanthropist Scott Griffin, the Griffin Poetry Prize has consciously attempted to become what its benefactor himself calls "a really premium, class act" (qtd. in Barber, "Literary Awards" par. 5), and by all standards it seems to have succeeded in *this* regard. Its annual awards gala boasts sold-out readings to audience members numbering in the thousands and attracts what John Barber calls the "Bohemian elite" for "the liveliest, dancingest event of the literary calendar" (par. 7). Suffice it to say, the Griffin Prize has managed literary celebrity somewhat more cannily than have the GGs—that is, it has acknowledged that literary celebrity exists and has embraced and enlisted its powers of consecration in several different ways. Most obviously, the Griffin Trust awards two annual prizes: one for the best Canadian collection of the year and one for the best single first edition collection of poetry written in or translated into English. The Griffin staffs itself—at least on the level of the prize's public trustees—with arguably CanLit's two most recognizable living celebrities—Atwood and Ondaatje—as well as former Coach House Press president David Young, American poetry celebrities Carolyn Forché and Robert Haas, and Scottish poet Robin Robertson. But more importantly, the prize has succeeded in establishing a system of evaluation that has drawn comparatively little criticism from poets, critics, and readers who seem quite happy to accept the authority of literary celebrity upon which the Griffin rests and who elsewhere seem only too eager to attack the GGs for their perceived *misrecognition* of the power that that same celebrity might wield on its juries.

Three years before the granting of the inaugural Griffin, *Toronto Star* critic Philip Marchand argued that a major poetry prize was not likely in the cards for CanLit because "[a] genuinely lucrative prize for poets would make the question of who would be on the jury for that prize a real dilemma. Choosing three people out of the telephone book at random would be at least as sensible as choosing three members of the Canadian League of Poets at random" ("Are Literary Prizes Necessary?" 66). The Griffin has responded with aplomb by insisting that its juries be composed of both Canadian and international poetry celebrities with very few exceptions. Every year the jury consists of one Canadian and two international poets who judge both the Canadian and the international candidates; past international judges have included the likes of Forché, Robert Creeley, Paul

Muldoon, Sharon Olds, Billy Collins, and Colm Tóibín. I would argue, then, that this internationalization of the jury invokes a necessary cosmopolitanism that simultaneously reinforces the value and quality of Canadian poetry as both independent and romantically distinct from the poetry of other nations and yet also aesthetically accomplished and universally excellent enough to have its excellence recognized and consecrated by a jury of internationally qualified judges—judges supposedly not privy or prone to CanLit politics and prejudices. It relies upon what Roberts calls "guest authorities in the host culture" (39) and perhaps reinforces a still deep-rooted colonial anxiety by acknowledging that "Canadians prefer their guest authorities to be firmly attached to national cultures that have long dominated our own" (Roberts 52). Critics have been largely silent on this evaluative structure—with a few notable exceptions, Carmine Starnino and Wells being two—and on the relative lack of scandal that each Griffin consecration has elicited. Even the consecrations of potentially controversial winners like Christian Bök and Sylvia Legris have been met and received with relative complacency. Ironically, then, with the increased public sexiness of the Griffin Prize, the machinations of the prize itself and its acts of consecration—the reinforcing and the creating of literary celebrity—remain relatively uncontroversial and, cynically, unremarkable compared to those of the GG. This is certainly not to denigrate the prize or the works that it celebrates in any way, but, in fact, to acknowledge that the Griffin Prize's greatest failing as a prize might actually be the successful and authoritative management of its operation—its delivering on its evaluative promises and its obviation of scandal, controversy, and conversation.

Not only has the Canadian literary economy proven that it can support a major poetry award, but the purses recently offered for Canadian verse are among the wealthiest in the English-speaking world. The Griffin's obvious prestige and panache has been supplemented by an emerging prize out of Montreal that aims, according to the prize's co-founder and Global Media Contact, Asa Boxer, to acknowledge and celebrate "the monetary value of poetry" (2) alongside that of other arts like fiction, photography, or sculpture, which command similar financial recognition. The Montreal International Poetry Prize, though, is not an exclusively Canadian prize; in fact, this would signal a failure of its ideals in the first place. Emerging out of Montreal's historically cosmopolitan poetry community, the prize is in fact a "deliberate response...to the deeply entrenched national or regional divisions usually applied to literature" (*Global* 11). Instead of aspiring to recognize the best poetry produced annually in a given sociocultural or political space, the MIPP is using the Internet and the advent of social media to "mark a fundamental moment in the exploration of the still nascent idea of 'global poetry'" (*Global* 10). Awarded biennially (and for the first time in 2011), the Montreal International Poetry Prize is the brainchild of Boxer, Len Epp, and Peter Abramowicz, who, building upon a one-time anonymous donation and defraying many administrative costs by running the contest primarily electronically, awarded $50,000 (CDN) to the poem "The Kingfisher" by Australian writer Mark Tredinnick in its first year. Unlike the GG or the Griffin, the MIPP evaluates individual poems, not entire collections or ōeuvres. Furthermore, it is the first major literary award to follow a completely blind submission process, thus allowing new voices to compete alongside consecrated and recognized ones without the weight of potential extra-textual baggage. Furthermore, the prize is open to—and in fact crowd-funded by—poets writing in English around the world, all of whom pay an entry fee (on a sliding scale depending on whether they submit from a developed or developing nation), which leads to what they call "a flat or fundamentally democratic structure" (*Global* 12) that has been absent from major poetry awards thus far.

Poems are submitted to the MIPP electronically, stripped of all identifying markers, and randomly allocated to one of internationally celebrated (and niche celebrity) judges who then read each poem sent to them. The stable of judges of the 2011 competition consisted of Jamaican poet and Member of the Order of the British Empire Valerie Bloom, GG winner Stephanie Bolster, celebrated Montreal-scene stalwarts Michael Harris and Eric Ormsby, British-Guyanese poet and multiple-prize-winning poet Fred D'Aguiar, Northern Irish prize winner Sinéad Morrissey, Hindustani poet and singer Anand Thakore, Nigerian poet and journalist Odia Ofeimun, Malawian poet and broadcaster Frank M. Chipasula, and celebrated Australian writer John Kinsella. The prize's Advisory Board is equally diverse and impressive, boasting, in addition to many of the above, the likes of Ben Okri, Don Patterson, and Richard Pound. But the judges are not judges alone. While the most obvious function of the Montreal Prize is to award a prize, its primary goal is in fact "to produce an annual anthology of previously unpublished poetry from around the world" that might reflect "the rhythms, flavours, preoccupations and tastes of a diverse, international collection of poets writing in English" (*Global* 11, 9), not just in a particular English, culture, or country. The five poems selected by each judge are submitted to the prize administrators and are published alongside one another in an anthology. The winner is later chosen from that anthology by an independent but internationally recognized niche celebrity judge, like Andrew Motion (2011), Don Paterson (2013), or Eavan Boland (2015). Thus, the anthology offers each editor/judge complete autonomy in recognizing and assessing excellence, and the winning poem itself must be judged worthy by at least two worthy readers independently. What this does, then, is offer all poets the chance to be read by a literary celebrity whose entire goal in reading is to assess quality devoid of external influence; that is, it attracts entrants based on the prestige of its celebrity judges, but it uses the judges themselves exclusively for the skill and expertise that led them toward their niche celebrity in the first place—the recognition and fostering of the power of poetry as art.

As Boxer points out, this editorial structure serves a number of different functions. First of all, it negates the common criticism that more traditionally structured processes of evaluation might cause judges to forego individual taste or evaluations of excellence in favour of the "jury-style compromise" (Boxer 1) required in the name of practicality and collegiality (precisely what could never have happened in Wells's nightmare scenario involving McCaffery). Secondly, the editorial board structure "is virtually impossible to rig. Even if one of the editors recognises something unpublished that came randomly through the electronic system, the prize judge has nothing to do with it" (Boxer 2). Most interestingly, though, the MIPP is a prize whose administrative structure resists the traditional funding model for literary prizes and the ensuing trappings of patronage and obligation. According to the front matter in the competition's 2011 *Global Poetry Anthology*, the "community-funding model inverts the ancient and venerable tradition of patronage funding for major literary awards. With the advent of the internet, poets and poetry lovers can now create literary awards directly by building a global community of individual supporters" (*Global* 11). Currently in its third iteration, the prize model has demonstrated signs of sustainability despite, perhaps because of, its unorthodox purview and its democratic idealism. The notion of recognizing individual poems instead of collections has generated much conversation and arguably engaged wider audiences of both writers and readers. By focusing on and celebrating individual poems, the MIPP aspires to the more primal (I hesitate to say "pure") act of acknowledging the power of the (comparatively) brief and singular poetic utterance (even in poems that might "do the police in different voices," as it were). According to Boxer, by circumventing the trappings of larger units of verse (books informed by editors, designers, marketing departments, and perhaps even sales and reviewers), the prize can better hit upon poetry's more visceral and immediate sublimity. He recognizes also, however, that this model of recognition is still susceptible to the obvious complications of celebrity-making and/or breaking: "Another issue at stake is the celebrity or star poet. When you select an oeuvre from a young poet, you engage in psychic prediction. When you select a mature oeuvre, you either get it right or engage in cronyism. Any oeuvre is uneven, so why do we award prizes to poets rather than to poems?" (Boxer 4). By shirking the market-sanctioned product of the book itself, the prize proffers yet another challenge to what has become prize-giving orthodoxy by refocusing on the unalienated labour that we like to believe is at the core of the poetic act in the first place. Indeed, on account of the prize's celebrity editorial board, the bestowing of the prize immediately carries with it the trappings of some degree of literary celebrity via its symbolic capital (which York reminds us "is capital in denial; it is the economic capital that dare not speak its name" [*Literary Celebrity* 29]) but for the poem itself moreso than for the poet. Perfectly, Platonically, the poets might be booted from the Republic, but the truth and beauty of their words might remain etched on the cave wall for all to read as beginnings and ends in and of themselves. As Boxer puts it, "[t]he whole idea of prestige and reputation and high society confuses what we're after, great poems. So the Montreal Prize is trying to shift the discussion. We don't want a gala. We don't want to be in the business of making star poets. We want to share great poems with the world" (Boxer 4).

The marked internationality of the Montreal Prize is perhaps in part a reaction to the very kind of culturally inward gaze that the GGs and the Canadian Griffin Prize foster in their bordered purview. In a recent interview, Boxer suggested that the prize was in fact conceived in part as "a reaction to the Toronto poets' navel gazing, confused provincialism, and puritanical piety" (Boxer 2), which he believes fosters a short-sighted poetry community "dominated by 20-something fashionistas" (Boxer 8) that too often becomes a synecdoche for contemporary Canadian poetry— or at least poetry available to Canadian readers—as a whole. This is certainly not to suggest that the Montreal Prize shirks literary celebrity as a matter of course. Like all major prizes, consecration and celebration are inextricable from the power of cultural celebrity and literary prestige. What it does differently, though, is narrow the focus of that celebrity more directly onto the poetic act and utterance itself above and beyond the trappings that might be said to accompany poems. According to Boxer, aside from the notable purse, "[w]hat makes the Montreal Prize prestigious is of course the poets on our advisory and editorial boards" (Boxer 4), not the scandal that might arouse discussion for reasons outside of aesthetics and craft.

As a result, the Montreal Prize is an award that works very hard to defy the very tenets of prize-giving success as James English lays them out by operating in a comparatively scandal-resistant way beside its fellow poetry awards in this country; its beauty as a prize is that it still manages to inspire the enthused conversations that big names and large sums of cash in the arts tend to inspire without steering those conversations into the "inside baseball" tabloid aisle. There is little scandal to be gleaned, so far at least, in how the prize is funded or awarded, yet, in addition to its significant purse, it manages to be remarkable and newsworthy because of the opportunity it affords writers from all ranks and stations a democratic shot at being recognized. In Boxer's words, then, it appears in fact to be "a grassroots effort... about community building, not about galas and TV spots" (Boxer 5). As a result, it presents us with an interesting counterpoint to both the GGs and the Griffin, which respectively manage celebrity not at all and impressively; the Montreal Prize signals a new structural funding model for literary prizing that obviates the circulation of celebrity-driven cultural capital that fuels most other major awards. This is not to say that it refuses the trappings of niche celebrity, but that it deigns to strip the trappings of that celebrity away in order to engage the qualities and talents for which that celebrity has supposedly been bestowed. By evaluating and consecrating poems individually (i.e., independent of their larger collections) and blindly, it has the ability to create celebrity and prestige by in fact shirking both forces as valued currencies in the economy of prestige that undergirds most other major literary prizes in and of Canada.

In the years to come, discussions about the structure and scope of the Montreal Prize are bound to heat up as the prize stabilizes its funding system and becomes an annual event. Critics of the Griffin Prize are bound to grow from their current lean numbers into a thriving chorus, and celebrity-fuelled scandal is sure to emerge at regular intervals. And the GGs seem bound strongly enough to bureaucratic and administrative tradition to continue to spark vitriolic columns, blog posts, and pub conversations with each annual mishandling of literary celebrity. Put quite simply, more is, and always will be, expected of the GGs because of their public institutional patronage and ownership. But herein lies the wonderful ambiguity of prize culture in Canada as a whole; as Roberts suggests, "[p]rizes connected to the nation-state (through funding, for example) are most explicitly tied to national projects, and therefore suggest that winning texts, on some level, benefit the nation" (6). And even though the Griffin is a private award, it insists on speaking (very publically) on behalf of an imagined or construed public constituency. The promise of both the GGs and the Griffin remains the same—to evaluate and consecrate a collection of Canadian poetry as worthy and excellent and exemplary—and their tasks remain similarly improbable in both theory and practice. But the GGs are bound to remain successfully controversial because of their refusal to acknowledge or manipulate literary celebrity in the same register that the Griffin has. The GGs will keep the CanLit conversation going in this way, while the Griffin—with its celebrity-fuelled authority—will continue to recognize and reinforce the national habitus ("the legitimizing force behind national culture" [Roberts 14]) that has built and maintained its own standards of celebrity in the first place. The Montreal Prize, Canadian as it may be, remains unique in that it is exempt from the confines of CanLit, and also from the scope of the single-authored book of poems as a marker of poetic success; as such, it poses a challenge to our present scandal-driven prize economy by proffering a return to the less evidently compromised evaluative model of the ancient Greek festivals to which we might trace the very notion of prizing literature in the Western tradition—the celebration of the poetic utterance and expression in all its succinctness, the celebrity of language that might possibly incite subsidiary forms of intellectual and emotional circulation and feed back into future experiences and celebrations of the word and world itself.

11

Bureaucratic Celebrity

Ira Wagman

This chapter contributes to a discussion about the production of celebrity in Canada by exploring the relationship between artists and bureaucrats. This is a difficult subject to broach. There are many institutions that oversee culture in this country at different levels. Sheryl Hamilton recently characterized the elements of the Canadian celebrity apparatus as "disparate, diverse, and disorganized," composed of *Maclean's* magazine, Canadian content regulations, the Scotiabank Giller Prize, and others. While these mechanisms, institutions, and initiatives cannot be easily brought together, Hamilton explains, "taken together, the contours of a notion of Canadian celebrity apparatus can begin to be mapped" (201). It is more than this, of course. Few artists openly discuss their interfaces with the state, and much of what we know of this relationship is usually presented in the pages of official documents.[1] More fundamental is the fact that any intimation that achievement and celebrity status may have to do with state involvement runs counter to ideas about the autonomous and independent acts of creativity that are so much part the mythology associated with artistic pursuits. Would a softer set of terms be useful for engaging in such a study? Could we say that many forms of cultural work have built within them an expertise in "government relations"? Our tendency to ignore such a discussion says more about the inadequate ways we have of talking about how artists can work within predominantly state-sponsored systems. More importantly, greater attention to the relationship between artistic production and the bureaucratic apparatus draws us a little closer to the ways in which notions of celebrity have historically existed within environments characterized by cultural nationalism, a prominent force in the construction of celebrity status in Canada that is widely acknowledged but rarely reflected upon. It is against the backdrop of support programs that aid in the publication, marketing, and distribution of a range of Canadian texts—from films to books to artworks and television shows—that produce those celebrities who are supposedly reflective of "Canadian" values.

A major theme that emerges in this chapter concerns the role played by various kinds of administrative work in constructing and mediating celebrity status in Canada. For P. David Marshall, celebrity "is best defined as a system for valorizing meaning and communication" (x). Marshall's conception of celebrity as a mode of communication is useful here because it reminds us that celebrity is a form of status that is channelled *through* media, and not just something which is represented *by* media. However, we need to start to think about media beyond its conception as mass media (such as newspapers or television programs) or social media (such as blogs or Twitter). In Canada, one of the primary media for the communication of celebrity is governmental paperwork: grant applications, annual reports, White Papers, and other official documents. Such paperwork is part of the ways in which celebrities are afforded legitimacy, and more importantly, it is a primary medium through which ideas about "celebrity" itself are communicated.

If we pause to consider this in some detail we can consider how discourse about celebrity freely flows between the pages of policy documents and tabloids. We are reminded that our music awards—the Junos—are named after the bureaucrat who brought us Canadian-content regulations, Pierre Juneau; that the presence of programs like *ET Canada* are the products of initiatives coming from the drab offices of the Canadian Radio-television and Telecommunications Commission in Gatineau; and that our description of the sector that produces our film, television, radio, and so on is called "the cultural industries," itself a concept borrowed from the fields of policy-making.

Many of the terms used to study celebrity that we see in the wider literature either do not apply in the Canadian case or apply in very different ways. Some might suggest that our biggest international celebrities—at least in English Canada—are institutions, such as the CBC and NFB, both subjects of considerable downsizing through government cuts. On an individual level, many of our most celebrated artistic talent yearn for their fifteen minutes of fame in a country that has historically ignored its artists or that affords celebrity status to those who have made it "elsewhere" first. The notion of "star power," a status accrued through an ability to attract and influence audiences, is a complex concept in a country where ratings for things like Canadian dramatic television programs are low, sales of Canadian books are seen as problematic, and box-office attendance for Canadian films has always been lacklustre. The idea that celebrity is a phenomenon associated with the expansion of media may be true in some places, but in Canada the development of telecommunications only served to improve the exposure of celebrities from other places. A stable of domestic paparazzi, gossip columnists, or "gawker stalkers" tracking the shopping habits, dieting fads, and nocturnal affairs of Sarah Polley or the members of the Tragically Hip would be a refreshing departure for a media culture that largely ignores prominent figures except for those who are usually seen wearing hockey equipment or who advocate for social issues like the environment. Such coverage is part of the give and take of American celebrity life, in which creative performers simultaneously despise the intrusion into their private lives while at the same time requiring it for continued exposure in a crowded media landscape.

We commonly hear the refrain that celebrity carries with it a weight that is often too much to bear, and that this is somehow reflective on an inherent cultural sensibility. Commenting on Alice Munro's recent winning of the Nobel Prize, Sheila Heti explained that "In Canada, you can't make a spectacle for yourself. You have to let others make a spectacle of you for you" ("Writers on Munro"). Here Heti communicates the truism that there is very little to celebrate about being a Canadian celebrity: The country lacks the apparatus to produce the spectacles that would celebrate Canadian achievements, and yet those who want those achievements to be celebrated often don't want to say that they do for fear of revealing a set of characteristics that may be interpreted as being "too American" or, even worse, "a sellout."

Such claims more broadly reflect internal tensions within creative communities around upward mobility. Artists who may start by forming a group in one place (art school, writing program, affiliation with a television show) will invariably separate due to their respective successes or failures. Since the community is relatively small, there is a great deal of self-monitoring and tracking of others' activity. As Robert Faulkner put it in his study of Hollywood composers, "Comparison is inevitable and, as the composer watches others move past him on their way to better opportunities, he starts to feel like a failure, not an absolute loser, but a comparative loser" (Faulkner qtd. in Giuffre 818). In the digital world, those successes and failures—from winning awards to winning grants—are there for everyone to see, adding a strong public component to the social dynamics that Faulkner discusses.

The bureaucratic nature of celebrity attempts to bridge overtly romantic and nationalistic conceptions of celebrity and the one mentioned above that is centred around an understanding of artistic careers in the Canadian context. It is part of the everyday experience of so many creative talents, an experience typified by the constant demands—both financially and in terms of the invisible labour of a career in culture—of having to apply for grants or complete reams of administrative work to get things off the ground, published, produced, distributed, and exhibited. Those who dole out the grants—program administrators, clerks, and analysts—are very much part of what Katherine Giuffre describes as the shifting sets of relations that are part of many artistic careers (815). A complex part of those shifting relations is that many artists who apply for support from institutions like the Canada Council also serve that very system. Another performer is at the same time one's colleague, peer, and judge whose decisions have financial consequences. Moreover, the results of competitions are made public, so other artists are able to see the winners and losers of recent competitions. Philip Drake and Andy Miah recently characterized celebrity as "a form of public performance, describing both an individuals' mediated persona as well as the qualities (fame, glamour and so on) that they are perceived by an audience to possess" (52). The "and so on" part of that quotation is where the Canadian characteristics come into play—ones marked by detailed engagement with the state and the political consequences of that engagement. The notion of "achieved celebrity" (Rojek 17), status gained through success in open competitions, then, carries a particular connotation in the Canadian case.

To illustrate, I offer three discussions about the bureaucratic nature of celebrity culture in Canada. First, I follow Lorraine York's lead about the labour of celebrity by focusing on the role played by paperwork—grant applications, government reports, and the publication of grant recipients—in constructing aspects of the celebrity apparatus having to do with success. Based on some recent work by Ben Kafka, I want to suggest that paperwork represents, in Marx's term, the "bureaucratic medium" through which celebrity is understood and produced in Canada. Second, I want to suggest that the heavy emphasis on administrative logic along with the public nature of grant competitions produces a series of minor affective states that we commonly call envy, jealousy, or *schadenfreude*, which stem from disappointment from different individuals about the inability of "the system" to achieve its desired cultural or artistic objectives. Finally, I interrogate a common line of argument about the existence or non-existence of a "star system" that exists in the pages of policy documents, a concept that is almost always offered without definition or details. I conclude by noting the movement of celebrated Canadians into administrative positions at a time when so much of the cultural policy apparatus appears to be under attack to ask what this development reveals about the distance between celebrities and bureaucrats in Canada.

Paperwork: Where the Faces Interface with the Faceless

Many of Canada's most successful artists are also incredibly good grant writers (can we not say the same thing about academics?). While some perform the work themselves, others employ talented administrators, agents, accountants, or, in more corporate settings, government relations officials who perform the work on their behalf. If artistic skill is something developed through formal training, grant writing is often a skill learned with what we might call "real-world experience," through trial and error. Lorraine York's *Margaret Atwood and the Labour of Literary Celebrity* details the work of agents in the production of celebrity status; however, there was little reference to Atwood's engagement with the various state agencies and programs that make book publishing initiatives from fictional works to scholarly monographs possible in Canada. Yet the evidence of successful paperwork is usually present in the marginal areas of Canadian cultural texts. The presence of the logo of various granting agencies, like the Canada Council or Ontario Arts Council, is a prominent feature on the front matter of many publications, while the phrase "Canadian Film or Video Production Tax Credit" or the Canada Wordmark typically occupies the bottom 10 per cent of the space of most movie posters, or in the credits of films and television programs. This is also true in many other countries, where state support is an important part of national cultural policies. In these cases we are reminded that what we are reading or seeing was not possible without the support of various agencies that represent the state, province, or municipality in which that creative expression was produced. At the same time, those banal reminders of support, even now in dwindling sums, are also a reminder of the additional paperwork required to bring a creative work to fruition. Still further, they also remind us of Shyon Baumann's observation that "art world success depends on gaining power and savvy art world members will recognize the necessity of strategies and tactics" (56).

Broadly speaking, these initiatives are part of a cultural policy apparatus that has attempted to compensate for what we might call a "promotional gap" in Canada's entertainment industries for nearly a century. By this I mean that Canada's cultural policies have represented sustained efforts in the promotion of Canadian creative expression based on a belief that various structural forces would prevent those things from occurring without significant intervention. That stance is clearly nationalistic; since culture has been tied to sovereignty and expressive of a distinctive set of Canadian values, the policy apparatus has conceived of its efforts, and of those who take advantage or engage with them, as working in the national interest. As Kevin Dowler once noted, the establishment of a cultural policy apparatus comes in large part as a response to the recognition that independence

would have to come through metaphysical, rather than economic, impera-
tives. The establishment of key institutions ranging from the NFB to the
CBC to the Canada Council and emboldening the Department of Canadian Heritage to develop a range of cultural programs "would establish the
coherence required for the development of a Canadian culture" (334). The
effect of this was a conflicted relationship to the marketplace, where "success" would not necessarily be measured in terms of sales. This is reflected
in the ways many of the techniques of celebrity—like publicity law—are
different in Canada and reflect, in Sheryl Hamilton's terms, "a distrust of
the persona within a marketized economy and a desire to keep it closely
sutured to the person, often configured as a national citizen" (200).

"To be Canadian," write Geoff Pevere and Greig Dymond, "is to exist
in a state of constant becoming" (1). It is also about being "in-between"
or uncertain, or full of doubt. This particular characterization is common within cultural nationalist rhetoric. As John Hutchinson explains
in the case of Ireland, cultural nationalism perceives the nation not as a
state but as a distinctive historical community in a constant state of evolution, embodying "a higher synthesis of the 'traditional' and the 'modern'"
("Cultural Nationalism" 468). However, the efforts to produce that higher
synthesis through the efforts of educated elites and powerful mythmaking
frequently fail. As a result, the state is left with little choice but to pick up
the slack, adopting strategies "by which to institutionalize its ideals in the
social order" (Hutchinson, *Dynamics* 17).

We see these ideas throughout the discursive and institutional construction of the Canadian cultural system. It usually begins with a story about
failed potential. Canadians need to "hear their own stories" in order to stand
together as a cohesive nation. However, there lacks a strong entertainment
industry to meet that need, and a weak private sector to establish and invest
in infrastructure, therefore the state and many of its various agencies have
stepped in as a support system to bring that into existence, a process Maurice
Charland has referred to as "technological nationalism" (Charland).

The remedies offered to meet this perceived lack are well known by analysts of the Canadian situation. We have a vast and elaborate policy apparatus that influences the ways in which cultural production takes place.
We have a web of policies, programs, and techniques that operate in the
name of the promotion of Canadian culture. Foreign ownership restrictions remain in place for newspapers, magazines, film distribution companies, book publishers, and radio and television networks in part because
of the belief that there must be a solid infrastructure in place for the distribution of Canadian creative work to Canadians. The presence of various
kinds of subsidy programs to support an artist's first album, the marketing

of books, the distribution of films, and the exhibition of television programs reflects the perception that audiences in Canada are either small or dispersed, and that Canadian firms do not have the financial strength to compete with American entertainment companies that can easily and cheaply access the Canadian market. Content regulations stimulate activity within the independent production sector by forcing broadcasters to devote a certain percentage of their airtime to local content. Those same broadcasters, as well as cable and satellite providers, contribute a portion of their revenues to funds that support the production of film and television programs later to be aired on their networks. As those funds have dwindled at the federal level, provinces and municipalities have become more active. Recently, the Ontario government announced the creation of a fund to support the music industry, including providing funds to record companies to help defray the costs associated with touring (Rayner).

These support initiatives have obviously had the effect of helping to sustain and develop the cultural industries, and to allow for many artistic careers to develop within Canada. It has also come with serious consequences: in return for this support we continue to maintain a strong belief in the role that state institutions can play in creating conditions that are favourable to the cultural industries; but in fact it is state institution that are presented as solely responsible for the success of Canadian culture as a whole. Paul Attallah has observed that this is important for the ways in which we understand the concept of the audience in the Canadian context; since "Canadians" are presented in cultural nationalist terms and not based on actual behavior, various interested parties in policy debates can easily speak on their behalf in the name of a mythologized and administrative version of a Canadian nation (Attallah 343–345). For our purposes, though, the main result has been the heavy emphasis on bureaucratic work as part of the Canadian artistic experience. Since the cultural apparatus represents so many agencies operating at the federal, provincial, and municipal levels where jurisdictional issues are at play, what results, according to Michael Dorland, is that "primarily administrative norms and practices prevail – because there are no other norms" ("Policing Culture" 147).

Recent scholarship inspired by an increased interest in the materiality of communication has focused on the role played by paperwork within modern bureaucratic systems (Vismann; Guillory; Kafka). For Ben Kafka, paperwork represents a set of practices that are "full of surprises," that although we associate paperwork with monotony or with state control, there are always unintended consequences produced by the production, distribution, and distribution of paper. For Kafka, the primary characteristic of paperwork is that it is unpredictable and that unpredictability creates frustration (10–11). A turn to the function of paperwork and the feelings associated with it would also be a welcome use in the study of cultural policy, where so much appears to occur in an environment characterized by secrecy and mystery and where there are few venues for the expression of frustration such a system produces.

Paperwork serves a range of different functions within the celebrity apparatus. In one sense, the state is easily the largest producer of knowledge about the cultural sector and its activities. There is a raft of paper in the form of reports, documents, White Papers, committee meetings, Royal Commissions, witness testimony at CRTC hearings, expert submissions, and other supplementary policy documents used as part of the process. In a different context, that of nineteenth-century Britain and the United States, Oz Frankel characterized the efforts of states to commission and collect knowledge through expert reports, commissions, and censuses as an act of "print statism" that equates state power with the possession and deployment—or denial—of forms of social knowledge. A major consequence of this, Frankel writes, "was that investigations and reports incorporated less powerful groups into the national conversation by rendering them presentable and representable political subjects" (2).

This description applies to the Canadian cultural sector, and it has dominated the environment in which both the famous faces and "faceless" bureaucrats interact.[2] It also raises important methodological questions; recent work on Truth and Reconciliation Commissions and governmental apologies has revealed how little critical or literary analysis has ever gone into interrogating how best to read these kinds of documents, even as they serve as such prominent sources of information about how we understand cultural activity in Canada and as an arena in which the artists engage with the state (see Henderson and Wakeham). Much of that interaction appears to go on in silence, as very little knowledge about the forms of knowledge that goes into grant writing is shared with others. This is not only for competitive purposes, a resistance to share among people going after the same pots of money. Part of this is for legal reasons: many decisions on funding are based on peer-review systems that are secretive and whose deliberations are *in camera*. Many cultural statistics are collected in aggregate, in order to respect privacy concerns and mitigate against intra-industry competition.

If many of the processes occur in respect for privacy, others take place in highly formalized forms of interaction. For example, the CRTC hearing is truly a must-see event for those interested in understanding the nature of official discourse in this country, in what qualifies as the public sphere. The event is set up as a quasi-judicial inquiry, with testimony, the presentation of evidence, submissions from interested groups and members of the public, cross-examination, deliberation, with the release of a final decision, and dissenting reports often attracting considerable, albeit evanescent, media attention, followed by appearances by the chairperson of the CRTC giving interviews to members of the Ottawa press corps. The event is occasionally covered on CPAC and, as I have written elsewhere, the broadcast typically cuts off when a recess is announced, and just before those sitting in an adversarial relationship cross over the imaginary fourth wall and shake each other's hands, and where some of the real business takes place (Wagman).

In her discussion of the precarious labour conditions of freelance writers in Canada, Nicole Cohen explains, "To understand why work is experienced in particular ways requires broadening the forms from individual experiences to consider cultural workers as part of a class or workers struggling over the terms of the commodification of their labour" (144). The paperwork trail outlined in this discussion contributes to that discussion about why "cultural work" is experienced in the way that it is in Canada. The fact that this is part of the job means that there exists an intermediate location between "art" and "industry" that many within the cultural industries will be quite familiar with. This fact of cultural life is also a reminder that we likely need to develop more complex terms to define the nature of the work on display here. The paperwork many artists "submit" is about the struggle over the conditions under which they will labour in the most basic sense: whether or not their creative project will be financed. However, so much about the nature of that struggle concerns the peculiar nature of how that artistic output must negotiate its commodity status, how triangular relations between private firms, government institutions, and artistic institutions are also a part of a broader struggle over the form the "commodity" will ultimately take in the end.

Grant Envy?
From the previous discussion we can see how paperwork stands as the medium between artists and their work and is a part of the territory that separates the fundable from the unfundable. Since much cultural discourse in this country appears caught between aesthetic judgments about the quality of creative work and the politics of the system that assists, to varying degrees, in making that work possible, this has an effect on the nature of discourse around those who occupy celebrity status in Canada. How does this environment impact upon how creative talent feels about being an artist in Canada?

A former punk rock musician and now proprietor of Mammoth Cave Records, Paul Lawton, recently attracted a considerable amount of attention for comments published on his Tumblr page, Slagging Off. On

Slagging Off, Lawton provided a series of reviews of musical acts appearing during Canadian Music Week, a festival of national musical talent that takes place in Toronto. Artists supported by the Fund to Assist Canadian Talent on Record (FACTOR) were the primary targets of those attacks. The fund was started in 1982 in order to provide support to emerging Canadian music talent. However, Lawton attracted attention by suggesting that the fund actually directs much of its money to a small number of musical acts, such as The Trews, Metric, and Stars, which have already achieved a certain measure of success. For Lawton, this money supports what he called "middle-of-the-road indie rock" and "more specifically, the business-class individuals who have set themselves up to live off the profits of middle of the road indie rock" ("The Trouble with FACTOR"). Lawton's comments echoed similar statements uttered a few years earlier by the founder of Unfamiliar Records, Greg Ipp, who complained about the disconnect between the critical attention garnered by his musical talent and their inability to access support funds from federal granting programs. Established bands, such as Metric, on the other hand, received funds from FACTOR and VideoFACT (two bodies which support the production and distribution of Canadian music and music videos). Moreover, Ipp claims to have received advice from "industry insiders" that he should "get to know the judges" who oversee these competitions "so our bands can 'earn' the right to have them as benefactors" (Hughes). Such practices, Ipp claimed, were part of the "well-funded mediocrity" that dominates the Canadian music industry.

Lawton's comments attracted attention from many within the music industry, including artists who have been recipients of FACTOR funding. Some accused Lawton of sour grapes; since he didn't receive FACTOR funding he was jealous of those who did. Others claimed his rant was unproductive, that it didn't help an already struggling industry. Still others claimed it was naive, not taking into account the benefits the system has had for Canadian artists. The response that seemed to attract the most attention came from indie rock musician Dan Mangan, who took to his website to write an "open letter." Mangan replied that FACTOR does not in fact give money to "bands to line their pockets" but rather to "2-star hotels, shitty diners, toll-road attendees, gas stations, publicists, record stores, record distributors, record labels (including small 'true' indies), van mechanics, guitar shops, camera operators, recording engineers, dingy basement recording studios, graphic designers, poster illustrators, and a billion other variables in a world of a touring band." Mangan continued by telling Lawton that FACTOR's activities "should be the least of your worries," that "they're doing everything they can to maybe make an impact for the better given the inherent institutional/societal boxes that surround them" ("An Open Letter"). Then he wondered whether Lawton could do a better job of juggling the various pressures placed upon the organization from within the industry and government.

The debate attracted considerable media attention in Canada that Lawton was clearly not prepared for. By the time he appeared on CBC Radio One's *DNTO* Lawton took a much more diplomatic position: "Sometimes when you focus on the numbers, the people get lost." Later, Lawton explained that after consideration and discussion with Mangan, he was able to conclude that the musician "didn't get that automatically, he worked for it" ("Slagging Off"). He went on to say that this gave him a greater appreciation of the work of Canadian musicians, and that he and Mangan are now friends. Then host Sook-Yin Lee asked Lawton what the take-away would be from the skirmish with Mangan:

> It's really draining and exhausting and it's, like, I'm sick of myself. All of this negative energy that's surrounded this blog.... Just the title of it "Slagging Off." I hate it now. It's so ugly. It's where I was at when I started the journey. It's not where I am at now, and I feel myself softening and feeling less hostile towards what I see as the bigger problem because it's far more nuanced than I could even imagine. ("Slagging Off")

At first glimpse this would seem to be an odd way to answer the question, the punk rocker answering in the language of self-help. And indeed, it may have been the case that raising questions about the system may well have been for selfish reasons or out of jealousy. However, there is much more productive thinking we can do with this when our attention turns to a consideration of the relationship between administration and cultural production, namely, about the kinds of frustration such a relationship produces in so many of its participants. Seen a different way, Lawton's expressions of envy, jealousy, and ugliness shed light on what Sianne Ngai calls "obstructed agency," which produces the conditions on which those ugly feelings emerge (3). For Ngai, emotions such as these represent "unusually knotted or condensed 'interpretations of predicaments'" (3). That such a reaction should come from the questioning of a policy measure should serve as a reminder of the administrative politics of culture in Canada, and that it is in the cultural realm where some of the harshest forms of discourse exist and are encouraged because so many different characters in the tableau exist under feelings of persistent threat.

It also reminds us that much celebrity culture is shot through with auditing discourse, with uncovering where the money has been dispensed, how it was spent, and how those that receive support attempt to justify it.

Of course, the biggest problem is that most of the arguments in the debate are virtually impossible to prove. Mangan may claim that the money is distributed to all of these different people in his touring operation, but there is no way of knowing since that material is not publicly available. It is perfectly reasonable for Mangan to claim that his professional career would not have developed without FACTOR support; however, we have no real way of knowing if this was the case. Lawton's "ugly feelings," to use Ngai's terms, derive in large part from this, I believe. However, it is also indicative of the firm contours of the way these conversations unfold, where criticism is interpreted as jealousy, or a plea for more funding for your project, or part of a wider plot to get rid of the system and replacing it with an American one. More importantly, however, we can also see this exchange—about who gets grant money and how good or bad they are as artists as standing in for the absence of a broader discussion about how the system itself is structured in such a way to produce political discourses over ones that may be more professional in nature.

A related affective response associated with the administration of culture is public acts of shaming. We see this in the celebrated case between Sun News presenter Krista Erickson and dancer Margie Gillis. During the interview, which aired on June 1, 2011, Sun News displayed a list of grants received by the Margie Gillis Dance Foundation over the past ten years, followed by Erickson asking Gillis, "Why is the price tag for research, reflection and the study of human adventure, uh, through interpretive dance costing 1.2 million dollars a year?" (Canadian Broadcast Standards Council). The interviewer continued by badgering Gillis, calling on her to justify her expenses, querying why money was going to her and not others, and why a small group of elites get to decide what to do with public monies. A social media campaign was launched and more than six thousand complaints came into the Canadian Broadcast Standards Council, which reviewed the case and determined that while many of the facts posted on the screen were accurate, Gillis was treated unfairly by Erickson over the course of the interview.

Such confrontations are long- standing in the Canadian context. They usually combine feelings of hostility (*how could that happen?*) with astonishment (*they gave you that much* for *that?*) and resentment (*why couldn't I get that?*). The confrontation and subsequent squirming it produces give the initiator a feeling of *schadenfreude*, a sense that, when applied to celebrities, serves as a kind of "leveling through humiliation" (Cross and Littler 397). In Canada, such sentiments come from the libertarian side of the political spectrum, usually as part of anti-welfare rhetoric that artists are getting rich "off the system" and need to produce their work for the marketplace rather than for themselves or for "elite" audiences. However, there is more to the story here. In writing about popular music in Canada, Will Straw explains that status anxiety and envy are representative of the less exciting but more practical affective responses for a country like Canada that emerges out of a colonial relationship and exists outside of centres of power (Straw, "Dilemmas" 101).

Star System Determinism

Another condition created by the heavy role of the state, a relatively weak public sphere, and the prominence of government as a leading disseminator of information has been relatively easy leakage of policy concepts into broader cultural discourses. Discourses on celebrity, and particularly around the "star system," are a perfect illustration of this. To say that celebrity is a policy matter is not an understatement or an exercise in hyperbole. In 2001, the CRTC declared that entertainment news programming represented "priority programming," a move that allowed broadcasters to air programming and receive credit toward their Canadian content regulations. This is the major force behind the creation of *Etalk Daily* (CTV, 2002–present, now called *Etalk*), *Entertainment Desk*, and *Entertainment Tonight Canada* (Global, 2005–present). Until the regulations were changed in 2010, at least two-thirds of the programming had to be Canadian-based entertainment news. One of the reasons behind that initiative was the belief that English Canada lacked the promotional apparatus to support its domestic talent and publicize the life and activities of its homegrown celebrities. A major part of that argument is the belief that the situation is very different in Quebec because it has its own star system, which is one of the primary factors explaining the health of its cultural sector.

This is an argument that is regularly found in policy documents assessing the state of the Canadian broadcasting system. One example will suffice here, from a major review of the state of Canadian broadcasting published in 2003. It begins with a nod to Quebec's cultural sovereignty, noting that, along with a need to protect a distinct language, "French-language broadcasters realized in the mid-1980s that the way to break the dependence on American programming was to develop a star system and to produce programming which would permit French-speaking Canadians to see their stories and their communities" (Canada, Standing Committee on Canadian Heritage 121). The report later elaborates this point by placing Quebec's star system in a sidebar note:

> Nonetheless it is the central role played by artists, particularly performing artists and writers, in the development of broadcasting in Quebec that is remarkable and probably unique in Canada, and we can conclude that the

> high levels of viewership attained by indigenous French-language programs
> is closely aligned with identification, encouragement and promotion of well-
> known and popular stars in the Quebec broadcasting and entertainment
> industries.... Over the years, a symbiosis has developed between the viewing
> public in Quebec and the performers and writers who entertain them. The
> bond goes well beyond admiration and appreciation. It can best be described
> as an ongoing love affair and a celebration between the public and their art-
> ists. (Canada, Standing Committee on Canadian Heritage 149)

Here we have an example of what I would call "star-system determinism,"
in that it attributes the success of the industry to its celebrity apparatus. The
rhetorical claim here—that Quebec's star system is successful and this is
something that the rest of country is deeply envious of—is a powerful feature of cultural arguments made at the policy level and by those who study
it. Robert Armstrong's recent study of Canadian broadcasting claims that
unlike English-language broadcasting, "French-language entertainment
programs benefit from a 'star system' that is maintained by the local media,
with the result that domestic drama and variety programs are capable of out-
performing US programs in many situations" (105, emphasis mine). Notice
the way this argument unfolds, starting from a definitive statement about
causality to a less definitive set of statements that undercut the strength of
the original claim. Here we see that the existence of a star system creates
results that make programs capable (although it is not clear how) in many
situations (without saying which ones work and which ones do not).

What is striking about star-system determinism within policy circles
is how the idea circulates unchallenged either on its premises or its terms.
Most say it so often that they routinely fail to mention the terms, as if "star
system" represented a clear and organized set of institutions, individuals,
and practices. No definition of a star system is ever offered. The term itself,
as many of us know, derives from Hollywood and the particular production environment characterized by the major movie studios of the 1920s
and 30s. The structural characteristics of the Canadian system are a far
cry from that one, with the exception of high levels of vertical and hori-
zontal integration of media companies. The peculiarities of the Quebec
media system are also offered without specific references to institutions,
industries, players, publications, venues, and so on. Of course, not all performers in Quebec are stars, even if they are participants in the province's
promotional system.

The tendency to reiterate this argument is due to a number of factors.
One of them may be a case of ignorance; many anglophones assessing the
national situation do not understand French, do not live in Quebec, and

lack both the linguistic knowledge and exposure to be able to offer a more nuanced account of cultural production in the province. Here we may also have another case of envy driven by frustration, at the inability to create the kind of popular symbolic order that is present and popular a province or two away. But still another reason may be that the imprecision of terms does not matter, since the language of the celebrity apparatus—that of "system"—is one that resonates with a larger cultural apparatus that uses similar terms. The fact that Quebec's entertainment industries are integrated across platforms, producers, and venues—the fact that they constitute a system is more important than matters of definition, measures of effectiveness, or the existence of case studies to prove them.[3]

We see these kinds of truisms all the time when it comes to cultural policy. One of the most popular one links the establishment of Canadian content regulations with the development of Canada's music industry. Without these regulations, we would not have our Arcade Fires that are now trumpeted around the world today. But like the case of the star system, the argument about content is one that is both impossible to test and tautological in nature. Since we cannot actually say how the industry would have developed we can't really know that content regulations "saved" it. We also cannot say if industrial survival was based solely on account of content regulations or other measures, such as touring. But at the same time, we can also say that the claim itself is self-evident. The policy was put in place to artificially create a demand for which an industry emerged to produce it. We cannot say that no industry would have developed in the absence of content regulations, only that the shape of the current industry, with its current players, discourse, and interest, developed in the way that it did because of content regulations that brought it into being.

Taken together, the prominence of these measures in the discourse relating to culture in Canada is part of a rhetoric of cultural nationalism, particularly in English Canada, which privileges measures that highlight elements of cultural weakness. As we have seen so far, the precision of the terms is really beside the point; such terms "mean" in and of themselves to those who most need them, namely, the policy-makers, industries, and interested parties who trade paperwork back and forth with various state agencies.

Perhaps a place to conclude this discussion on the relationship between celebrity and the bureaucracy would be at the offices of the Canada Council for Arts. From 2004 to 2008 the celebrated ballerina Karen Kain served as the Council's Executive Director, replacing James Kudelka. Kain's move from the stage to administration was one of a flood of similar moves that have taken place in the Canadian creative world over the last decade and a half. A different kind of interface might be the one that sees former journalists crossing the imaginary line to work for the government they once subjected to objective reportage. This could include the tenures of former broadcasters Adrienne Clarkson and Michaëlle Jean in Rideau Hall as Governors General of Canada, the work of people like Liza Frulla or Peter Kent on the backbenches of their respective political parties, and of the now dubious careers of Pamela Wallin and Mike Duffy in Canada's upper chamber. Radio-Canada's former Ottawa parliamentary correspondent Bernard Drainville once served in the Quebec government as the government's point person for its controversial Charter of Values legislation. In the riding of Toronto-Centre a compelling political story played out with author Linda McQuaig, the journalist Jennifer Hollett, and writer Chrystia Freeland vying for a seat in Parliament once held by Bob Rae, with Freeland coming away with the win.[4]

In his account of stardom, Richard Dyer argued that stars operate as an array of signs and signifying discourses that gave them particular meaning for audiences. More than this, stars serve the function of managing contradictions by underscoring certain kinds of myths and values. Given what has been said in the few examples discussed in this chapter, how can we account for the constant movement of celebrities into political or administrative positions in government? Of course, there are different answers and motivations, but many of them have to do with the perceived limits of a career in journalism or the arts in Canada. In one sense you reach the point where there is nowhere else you can go but out. In another you may have achieved the status that allows you to influence the future development of your field. In still another you determine that you are unable to achieve upward mobility through one sphere of work, resulting in a moderate change of course. In the turbulent times experienced by the journalistic community, a government job still signifies a relatively safe place to land.

For our purposes, however, it signifies something more important: in the end, the government and its institutions remain the real celebrities in this country, the state remains the most powerful producer of a nation, and since cultural issues are also political ones, and since most creative work is so closely engaged with the administrative work of government bureaucracy, the movement between the two spheres is not as difficult as it may seem to be.

However, we know that things are changing. The proliferation of social media has made it possible for creative talent in Canada to fashion personas in new and interesting ways. Indeed, it may be the case that a turn toward celebrity production within Canadian creative life is a function of the declining influence of those very support systems themselves. Before the 2015 election that brought the Liberals back to power, a visit to the website of the Department of Canadian Heritage was a sobering reminder of the quiet but consistent strategies to rebrand the federal government and the way it communicates itself to Canadians. The red and white colours of the flag had been replaced by the prominence of Tory blue across all government communications, and the website barely mentioned that this is the agency devoted to supporting culture, ensuring Canadians can tell stories, and developing a positive cultural identity.

Noticeable was a striking absence of cultural nationalist discourse, replaced with the rhetoric of job creation and innovation. A contemporary funding announcement for support of the sixteenth annual FestiBlues International de Montréal was justified by then-new Heritage Minister Shelley Glover as helping to improve "the vitality of Canada's economy" and the overall quality of life (Canada, "Minister"). This was on the heels of numerous policy announcements that either decreased funding to various funding programs, politicized those programs to turn them into contributors to youth employment strategies, or increased involvement of the private sector, or encouraged individual or corporate philanthropy. In other cases, such as the CBC, the government increased the amount of federal government oversight into business affairs or forced it to cut services, such as Radio Canada International. In other cases, such as cultural affairs programs once administered by the Department of Foreign Affairs and International Trade, they were cancelled altogether. At the same time, however, many of the basic building blocks of the policy apparatus were still in place. We still have Canadian content regulations, we still have restrictions on foreign ownership of most forms of cultural production, and we still participate in global copyright regimes that impinge upon our ability to watch Hulu, listen to Pandora, or access the same catalogue of films on Netflix as our neighbours to the south.

It is too early to say how these developments will affect the way we understand celebrity culture in Canada. The reorientation of the cultural portfolio along the lines of economic development is simply another part of the rewriting of the paper on which nationalism in this country is understood, placing a version of the nation that is more militaristic, more economically minded, and more consumer-friendly than previous government administrations. Is this the way we can understand the production of some of the country's current media celebrities like Kevin O'Leary, Arlene Dickinson, and the other judges on *Dragon's Den*? Or will we continue to prize the modesty of Alice Munro or the collaborative culture of bands like Arcade Fire or Broken Social Scene? If federal cultural policy measures are now presented explicitly in economic terms, will that change the ways artists interface with the state? Will they become more impolite, more frustrated, even more jealous? Or will they throw the grant application in the trash?

Notes

I would like to thank Derek Antoine for his research assistance with this paper. The final version is my own responsibility.

1 An important exception here is Dobson and Kamboureli's collection of interviews with Canadian writers, some of which end up discussing their interactions with cultural institutions.

2 The administrative nature of cultural policy made Michel Foucault's writing on governmentality so attractive to many observers of Canadian cultural policy (Foucault; Allor and Gagnon; Dowler; Druick). For Foucault, the transition from sovereign to democratic societies brought about new ways of thinking about the nature of government, one that is exercised through a series of tactics—or "techniques"—rather than the brute exercise of force. To accomplish this, the state produces various kinds of subject populations through devices like the census in order that they may be amenable to government. Thinking about governmentality offered many scholars an opportunity to see the relationship between the state and the cultural sector as a series of programs, populations, and techniques, rather than as the actions of a monolithic state. As much as this work benefited and enriched the understanding of cultural policy, it offered very few specific case studies of the role of specific techniques of governing over the cultural apparatus.

3 This is a common problem; Charles Acland has talked at length about the troubled and confused history of the notion of "screen time" in discussions about Canadian cinema. He notes that figure of 2 per cent used to describe the status of Canadian films vis-à-vis American ones often mixes two different notions—screen time and screen space—intermittently, and usually deploys those figures without reference to where such numbers derive, and privilege theatrical consumption over other ways of watching Canadian cinema (Acland).

4 Of course, there are other, more small-scale examples of movement; CBC television's former chief political correspondent Jason Moscovitz joined the Business Development Bank of Canada as its vice-president of public affairs, while his former radio colleague Susan Murray became the communication director for Liberal MP Scott Brison before moving to the International Development Research Centre

Bibliography

Abbott, Larry. "A Time of Visions." Interview with Shelley Niro. Britesites. Web. 18 Apr. 2014.

"About BookThug." *BookThug.ca*. 2011. John Schmidt Web Marketing. 5 Feb. 2013. Web.

"About Us." *Canada's Walk of Fame*. 2014. Web. 16 Feb. 2014.

Acland, Charles. *Screen Traffic: Movies, Multiplexes, and Global Culture*. Durham & London: Duke UP, 2003. Print.

———. "Screen Space, Screen Time, and Canadian Film Exhibition." *North of Everything; Canadian Cinema since 1980*. Ed. William Beard and Jerry White. Edmonton: U of Alberta P, 2002. 2–18. Print.

Albani, Emma. *Forty Years of Song*. London: Mills & Boon, 1911. Print.

Aleiss, Angela. *Making the White Man's Indian: Native Americans and Hollywood Movies*. Westport: Praeger, 2005. Print.

Allain, Kristi A. "'Real Fast and Tough': The Construction of Canadian Hockey Masculinity." *Sociology of Sport* 25.4 (2008): 462–482. Print.

Allan, Maud. *My Life and Dancing*. Special Souvenir Edition. London: Everett, 1908. Print.

Allen, Barry. "Foucault's Nominalism." *Foucault and the Government of Disability*. Ed. Shelley Tremain. Ann Arbor: U of Michigan P, 2005. 93–107. Print.

Allor, Martin, and Michelle Gagnon. *L'État de Culture: Généologie Discursive des Politiques Culturelles Québécoises*. Montréal: GRECC, 1994. Print.

Ammirante, Julian. "Manufacturing Players and Controlling Sports: An Interpretation of the Political Economy of Hockey and the 2004 NHL Lockout." *Canada's Game: Hockey and Identity*. Ed. Andrew C. Holman. Montreal: McGill-Queen's UP, 2009. 180–210. Print.

"An Open Letter to Paul Lawton (the man behind the 'Slagging off" Blog)." *Dan Mangan*. 11 Apr. 2013. Web. 15 May 2013.

Armatage, Kay. *The Girl from God's Country: Nell Shipman and the Silent Screen*. Toronto: U of Toronto P, 2003. Print.

Armstrong, Robert. *Broadcasting Policy in Canada*. Toronto: U of Toronto P, 2010. Print.

Attallah, Paul. "A Usable History for the Study of Television." *Canadian Review of American Studies* 37.3 (2007): 325–349. Print.

Atwood, Margaret. *The Year of the Flood*. Toronto: Vintage Canada, 2010. Print.

Bachman-Turner Overdrive. "You Ain't Seen Nothing Yet." *Not Fragile*. Comp. Randy Bachman. Mercury, 1974. LP.

Bailey, Steve. *Media Audiences and Identity: Self-Construction and the Fan Experience*. Houndmills, Basingstoke: Palgrave Macmillan, 2005. Print.

Baldwin, M. Page. "Subject to Empire: Married Women and the British Nationality and Status of Aliens Act." *Journal of British Studies* 40.4 (2001): 522–556. Print.

Banet-Weiser, Cynthia Chris and Anthony Freitas, eds. *Cable Visions: Television Beyond Broadcasting*. New York: New York UP, 2007. Print.

Banff Television Festival. Interview with Colm Feore. http://blip.tv/banff-world -television-festival/colm-feore-actor-824466. n . Web. 30 June 2012.

Barber, John. "Why Canada's A-list Wants to Save Al Purdy's A-frame." *Globe and Mail* 5 Feb. 2013. Web.

———. "Literary Awards Are Abundant in Canada, but Some See a Downside." *Globe and Mail* 28 May 2011. Web.

Baumann, Shyon. "A General Theory of Artistic Legitimation: How Art Worlds Are Like Social Movements." *Poetics* 35.7 (2007): 47–65.

"B.C. Film Industry Seeking Ways to Survive." *CBC News*. Canadian Broadcasting Corporation. 22 Jan. 2013. Web. 5 Aug. 2103.

Beaty, Bart, and Rebecca Sullivan. *Canadian Television Today*. Calgary: U of Calgary P, 2006. Print.

Beck, Andrew. "Introduction: Cultural Work, Cultural Workplace—Looking at the Cultural Industries." *Cultural Work: Understanding the Cultural Industries*. Ed. Andrew Beck. London and New York: Routledge, 2003. 1–12. Print.

Bennett, James. *Television Personalities: Stardom and the Small Screen*. New York: Routledge, 2011. Print.

———. "The Television Personality System: Televisual Stardom Revisited after Film Theory." *Screen* 49.1 (2008): 32–50. Print.

Berland, Jody. *North of Empire: Essays on the Cultural Technologies of Space*. Durham, NC: Duke UP, 2009. Print.

Berlant, Lauren. *The Female Complaint*. Durham: Duke UP, 2008. Print.

Bishop-Gwyn, Carol. "Willing to Be Thrilling: Her Skirt Was Transparent, Her Midriff Was Bare. Canadian-born Pioneer of Modern Dance Maud Allan Scandalized Edwardian London. In More Ways Than One." *The Beaver: Exploring Canada's History* 86.6 (2006): 32–38. Print.

Black, Martha. *My Seventy Years*. London: Thomas Nelson, 1938. Print.

Bociurkiw, Marusya. *Feeling Canadian: Television, Nationalism, and Affect*. Waterloo: Wilfrid Laurier UP, 2011. Print.

Boorstin, Daniel. *The Image: A Guide to Pseudo-Events in America*. New York: Athaneum, 1971. Print.

———. *The Image*. 50th Anniversary ed. New York: Vintage Books, 2012. Print.

———. "From Hero to Celebrity: The Human Pseudo-Event." *The Celebrity Culture Reader*. Ed. P. David Marshall. New York: Routledge, 1993. 72–90. Print.

Boshra, Basem. "'We Knew Him When': Majumder Is Host of New CBC Series." *Montreal Gazette* 10 Oct. 2002: D7. Print.

Bourdieu, Pierre. *The Field of Cultural Production: Essays on Art and Literature.* Trans. Rupert Sawyer. New York: Columbia UP, 1993. Print.

Boxer, Asa. Personal interview. 2–6 Nov. 2012. Email.

Braz, Albert. "The Modern Hiawatha: Grey Owl's Construction of his Indigenous Self." *Auto/biography in Canada: Critical Directions.* Ed. Julie Rak. Waterloo, ON: Wilfrid Laurier UP. 53–68. Print.

Bredin, Marian. "Producing Aboriginal Television in Canada: Obstacles and Opportunities." *Canadian Television: Text and Context.* Ed. Marian Bredin, Scott Henderson, and Sarah A. Matheson. Waterloo, ON: Wilfrid Laurier UP, 2012. Print.

———— and Sigurjon Baldur Hafsteinsson, ed. *Indigenous Screen Cultures in Canada.* Winnipeg: U of Manitoba P, 2010. Print.

Brennan, Edward. "Not Seeing the Joke: The Overlooked Role of Humour in Researching Television Production." *Media Culture Society* 33 (2011): 819–833. Print.

Brennan, Timothy. "Cosmopolitans and Celebrities." *Race & Class* 31.1 (1989): 1-19. Print.

Brownlow, Kevin. *The Parade's Gone By...* Los Angeles: U of California P, 1976. Print.

Buddle, Kathleen. "Media, Markets and Powwows: Matrices of Aboriginal Cultural Mediation in Canada." *Cultural Dynamics* 16.1 (2004): 29–69. Print.

Butler, Judith. *Bodies That Matter.* New York: Routledge, 1993. Print.

————. "Imitation and Gender Insubordination." *The Critical Tradition: Classic Texts and Contemporary Trends.* Ed. David H. Richter. Boston: Bedford/St. Martin's, 2007. 1707–1718. Print.

Byers, Michele. "On the (Im)possibility of Canadian Celebrity." *Reconstruction: Studies in Contemporary Culture* 12.1 (2012). Web. 2 Apr. 2013.

Cain, Steven. "Ashby's World..." Product review of *Californication: The Complete Second Season. Amazon.* July 2010. Web. 5 Aug. 2013.

Californication. Season 2. Prod. David Duchovny, Tom Kapinos, and Stephen Hopkins. Totally Commercial Films. 2008.

Californicationwiki. Wikifoundry. n.d. Web. 4 Mar. 2014.

"Callum Keith Rennie. Interview by CITY TV." *YouTube.* 16 Aug. 2006. Web. 4 Mar. 2014. *callumkeithrenniefanfusion.* Word Press. 2007–2009. Web. 4 Mar. 2014.

Canada. Department of Canadian Heritage. "Minister Shelley Glover Announces Funding for FestiBlues International de Montréal." 6 Aug. 2013. Web. 7 Aug. 2013.

Canada. Parliament. House of Commons. Standing Committee on Canadian Heritage and Clifford Lincoln. *Our Cultural Sovereignty : The Second Century of Canadian Broadcasting.* [Ottawa]: Standing Committee on Canadian Heritage, 2003. Print.

Canadian Broadcast Standards Council. "Appendix A: CBSC Decision 10/11 – 1803+ Sun News Network re: *Canada Live* (Margie Gillis Interview)." 15 Dec. 2011. Web. 31 Mar. 2014.

"Canadian Institutes of Health Research Act." Government of Canada. Justice Laws. Web. 12 May 2015.

"Canadian Photoplays, Limited: Prospectus." *Nell Shipman Collection,* Boise State University (MSS 99, Box 10, Folder 6). Print.

Canuel, Érik. dir. *Bon Cop, Bad Cop.* Perf. Patrick Huard, Colm Feore. Park Ex Pictures, 2006. Alliance Atlantis Vivafilm. DVD.

Carr, Jimmy, and Lucy Greeves. *Only Joking: What's So Funny about Making People Laugh?* New York: Gotham Books, 2006. Print.

Carter Flinn, Sue. "Canada Council defends GG poetry shortlist." *Quill & Quire.ca.* 14 Oct. 2011. Web.

CBC Sports. "CBC wins rights to 2014, 2016 Olympic Games." 1 Aug. 2012. Web. 17 Jan. 2014.

———. "Hockey Night in Canada, a History of Excellence." 2013. Web. 17 Jan. 2014.

Charland, Maurice. "Technological Nationalism." *Canadian Journal of Politcal and Social Theory* 10. 1–2 (1986): 196–220. Print.

Cherniavsky, Felix. *The Salome Dancer: The Life and Times of Maud Allan.* Toronto: McClelland & Stewart, 1991. Print.

———. *Maud Allan and Her Art.* Toronto: Dance Collection Danse, 1998. Print.

Cherry, Don, with Al Strachan. *Don Cherry's Hockey Stories and Stuff.* Toronto: Doubleday Canada, 2008. Print.

Chivers, Sally. "Ordinary People: Reading the TransCanadian Terry Fox." *Canadian Literature* 202 (2009): 80–94. Print.

The CKR Files. Live Journal. n.d. Web. 4 Mar. 2014.

Clark, Andrew. *Stand and Deliver: Inside Canadian Comedy.* Toronto: Doubleday, 1997. Print.

———. "The Land of Laughs." *Canadian Communication: Issues in Contemporary Media and Culture.* Ed. Bohdan Szuchewycz and Jeannette Sloniowski. Scarborough, ON: Prentice-Hall, 2002. 124–126. Print.

Clarke, Robert, ed. *Celebrity Colonialism: Fame, Power and Representation in Colonial and Postcolonial Cultures.* Newcastle upon Tyne: Cambridge Scholars, 2009. Print.

Cohen, Andrew. *The Unfinished Canadian.* Toronto: McClelland & Stewart, 2007. Print.

Cohen, Nicole. "Cultural Work as a Site of Struggle: Freelancers and Exploitation." *tripleC* 10.2 (2012): 141–155. Web. 13 Feb. 2014.

"Colette Bourgonje." Canadian Paralympic Committee. Web. 20 Feb. 2013.

Conyers, Claude. "Courtesans in Dance History: Les Belles de la Belle Époque." *Dance Chronicle* 26.2 (2003): 219–243. Web. 17 July 2013.

Cormack, Patricia. "Double-Double: Branding, Tim Hortons, and the Public Sphere." *Political Marketing in Canada.* Vancouver: U of British Columbia P, 2012. 209–223. Print.

Corner, John. "Mediated Persona and Political Culture." *Media and the Restyling of Politics*. Ed. John Corner and Dick Pels. London: SAGE, 2003. 67–84. Print.

Corner, John, and Dick Pels. Introduction. *Media and the Restyling of Politics*. Ed. John Corner and Dick Pels. London: SAGE, 2003. 1–18. Print.

Cowan, Stu. "Are Fans Tuning Out Don Cherry?" *Montreal Gazette* 2 Dec. 2011. n.p. Print.

Cross, Steve, and Jo Littler. "Celebrity and Schadenfreude: The Cultural Economy of Fame in Freefall." *Cultural Studies* 24.3 (2010): 395–417. Print.

CRTC. "A Policy Framework for Canadian Television." *Canadian Radio-television and Telecommunications Commission Performance Report*. 1999. Web. 25 May 2013.

Czach, Liz. "Television, Film and the Canadian Star System." *Canadian Television: Text and Context*. Ed. Marian Bredin, Scott Henderson, and Sarah A. Matheson. Waterloo, ON: Wilfrid Laurier UP, 2011. 59–72. Print.

———. "The Transnational Career of Geneviève Bujold." *Transnational Stardom: International Celebrity in Film and Popular Culture*. Ed. Russell Meeuf and Raphael Raphael. New York: Palgrave Macmillan, 2013. 95–114. Print.

Dallaire, Christine, and Claude Denis. "'If You Don't Speak French, You're Out': Don Cherry, the Alberta Francophone Games, and the Discursive Construction of Canada's Francophones." *Canadian Journal of Sociology* 25.4 (2000): 415–440. Print.

Davey, Frank. *Post-National Arguments: The Politics of the Anglophone-Canadian Novel since 1967*. Toronto: U Toronto P, 1993. Print.

David, Jennifer. "Seeing Ourselves, Being Ourselves: Broadcasting Aboriginal Television in Canada." *Cultural Survival Quarterly* 22.2 (1998). Web. 4 Apr. 2014.

Davis, Lennard J. *Bending Over Backwards: Disability, Dismodernism and Other Difficult Positions*. New York: New York UP, 2002. Print.

Day, Karen. "Nell Shipman: Girl from God's Country Film." *Kickstarter* Web. 22 Mar. 2014. Web.

deCordova, Richard. *Picture Personalities: The Emergence of the Star System in America*. Urbana: U of Illinois P, 2001. Print.

———. *Picture Personalities: The Emergence of the Star System in America*. Champaign: U of Illinois P, 1990. Print.

Den Tandt, Michael. "Justin Trudeau on the 'Tremendous Hill' Facing the Liberals, His Platform Deficit, and Those Tory Attack Ads." *National Post* 12 Apr. 2013. Web. 26 June 2013.

Deshaye, Joel. *The Metaphor of Celebrity: Canadian Poetry and the Public, 1955–1980*. Toronto: U of Toronto P, 2013.

Deuze, Mark. *Media Work*. Cambridge: Polity, 2007. Print.

Dickinson, Peter. "Being at Home with Roy Dupuis and Pascale Bussières: Or, Star-Gazing In and Out of Québec." *Cinéaction* 73–4 (Summer 2007): 38–43. Web. 17 Feb. 2014.

———. "Subtitling CanLit: Keywords." *Trans.Can.Lit.: Resituating the Study of Canadian Literature*. Ed. Smaro Kamboureli and Roy Miki. Waterloo, ON: Wilfrid Laurier UP, 2006. 45–54. Print.

Dobson, Kit, and Smaro Kamboureli. *Producing Canadian Literature*. Waterloo, ON: Wilfrid Laurier UP, 2013. Print.

"Don Cherry." *The Greatest Canadian*. Senior Producer, Jim Williamson. CBC Home Video, 2004. CD-Rom.

Don We Now Our Gay Apparel. 2013. Web. 17 Jan. 2014.

Dorland, Michael. "A Thoroughly Hidden Country: *Ressentiment,* Canadian Nationalism, Canadian Culture."*Canadian Journal of Political and Social Theory* 7.1-2 (1988):130–164. Print.

———. "Policing Culture: Canada, State Rationality, and the Governmentality of Communication." *Capital Culture: A Reader on Modernist Legacies, State Institutions, and the Value(s) of Art*. Ed. Jody Berland and Shelley Hornstein. Montreal: McGill-Queen's UP, 2000. 142–151. Print.

"Douglas and Mary Back from Europe." *New York Times* 29 July 1920: 16. Web. 20 Apr. 2013.

Dowbiggin, Bruce. "Cherry's Salary Makes Him a Big, Fat Target for Cuts." *Globe and Mail* 5 Apr. 2012. Web. 17 Jan. 2014.

———. "Don Cherry's Ratings Take a Hit." *Globe and Mail* 1 Dec. 2011. Web. 17 Jan. 2014.

Dowler, Kevin. "The Cultural Industries Policy Apparatus." *The Cultural Industries in Canada*. Ed. Michael Dorland. Toronto: James Lorimer and Company, 1996. 328–346. Print.

Drake, Philip, and Andy Miah. "The Cultural Politics of Celebrity." *Cultural Politics* 6.1 (2010): 49–64. Print.

Drake, Philip, and Michael Higgins. "Lights, Camera, Election: Celebrity, Performance and the 2010 UK General Election Leadership Debates." *British Journal of Politics and International Relations* 14.3 (2012): 375–391. Print.

Dressler, Marie. *The Eminent American Comedienne Marie Dressler in The Life Story of an Ugly Duckling: An Autobiographical Fragment in Seven Parts*. New York: Robert M. McBride, 1924. Print.

——— with Mildred Harrington. *My Own Story*. Boston: Little, Brown, 1934. Print.

Driessens, Olivier. "The celebritization of society and culture: Understanding the structural dynamics of celebrity culture." *International Journal of Cultural Studies* 16.6 (2012): 641–657. Web. 28 June 2015.

Druick, Zoë. *Projecting Canada: Government Policy and Documentary Film at the National Film Board*. Montreal: McGill-Queen's UP, 2007. Print.

Dyer, Richard. *Heavenly Bodies: Film Stars and Society*. 2nd ed. London: BFI Macmillan, 1986. Print.

———. *Heavenly Bodies: Film Stars and Society*. 2nd ed. London and New York: Routledge, 2004. Print.

———. *Only Entertainment*. 1992. 2nd ed. London: Routledge, 2002. Print.

———. *Stars*. 1979. London: BFI, 1998. Print.

———. "Stars as Images." Marshall 153–76.

———. "Stars." In *Stardom and Celebrity, a Reader.* Edited by Sean Redmond and Su Holmes. London: Sage, 2007. 78–84. Orig. published as *Stars.* London: BFI Publishing, 1998. Print.

Egan, Kate and Sarah Thomas, ed. *Cult Film Stardom: Offbeat Attraction and Processes of Cultification.* Houndmills, Basingstoke: Palgrave Macmillan, 2013. Print.

Elcombe, Tim. "The Moral Equivalent of Don Cherry." *Journal of Canadian Studies* 44.2 (2010): 194–218. Print.

Elliot, Robin. "Constructions of Identity in the Life Stories of Emma Albani and Glenn Gould." *Journal of Canadian Studies* 39.2 (2005): 105–126. Print.

Ellis, John. "Stars as a Cinematic Phenomenon." *Star Texts: Image and Performance in Film and Television.* Ed. Jeremy G. Butler. Detroit: Wayne State UP, 1991. 300–315. Print.

English, James. *The Economy of Prestige: Prizes, Awards, and the Circulation of Cultural Value.* Cambridge, MA: Harvard UP, 2005. Print.

English, John. *Citizen of the World: The Life of Pierre Elliott Trudeau Volume One: 1919–1968.* Toronto: Alfred A. Knopf Canada, 2006. Print.

———. *Just Watch Me: The Life of Pierre Elliott Trudeau Volume Two: 1968–2000.* Toronto: Knopf Canada, 2009. Print.

English, Susan. "Local Heroine." *Pacific Northwest* January 1991: 32–33. Print.

Erevelles, Nirmala. "The Color of Violence: Reflecting on Gender, Race, and Disability in Wartime." Hall 117–135.

"Facts." The Terry Fox Foundation. Web. 26 Feb. 2013.

Feuer, Jane. "The MTM Style." *MTM: Quality Television.* Ed. Jane Feuer, Paul Kerr, and Tise Vahimagi. London: BFI, 1984. 32–60. Print.

"First Public Stock Offering by Canadian Photoplays, Limited." *Calgary Herald* March 1919: n.p. Print. (Copy of notice in *Nell Shipman Collection.* Boise State University, MSS 99, Box 10, Folder 6.)

Fiske, John. "The Cultural Economy of Fandom." *The Adoring Audience, Fan Culture and Popular Media.* Ed. Lisa A. Lewis. London and New York: Routledge, 1992. 30–49. Print.

Fitz-gerald, Sean. "George Stroumboulopoulos to host 'Hockey Night in Canada,' Don Cherry and Ron MacLean to remain 'cornerstones' of NHL coverage: Rogers." *National Post.* 14 March 2014. Web. 13 May 2014.

Flint, Kate. *The Transatlantic Indian 1776–1930.* Princeton: Princeton UP, 2009. Print.

Foucault, Michel. *The Birth of the Clinic.* Trans. A.M. Sheridan Smith. New York: Vintage, 1994. Print.

———. "Governmentality". *The Foucault Effect.* Ed. Graham Burchell, Peter Miller, and Colin Gordon. Chicago: U of Chicago P, 1991. 87–104. Print.

"Foundation Policies & Guidelines." Terry Fox Foundation. Web. 26 Feb. 2013.

Francis, Daniel. *The Imaginary Indian: The Image of the Indian in Canadian Culture.* 1992. 2nd ed. Vancouver: Arsenal Pulp P, 2011. Print.

Frankel, Oz. *States of Inquiry: Social Investigations and Print Culture in Nine-teenth-Century Britain and the United States*. Baltimore: Johns Hopkins UP, 1998. Print.

Frick, Caroline. *Saving Cinema: The Politics of Preservation*. London: Oxford UP, 2011. Print.

Friesen, Andrew. "A Tribe Called Red Asks Fans to Stop Showing up in 'Red-face.'" cbc.ca. Web. 22 Apr. 2014.

Frye, Northrop. "Conclusion to the *Literary History of Canada*." Ed. Carl F. Klinck. Toronto: U of Toronto P, 1965. Print.

Fulbright, Thomas. "New State Park to Honor Silent Film Star." *The World of Yesterday* July 1976: 5. Print.

"Funding Model." *MontrealPrize.com*. 2011. 5 Feb. 2013. Web.

Gamson, Joshua. *Claims to Fame: Celebrity in Contemporary America*. Berkeley: U of California P, 1994. Print.

———. "The Assembly Line of Greatness, Celebrity in Twentieth-Century America." *Critical Studies in Mass Communication* 9 (1992): 1–24. Print.

Gasher, Mike. *Hollywood North: The Feature Film Industry in British Columbia*. Vancouver: U of British Columbia P, 2002. Print.

Gatehouse, Jonathon. "Justin Trudeau on his own terms." *Maclean's* 11 Oct. 2012. Web. 12 Jan. 2013.

———. "Justin Trudeau (Profile)." *The Canadian Encyclopedia: Maclean's* 17 Mar. 2007. Web. 12 Jan. 2013.

Gauntlett, David. "Media Studies 2.0." Theory.org.uk. Web. 15 Jan. 2014.

Geddes, John. "In Conversation: Justin Trudeau." *Maclean's* 27 Feb. 2012. Web. 12 Jan. 2013.

Genette, Gérard. *Palimpsests*. Trans. Channa Newman & Claude Doubinsky. Lincoln: U of Nebraska P, 1997. Print.

Gerson, Carole, and Veronica Strong-Boag, ed. *Paddling Her Own Canoe: The Times and Texts of E. Pauline Johnson (Tekahionwake)*. Toronto: U of Toronto P, 2000. Print.

Giardina, Michael D. "Global Hingis: Flexible Citizenship and the Transnational Celebrity." *Sports Stars: The Cultural Politics of Sporting Celebrity*. Ed. David Andrews and Steve Jackson. London: Routledge, 2001. 201–217. Print.

Giasson, Thierry, Jennifer Lees-Marshment, and Alex Marland. "Challenges for Democracy." *Political Marketing in Canada*. Vancouver: U of British Columbia P, 2012. 241–255. Print.

———. "Introducing Political Marketing." *Political Marketing in Canada*. Vancouver: U of British Columbia P, 2012. 3–21. Print.

Gibbs, Anna. "Contagious Feelings: Pauline Hanson and the Epidemiology of Affect." *Australian Humanities Review* 24 (2001). 7 Feb. 2013. Web. June 2013.

Gilbert, Joanne. *Performing Marginality: Humor, Gender, and Cultural Critique*. Detroit: Wayne State UP, 2004. Print.

Giuffre, Katherine. "Sandpiles of Opportunity: Success in the Art World." *Social Forces* 77.3 (1999): 815–832. Print.

Giulianotti, Richard. "Scotland's Tartan Army in Italy, the Case for the Carni-valesque." *Sociological Review* 39 (1991): 503–527. Print.

Global Poetry Anthology. Ed. Valerie Bloom et al. Montreal: Véhicule/Signal. 2012. Print.

Gordon, Sean. "Don Cherry to Rogers: Leave Coach's Corner Alone." *Globe and Mail* 30 Nov. 2013. Web. 17 Jan. 2014.

Gorton, Kristyn. *Media Audiences: Television, Meaning and Emotion.* Edinburgh: Edinburgh UP, 2009. Print.

Grace, Sherrill. *Canada and the Idea of North.* Montreal: McGill-Queen's UP, 2007. Print.

Gray, Jonathan, Jeffrey Jones, and Ethan Thompson, eds. *Satire TV: Politics and Comedy in the Post-Network Era.* New York: NYUP, 2009. Print.

Griffin, Scott. Personal interview. 16 Aug. 2012.

Griffiths, Rudyard. *Who We Are: A Citizen's Manifesto.* Vancouver/Toronto: Douglas and McIntyre, 2009. Print.

Grossberg, Lawrence. "Is There a Fan in the House? The Affective Sensibility of Fandom." *The Adoring Audience, Fan Culture and Popular Media.* Ed. Lisa A. Lewis. London and New York: Routledge, 1992. 50–68. Print.

Gruneau, Richard, and David Whitson. *Hockey Night in Canada.* Toronto: Gara-mond P, 1993. Print.

Guillory, John. "The Memo and Modernity." *Critical Inquiry* 31.1 (2004):108–132. Print.

Gunless. Dir. William Phillip. Alliance, 2010.

Hadley, Jo-Anne. "Translating the Québécois Sociolect for Cinema: The Creation of a Supertext in *Bon Cop Bad Cop.*" MA thesis. Concordia University. 2011. Print.

Hall, Kim Q., ed. *Feminist Disability Studies.* Bloomington: Indiana UP, 2011. Print.

———. "Reimagining Disability and Gender Through Feminist Studies: An Introduction." Hall 1–10.

Hallett, Hilary A. *Go West, Young Women: The Rise of Early Hollywood.* Berkeley: U of California P, 2013. Print.

Hamilton, Sheryl. *Impersonations: Troubling the Person in Law and Culture.* Toronto: U of Toronto P, 2009. Print.

Hard Core Logo. Dir. Bruce McDonald. Ed Festus Productions, 1996.

"Harper Says Meeting Bono Isn't His 'Shtick.'" *CBC News* 7 June 2007. Web. June 2015.

Harrison, Deborah. "The Terry Fox Story and the Popular Media: A Case Study in Ideology and Illness." *Canadian Review of Sociology and Anthropology* 22.4 (1985): 496–514. Print.

Hays, Matthew. "Police State." *Canadian Screenwriter* 9.1 (Fall 2006/Winter 2007): 12–15. Print.

Henderson, Jennifer, and Pauline Wakeham, eds. *Reconciling Canada: Critical Perspectives on the Culture of Redress.* Toronto: U of Toronto P, 2013. Print.

Henighan, Stephen. "Giller's Version." *When Words Deny the World: The Reshaping of Canadian Writing*. Erin: Porcupine's Quill, 2002. 83–89. Print.

"Hero." *Oxford Canadian Dictionary*. 2nd ed. Oxford: Oxford UP, 2006. Print.

Hills, Matt. *Fan Cultures*. New York: Routledge, 2002. Print.

"Hockey in Europe." 2013. NHL.com. Web. 17 Jan. 2014.

Holmes, Su, and Diane Negra, eds. *In the Limelight and Under the Microscope: Forms and Functions of Female Celebrity*. New York: Continuum, 2011. Print.

Holmes, Su, and Sean Redmond, eds. *Framing Celebrity: New Directions in Celebrity Culture*. London: Routledge, 2006. Print.

———. *Stardom and Celebrity: A Reader*. Los Angeles: Sage, 2007. Print.

Hoskins, Colin, Stuart McFadyen, and Adam Finn. "Refocusing the CBC." *Canadian Journal of Communication* 26.1 (2001): 17–30. Print.

"How the Presidential Candidates Use the Web and Social Media." *Journalism.org: Pew Research Center's Project for Excellence in Journalism* 15 Aug. 2012. Web. 12 Jan. 2013.

Howley, Brendan. "Sheila McCarthy." *Homemakers* (May 2007): 15–16. Print.

Huggan, Graham. *The Postcolonial Exotic: Marketing the Margins*. New York: Routledge, 2001. Print.

Hughes, Josiah. "Unfamiliar Records Head Slams Canada's Music Industry and Grant System, Calls Out 'Well-Funded Mediocrity' of Bands Such as Metric and MSTRKRFT." Exclaim.ca. 13 July 2009. Web. 17 Jan. 2014.

Hutchinson, John. *The Dynamics of Cultural Nationalism: Gaelic Revival and the Creation of the Irish Nation-State*. London: Allen and Unwin, 1987. Print.

———. "Cultural Nationalism, Elite Mobility and Nation-Building Communitarian Politics in Modern Ireland." *British Journal of Sociology* 38.4 (1997): 482–501. Print.

"I'm Good, but I'm Not the Greatest: Don Cherry." Interview. CBC News Online. 22 Oct. 2004. Web. 17 Jan. 2014.

Inglis, Fred. *A Short History of Celebrity*. Princeton and Oxford: Princeton UP, 2010. Print.

"*Intensities* interviews Henry Jenkins at Console-ing Passions Conference, University of Bristol". *Intensities: The Journal of Cult Media* 2 (2001): n.p. Web. 4 Mar. 2014.

Jackson, Naathan. *Bono's Politics: The Future of Celebrity Political Activism*. Saarbrucken: VDM Verlag, 2008. Print.

Japenga, Ann. "Nell Shipman: Silent No More." *Palm Springs Life* Nov. 1997: 39–42, 75. Print.

Kafka, Ben. *The Demon of Writing*. New York: Zone, 2012. Print.

Karim, Karim H. "The Elusiveness of Full Citizenship: Accounting for Cultural Capital, Cultural Competencies, and Cultural Pluralism." *Accounting for Culture: Thinking Through Cultural Citizenship*. Ed. Caroline Andrew, Monica Gattinger, M. Sharon Jeannotte, and Will Straw. Ottawa: U of Ottawa P, 2005. 146–158. Print.

Karr, Clarence. *Authors and Audiences: Popular Canadian Fiction in the Early Twentieth Century*. Montreal: McGill-Queen's UP, 2000. Print.

Kelly, Brendan. "Show Biz Chez Nous: 2012 a Bad Year at the Box Office for Québécois films." *Montreal Gazette* 9 Jan. 2013. Web. 5 Aug. 2013.

Kelly, Cathal. "CBC's Don Cherry, Female Reporters Don't Need Protection from Coach's Corner: Kelly." *Toronto Star* 8 May 2013. Web. 17 Jan. 2014.

Keohane, Kieran. *Symptoms of Canada: An Essay on the Canadian Identity.* Toronto: U of Toronto P, 1997. Print.

King, Robin Levinson. "Justin Trudeau Got Help from Youth, New Voters, Social Media in Election Win." *Toronto Star* 23 Oct. 2015. Web. Dec. 2015.

King, Samantha. *Pink Ribbons, Inc.: Breast Cancer and the Politics of Philanthropy.* Minneapolis: U of Minnesota P, 2006. Print.

King, Thomas. *The Inconvenient Indian: A Curious Account of Native People in North America.* Toronto: Anchor Canada, 2012. Print.

Knowles, R.E. "Mary Urges Women Become Guardian Angels of Peace." *Toronto Star* 19 May 1934: 3. Web. 15 Jan. 2013.

Koziski, Stephanie. "The Standup Comedian as Anthropologist: Intentional Culture Critic." *The Humor Prism in 20th-Century America: Humor in Life and Letters.* Ed. Joseph Boskin. Detroit: Wayne State UP, 1997. 86–114. Print.

Kristeva, Julia. *Powers of Horror: An Essay on Abjection.* Trans. Leon S. Roudiez. New York: Columbia UP, 1982. Print.

Kroetsch, Robert. *The Lovely Treachery of Words. Essays Selected and New.* Toronto: Oxford UP, 1989. Print.

Kubus, Stefan. "Power Ranking Don Cherry's Top 25 Most Obnoxious Suits of All Time." NHL.com. Web. 17 Jan. 2014.

LaCom, Cindy. "Revising the Subject: *Disability as 'Third Dimension' in* Clear Light of Day *and* You Have Come Back." Hall 159–174.

Lafleche, Grant. "Don Cherry Is as Wrong as Two Left Shoes." *St. Catharines Standard* 5 May 2013. Web. 17 Jan. 2014.

Lahey, Anita. "Rewards of Awards: Literary Prizes Result in Higher Sales and Greater Prestige, but Which Award's Worth Most?" *Quill & Quire* 62.12 (1996): 12–14. Print.

Langan, F.F. "He Could Laugh about Anything – Except Not Making It Big in Hollywood." *Globe and Mail* 8 Apr. 2010: S8. Print.

Langer, John. "Television's 'Personality System.'" *The Celebrity Culture Reader.* Ed. P. David Marshall. New York: Routledge, 2006. 181–195. Print.

Laroque-Poirier, Joanne. Personal interview. 22 May 2009.

"Leaders Honored by 12,000 Women: American Association Elects 49 as Typical of Nation in Business World. Mary Pickford Speaks." *New York Times* 19 Mar. 1926: 21. Web. 23 Apr. 2013.

Lee, Katja. "Women's Celebrity in Canadian Contexts and Memoirs, 1908–2011." Diss. McMaster University, 2014. Print.

Léger, Marc James. "The Non-Productive Role of the Artist: The Creative Industries in Canada." *Third Text* 24.5 (2010): 557–570. Print.

Lewis, Jason, and Tricia Skawennati Gragnito, "Aboriginal Territories in Cyberspace." *Cultural Survival Quarterly* 29.2 (2005). Web. 4 Apr. 2014.

Lombardi, Lisa. "The Picture! Anything for the Picture!" *Idaho Arts Journal* circa 1990. Print. (Undated copy included in The Nell Shipman Collection at the Boise State University Special Collection Archives.)

Loriggio, Paola. "Cherry's Special Talent Makes It Hard to Rebrand HNIC with Him, Marketers Suggest." 29 Nov. 2013. Web. 17 Jan. 2014.

Lowenthal, Leo. "The Triumph of Mass Idols." Marshall 124–152.

———. "The Triumph of Mass Idols." *Literature, Popular Culture and Society.* 1944. Palo Alto: Pacific, 1961. 109–140. Print.

Lucas, Ralph. "Mary Pickford." *NorthernStars.ca.* Web. 1 May 2013.

MacDonald, Tanis. "Terry Fox and the National Imaginary: Reading Eric Walters's *Run.*" *Studies in Canadian Literature.* 36.1 (2011): 18–35. *Erudite.* Web. 13 Feb. 2012.

Mackey, Eva. *The House of Difference: Cultural Politics and National Identity in Canada.* London, New York: Routledge, 1999. Print.

MacLean, Ron, with Kirstie McClellan Day. *Cornered, Hijinks, Highlights, Late Nights and Insights.* Toronto: HarperCollins, 2011. Print.

Majumder, Shaun. Just for Laughs Comedy Festival, 2008. Performance.

"Making a Suit with Don Cherry." *The Rick Mercer Report.* Canadian Broadcasting Corporation. First aired 18 November 2008. Web. 17 Jan. 2014.

Maloney, Ryan. "Trudeau Says Accessibility, Selfies 'Not about Image, It's about Substance." *Huffington Post Canada* 16 Dec. 2015. Web. Dec. 2015.

"Man in Motion World Tour." Rick Hansen Foundation. Web. 20 Feb. 2013.

Mangan, Dan. "Open Letter to Paul Lawton (the man behind the 'Slagging Off" blog). Website of Dan Mangan, 11 Apr. 2013. Web. 1 July 2013.

Manning, Erin. *Ephemeral Territories: Representing Nation, Home, and Identity in Canada.* Minneapolis: U of Minnesota P, 2003.

Manning, Frank E. "Reversible Resistance: Canadian Popular Culture and the American Other." *The Beaver Bites Back? American Popular Culture in Canada.* Ed. David H. Flaherty and Frank E. Manning. Montreal/Kingston: McGill-Queen's UP, 1993. 3–28. Print.

Marchand, Philip. "Quebec Fans' Loyalty Pays Off at the Box Office." thestar .com. 3 Mar. 2008. Web. 31 July 2013.

———. "Are Literary Prizes Necessary?" *Ripostes: Reflections on Canadian Literature.* Erin, ON: Porcupine's Quill, 1998. 63–69. Print.

Marcuse, Herbert. *One-Dimensional Man: Studies in the Ideology of Advanced Industrial Society.* Boston: Beacon, 1992. Print.

Marin, Richard. "Trying to Remember When America Wasn't Canadian." *Globe and Mail* 29 June 1993: D3. Print.

Marland, Alex. "What Is a Political Brand?: Justin Trudeau and the Theory of Political Branding." Annual meetings of the Canadian Communication Association and the Canadian Political Science Association, 6 June 2013, University of Victoria. Web. 26 June 2013.

Marland, Alex, Thierry Giasson, and Jennifer Lees-Marshment. Preface. *Political Marketing in Canada.* Vancouver: U of British Columbia P, 2012. xi–xiv. Print.

Marsh, David, Paul 't Hart, and Karen Tindall. "Celebrity Politics: The Politics of Late Modernity?" *Political Studies Review* 8.3 (2010): 322–340. Print.

Marshall, David. "Exceptional Canadians: Biography in the Public Sphere." *How Canadians Communicate IV: Media and Politics*. Ed. David Taras and Christopher Waddell. Edmonton: Athabasca UP, 2012. 233–257. Print.

Marshall, P. David. *Celebrity and Power: Fame in Contemporary Culture*. Minneapolis: U of Minnesota P, 1997. Print.

Marshall, P. David, ed. *The Celebrity Culture Reader*. New York: Routledge, 2006. Print.

Marshall, P. David, and Sean Redmond, eds. *Companion to Celebrity*. Boston: Wiley-Blackwell. 2015. Print.

Martin, Ruth. "The Political Canonization of the Canadian Anglophone Novel: An Examination of Governor General's Award Winners between 1980 and 2000." *Culture and the State: Nationalisms*. Ed. James Gifford and Gabrielle Zezulka-Mailloux. Edmonton: CRC Humanities Studio, 2003. 102–111. Print.

"Mary Pickford Interview with the CBC Canadian Television." CBC. 1959. *Mary Pickford Foundation*. Web. 15 Jan. 2013.

"Mary Pickford Quit Dolls at Five; 17 Years Actress; Makes $100,000 Year at 22." *Washington Post* 2 Apr. 1916: ES 12. Web. 23 Apr. 2013.

McCabe, Janet, and Kim Akass, eds. *Quality TV: Contemporary American Television and Beyond*. London/New York: Tauris, 2007. Print.

Mcdowell, Adam. "Giller Prize Lessons." *Vancouver Sun*. 11 Nov. 2008. Online Edition. Web.

McElroy, Ruth, and Rebecca Williams. "Remembering Ourselves, Viewing the Others: Historical Reality Television and Celebrity in the Small Nation." *Television and New Media* 12.3 (2011): 187–206. Web. 5 May 2015.

McEwan, Paul. *Bruce McDonald's Hard Core Logo*. Toronto: U of Toronto P, 2011. Print.

McFarlane, Brian. *The Best of It Happened in Hockey*. Toronto: Stoddart, 1998. Print.

McLuhan, Marshall. Letters to Pierre Elliott Trudeau. *Letters of Marshall McLuhan*. Ed. Matie Molinaro, Corinne McLuhan, and William Toye. Toronto: Oxford UP, 1987. Print.

———. "The Story of the Man in the Mask." Rev. of *Federalism and the French Canadians,* by Pierre Elliott Trudeau. *New York Times* 17 Nov. 1968: BR 36. Web. 12 Feb. 2014.

McRuer, Robert. *Crip Theory: Cultural Signs of Queerness and Disability*. New York: New York UP, 2006. Print.

Medd, Jodie. "'The Cult of the Clitoris': Anatomy of a National Scandal." *Modernism/modernity* 9.1 (2002): 21–49. Print.

Meeuf, Russell, and Raphael Raphael, eds. *Transnational Stardom: International Celebrity in Film and Popular Culture*. New York: Palgrave Macmillan, 2013. Web. 16 July 2013.

Meyer, David S., and Joshua Gamson. "The Challenge of Cultural Elites: Celebrities and Social Movements." *Sociological Inquiry* 65.2 (1995): 181–206. Print.

"Mission Statement and History." Terry Fox Foundation. Web. 26 Feb. 2013.

Monk, Katherine. "Coming Together for Actress's Swan Song. Production of Tracy Wright's Final Film Was Made Possible by a Close-knit Community." *Vancouver Sun* 14 Sept. 2010. Web. 31 Mar. 2013.

———. "Young Canadian Stars Opt for Better Roles This Side of the Border." *Vancouver Sun* 9 Oct. 2001. Web. 31 Mar. 2013.

Morin, Edgar. *The Stars*. New York: Grove, 1960. Print.

Morris, Peter. *Embattled Shadows: A History of Canadian Cinema: 1895–1939*. Montreal: McGill-Queen's UP, 1978. Print.

Moshovitz, Howie. "Arts Center Shows '20s Melodramas." *Denver Post* 2 Mar. 1991: 3E. Print.

Moss, Laura. "Margaret Atwood: Branding an Icon Abroad." *Margaret Atwood: The Open Eye*. Ed. John Moss and Tobi Kozakewich. Ottawa: Ottawa UP, 2006: 19–33. Print.

Mount, Nick. *When Canadian Literature Moved to New York*. Toronto: U of Toronto P, 2006. Print.

Murray, Anne, with Michael Posner. *All of Me*. Toronto: Vintage Canada, 2010. Print.

Musetto, V.A. "Recapturing Heart of the Wilderness," *New York Post* 10 Nov. 1989. Print.

National Council of Women of Canada. *Women of Canada: Their Life and Work*. 1900. Print.

Negra, Diane. *Off-White Hollywood: American Culture and Ethnic Female Stardom*. London: Routledge, 2001. Print.

Neilson, Shane. "Prize Culture: You're Next!" *Winnipeg Review* 21 Apr. 2011. Web. 28 Feb. 2013.

"Nell Shipman Is a Canadian." *Canadian Moving Picture Digest* 19 Oct. 1918: 5. Print.

Nesbitt-Larking, Paul. *Politics, Society, and the Media: Canadian Perspectives*. 2nd ed. Peterborough: Broadview, 2007. Print.

New, William H. *Borderlands: How We Talk about Canada*. Vancouver: U British Columbia P, 1998. Print.

"The News with Nikki Payne." *The Hour*. CBC, 2009. Television.

The Next Big Thing. Dir. Murray Battle. TVOntario, 2003; National Film Board of Canada, 2004.

Ngai, Sianne. *Ugly Feelings*. Cambridge, MA: Harvard UP, 2005. Print.

"niche." n. 3rd. def. *The Canadian Oxford English Dictionary*. 2nd ed. Don Mills, ON: Oxford UP, 2004. 1049.

Niro, Shelley. *The 500-Year Itch*. 1992. Photograph. National Gallery of Canada, Ottawa.

Olds, Jeremy, and Lyn Barnes. "'We look after our own': The Cultural Dynamics of Celebrity in a Small Country." *Pacific Journalism Review* 19.2 (2013): 86–106. Web. 5 May 2015.

Ong, Aihwa. "Flexible Citizenship among Chinese Cosmopolitans." *Cosmopolitics: Thinking and Feeling beyond the Nation.* Minneapolis: U of Minnesota P, 1998. 134–162. Print.

———. *Flexible Citizenship: The Cultural Logics of Transnationality.* Durham, NC: Duke UP, 1999. Print.

Orth, Maureen. *The Importance of Being Famous.* New York: Henry Holt, 2004. Print.

Palmer, Helen. "Just a Minute." *Toronto Star* 25 May 1963: 57. Web. 21 Jan. 2013.

———. "Mary Pickford: At 70, She's Still a Sweetheart." *Toronto Star* 22 May 1963: 51. Web. 21 Jan. 2013.

"Paraplegic Bungee Jumps Off B.C. Gorge in Wheelchair." CBC News. 23 Mar. 2012.

Parini, Jay. *Why Poetry Matters.* New Haven: Yale UP, 2008. Print.

Patterson, Kevin. "Mary Pickford: America's Sweetheart Born in Canada." *Canadian Story Collection.* Duenorth.net. Web. 28 Apr. 2013.

Paulson, Joanne. "It's a Laughing Matter: Majumder Says Just for Laughs 'a Really Big Thing.'" *Star-Phoenix* [Saskatoon] 9 November 2005: C1. Print.

Peters, Lloyd. *Lionhead Lodge: Movieland of the Northwest.* Fairfield: Ye Galleon Press, 1976. Print.

Pevere, Geoff. "A Joke in the Telling: On Canadian Comedy and the Missing Punchline." *Canadian Communication: Issues in Contemporary Media and Culture.* Ed. Bohdan Szuchewycz and Jeannette Sloniowski. Scarborough, ON: Prentice-Hall, 2002. 126–130. Print.

Pevere, Geoff, and Greig Dymond. *Mondo Canuck: A Canadian Pop Culture Odyssey.* Scarborough, ON: Prentice-Hall, 1996. Print.

Pickford, Mary. *Sunshine and Shadow.* New York: Doubleday, 1955. Print.

Pierre Elliott Trudeau: Memoirs. Dir. Brian McKenna. Writ. and Narr. Terence McKenna. 3 videocassettes. Les Productions La Fête, 1994. VideoCassette.

Pike, David L. *Canadian Cinema since the 1980s: At the Heart of the World.* Toronto: U of Toronto P, 2013. Print.

"Plenty of Cash Stashed in Coach's Corner." *Edmonton Journal* 3 Oct. 2007. Web. 17 Jan. 2014.

Ponce de Leon, Charles. *Self-Exposure: Human-Interest Journalism and the Emergence of Celebrity in America, 1890–1940.* Chapel Hill: U of North Carolina P, 2002. Print.

Pratt, Brooke. "Celebrity with a Cause: The Al Purdy A-frame Trust." ACCUTE 2011. University of Waterloo, Waterloo, ON. 28 May 2012. Conference Presentation.

"Quotes from Terry." Terry Fox Foundation. Web. 26 Feb. 2013.

Rak, Julie. "Canadian Idols? CBC's *The Greatest Canadian* as Celebrity History." *Programming Reality: Perspectives on English-Canadian Television.* Ed. Zoë Druick and Aspa Kotsopoulos. Waterloo: Wilfrid Laurier UP, 2008. 51–68. Print.

———. "Insecure Citizenship, Michael Ignatieff, Canada, Memoir." *Biography, an Interdisciplinary Quarterly* 32.1 (2010): 1–23. Print.

Rayner, Ben. "Ontario government to create $45M music fund." *Toronto Star*
1 May 2013. Web. 10 July 1013.
Red Hot Chili Peppers. "Californication." *Californication*. Warner Bros., 1998. CD.
"Reliving Terry Fox's Marathon of Hope: Day 79." CBC Digital Archives. Web. 10
Jan. 2014.
"Research Investment Portfolio." Terry Fox Foundation. Web. 9 Jan. 2014.
Reventon, Baron. "Will the Real Lew Ashby Please Stand Up..." *Matrix 2 A
Muse*. 10 Dec 2008. Web. 5 Aug. 2013.
Roberts, Gillian. *Prizing Literature: The Celebration and Circulation of National
Culture*. Toronto: U of Toronto P, 2011. Print.
Rojek, Chris. *Celebrity*. London: Reaktion, 2001. Print.
Roth, Lorna. "First Peoples' Television in Canada: Origins of the Aboriginal
Peoples Television Network." *Indigenous Screen Cultures in Canada*. Ed. Mar-
ian Bredin and Sigurjon Baldur Hafsteinsson. Winnipeg: U of Manitoba P,
2010. Print.
———. *Something New in the Air: The Story of First Peoples Television Broadcast-
ing in Canada*. Montreal: McGill-Queen's UP, 2005. Print.
Rush, Curtis. "NHL Signs 12-year TV, Internet Deal with Rogers; CBC Keeps
'Hockey Night in Canada.'" *Toronto Star* 26 Nov. 2013. Web. 17 Jan. 2014.
Sagan, Aleksandra. "Trudeau's Social-Media Playbook Looks a Lot like Obama's:
Liberal MP the Front-Runner in Party's Leadership Race." *CBC News* 11 Apr.
2013. Web. 26 June 2013.
Sampson, Mark. "My Kooky Ideas about Improving Literary Award Juries." *Free
Range Reading* 13 Oct. 2011. Web. 28 Feb. 2013.
Sandvoss, Cornel. *Fans: The Mirror of Consumption*. Cambridge: Polity, 2005.
Print.
Scales, Christopher. "The North American Aboriginal Music Industry." *Journal
of American Folklore* 126 (2013): 81–91. Print.
Schmidt, Christel. "American Idol: Mary Pickford, World War I, and the Making
of a National Icon." *Mary Pickford: Queen of the Movies*. Ed. Christel Schmidt.
Lexington: UP Kentucky, 2012. 145–62. Web. 6 June 2015.
Schroeder, Kirby. "Hypermasculinity." *Men and Masculinities, a Social, Cultural
and Historical Encyclopedia*. Ed. Michael Kimmel and Amy Aronson. Santa
Barbara: ABC-Clio, 2004. 417–418. Web. 17 Jan. 2014.
Scrivener, Leslie. *Terry Fox: His Story (Revised)*. Toronto: McClelland & Stewart,
2000. Print.
Senft, Teresa M. *Cam Girls: Celebrity and Community in the Age of Social Media*.
New York: Peter Lang, 2008. Print.
The Seven Year Itch. Dir. Billy Wilder. 20th Century Fox, 1955. Film.
Shattered. Prod. Laszlo Barna et al. Shaw Media, 2010.
Shildrick, Margrit, and Janet Price. "Breaking the Boundaries of the Broken
Body." *Feminist Theory and the Body: A Reader*. Ed. Janet Price and Margrit
Shildrick. New York: Routledge, 1999. 432–444. Print.
Shipman, Nell. *Abandoned Trails*. Lincoln Mac Veagh, 1932. Print.

————. *Get the Woman*. Dial Press, 1930. Print.

————. "The Movie That Couldn't Be Screened." *Atlantic Monthly* March, Apr., May 1925: 326–332; 477–482; 645–651. Print.

————. *The Silent Screen & My Talking Heart*. Boise, ID: Boise State UP, 1987, 2001. Print.

————. *Neeka of the North*. Collins, 1931. Print.

Siebers, Tobin. "Disability as Masquerade." *Literature and Medicine*. 23.1 (2004): 1–22. Web. 3 Mar. 2008.

Simpson, Jeffrey. *Star-Spangled Canadians: Canadians Living the American Dream*. Toronto: Harper Collins, 2000. Print.

"Slagging off." *DNTO*. Canadian Broadcasting Corporation Airdate: 7 Apr. 2013. Web. 15 Aug. 2013.

Small, Tamara A. "E-ttack Politics: Negativity, the Internet, and Canadian Political Parties" *How Canadians Communicate IV: Media and Politics*. Ed. David Taras and Christopher Waddell. Edmonton: Athabasca UP, 2012. 169–188. Print.

————. "Are We Friends Yet? Online Relationship Marketing by Political Parties" *Political Marketing in Canada*. Ed. Alex Marland, Thierry Giasson, and Jennifer Lees-Marshment. Vancouver: U of British Columbia P, 2012. 193–208. Print.

Smith, Judith. "Nell Shipman: Girl Wonder from God's Country." *Cinema Canada* 51 (Nov./Dec. 1978): 35–37. Print.

Smith, Laurajane. *Uses of Heritage*. London and New York: Routledge, 2006. Print.

Sontag, Susan. *Illness as Metaphor* and *AIDS and Its Metaphors*. New York: Doubleday, 1989. Print.

Stabile, Carol. "Resistance, Recuperation, and Reflexivity: The Limits of a Paradigm." *Critical Studies in Mass Communication* 12 (1995): 403–422. Print.

Stamp, Shelley. "Feminist Media Historiography and the Work Ahead." Women and the Silent Screen Conference. University of Melbourne, Melbourne. 1 Oct. 2013. Keynote Speech.

"Star of Silent Screen Was Born in Toronto." *Globe and Mail* 30 May 1979:13. Web. 23 Apr. 2013.

Stebbins, Robert. *The Laugh-Makers: Stand-up as Art, Business, and Life-Style*. Montreal: McGill-Queen's UP, 1990. Print.

Sterritt, Angela. "Do the Junos Still Need an Aboriginal Category?" cbc.ca. Web. 22 Apr. 2014.

Stone, Jay. "Maple-Western Misses; Mild, Mild West." *Montreal Gazette*, 30 Apr. 2010. Web. 31 Mar. 2013.

Stonechild, Blair. *Buffy Sainte-Marie: It's My Way*. Markham: Fifth House, 2012. Print.

Straw, Will. "Cross-Border Visualities and the Canadian Image." *Imaginations: Journal of Cross-Cultural Images Studies/Revue d'Études Interculturelles de l'Image* 1.1 (2010): 24–39. Print.

————. "Dilemmas of Definition." *Slippery Pastimes: Reading the Popular in Canadian Culture*. Ed. Joan Nicks and Jeanette Sloniowski. Wilfrid Laurier UP, 2002. 95–110. Print.

Street, John. *Politics & Popular Culture*. Philadelphia: Temple UP, 1997. Print.

————. "The Celebrity Politician: Political Style and Popular Culture." *Media and the Restyling of Politics*. Ed. John Corner and Dick Pels. London: Sage, 2003. 85–98. Print.

————. "Do Celebrity Politics and Celebrity Politicians Matter?" *British Journal of Politics and International Relations* 14.3 (2012): 346–356. Print.

Stringer, Arthur. "Our Mary: An Intimate Appraisement, in Four Parts, of the World's Most Widely Known Motion-picture Actress." *Maclean's* (Sept. 1918): 22–25, 98–104; (Oct. 1918): 19–22, 98-103; (Nov. 1918): 39–42; 75–82. Web. 28 Apr. 2013.

Stursberg, Richard. *The Tower of Babble, Sins, Secrets and Successes Inside the CBC*. Vancouver: Douglas & McIntyre, 2012. Print.

Sugars, Cynthia. "Marketing Ambivalence: Molson Breweries Go Postcolonial." *Canadian Cultural Poesis: Essays on Canadian Culture*. Ed. Garry Sherbert, Annie Gérin, and Sheila Petty. Waterloo: Wilfrid Laurier UP, 2006. 121–142. Print.

Sutcliffe, Mark. "CBC Must Decide What to Do with Don Cherry." *National Post*. 19 Mar. 19 2012. Web. 17 Jan. 2014.

"Swine Flu Hysteria and Making It in the USA." *The Debaters*. Season 4, Episode 1. CBC Radio One, 2009. MP3 File.

Szeman, Imre. "The Rhetoric of Culture, Some Notes on Magazines, Canadian Culture, and Globalization." *Cultural Studies: An Anthology*. Ed. Michael Ryan. Oxford: Blackwell Publishing, 2008. 82–98. Print.

Szeman, Imre, and Gail Faurschou. *Canadian Cultural Studies: A Reader*. Durham: Duke UP, 2009. Print.

Szuchewycz, Bohdan, and Jeannette Sloniowski, eds. *Canadian Communication: Issues in Contemporary Media and Culture*. Scarborough, ON: Prentice-Hall, 2002. Print.

Taft, Michael. "The Role of Hero-Making in Canadian National Identity: The Case of Terry Fox." *Artes Populares* 16/17.2 (1995): 761–766. Print.

Tanaka, Eisuke. "'Greek' Objects on Turkish Soil: A Link Between the Inalienability of 'Cultural Property' and Notions of Place in the Context of Turkish Claims for Repatriation." *Nationalism, Historiography and the (Re)construction of the Past*. Ed. Claire Norton. Washington, DC: New Academia Publishing, 2007. Print.

Taras, David. *Power and Betrayal in the Canadian Media*. Peterborough, ON: Broadview, 2001. Print.

————. "The Past and Future of Political Communication in Canada." *How Canadians Communicate IV: Media and Politics*. Ed. David Taras and Christopher Waddell. Edmonton: Athabasca UP, 2012. 1–25. Print.

Taras, David, and Christopher Waddell. "The 2011 Federal Election and the Transformation of Canadian Media and Politics." *How Canadians Com-*

municate IV: Media and Politics. Ed. David Taras and Christopher Waddell. Edmonton: Athabasca UP, 2012. 71–107. Print.

Tennant, Diane. "Hollywood ending." *Virginian-Pilot* 1 Mar. 2005. Print.

"Terry Fox Foundation Research." Terry Fox Foundation. Web. 9 Jan. 2014.

"Terry's Journal Entries and Map." Terry Fox Foundation. Web. 29 Oct. 2012.

Thacker, Robert. "Introduction: No Catlin without Kane: or Really Understanding the 'American West.'" *One West, Two Myths II. Essays on Comparison.* Ed. Robert Thacker and C.L. Higham. Calgary: U of Calgary P, 2006. 1–14. Print.

Thienpont, Eve. "A Re-Evaluation of Oscar Wilde's Homosexual Image." *Irish Studies Review* 13.3 (2005): 291–301. Print.

Thomas, Evan. *A Long Time Coming.* New York: Perseus, 2009. Print.

Thompson, Frank. "Letter to the Editor." *Idaho Arts Journal* vol. 4.4 (1987): 4. Print.

Thomson, Rosemarie Garland. *Extraordinary Bodies: Figuring Physical Disability in American Culture and Literature.* New York: Columbia UP, 1997. Print.

Tinic, Serra. *On Location, Canada's Television Industry in a Global Market.* Toronto: U of Toronto P, 2005. Print.

Titchkosky, Tanya. *Reading and Writing Disability Differently.* Toronto: U of Toronto P, 2007. Print.

"Traditional and Modern Makes a Tribe Called Red." local2 Sault Ste. Marie. Web. 2 May 2014.

Tremain, Shelley. "On the Subject of Impairment." *Disability/Postmodernity: Embodying Disability Theory.* Ed. Mairian Corker and Tom Shakespeare. London: Continuum, 2002. 32–47. Print.

Trigger. Dir. Bruce McDonald. New Real Films et al., 2010.

"The Trouble with FACTOR." *Slagging Off.* 2 Apr. 2013. Web. 1 July 2013.

Trudeau, Margaret. *Consequences.* Toronto: McClelland and Stewart, 1982. Print.

Trudeau, Pierre Elliott. *Memoirs.* Toronto: McClelland and Stewart, 1993. Print.

"Trudeau says counter-attack ads offer 'positive' message." *CBC News* 24 Apr. 2013. Web. 26 June 2013.

Trudelle Schwartz, Maureen. *Fighting Colonialism with Hegemonic Power: Native American Appropriation of Indian Stereotypes.* Albany, NY: SUNY P, 2013. Print.

Turner, Graeme. *Understanding Celebrity.* London: Sage, 2004. Print.

"Untitled, Newspaper coverage of *M'sieu Sweetheart* circa 1930." Print. Nell Shipman Collection. Boise State University: MSS99, Box 8, Folder 18.

Vance, Jonathan F. *A History of Canadian Culture.* Don Mills: Oxford UP, 2009. Print.

Veillette, Eric. "Toronto's Sweetheart Back in the Spotlight." *Toronto Star* 13 Jan. 2011: E3. Web. 30 Apr. 2013 .

Vérronneau, Pierre. "Genres and Variations: The Audiences of Quebec Cinema." *Self Portraits: The Cinemas of Canada since Telefilm.* Ed. André Loiselle and Tom McSorley. Ottawa: Canadian Film Institute, 2006. 93–127. Print.

"Victoria Girl Is Star at Columbia." *Vancouver World* 24 Apr. 1918: 9. Print.

Vismann, Cornelia. *Files: Law and Media Technology.* Palo Alto: Stanford UP, 2006. Print.

Waddell, Christopher. "Final Thoughts: How Will Canadians Communicate about Politics and the Media in 2015." *How Canadians Communicate IV: Media and Politics.* Ed. David Taras and Christopher Waddell. Edmonton: Athabasca UP, 2012. 369–377. Print.

———. "Berry'd Alive: The Media, Technology, and the Death of Political Coverage." *How Canadians Communicate IV: Media and Politics.* Ed. David Taras and Christopher Waddell. Edmonton: Athabasca UP, 2012. 109–128. Print.

Wagman, Ira. "On the 'Policy Reflex' in Canadian Communication Studies." *Canadian Journal of Communication* 35.4 (2010): 619–630. Print.

Walden, Keith. "Toronto Society's Response to Celebrity Performers, 1887–1914." *Canadian Historical Review* 89.3 (2008): 373–397. Print.

Walker, Alexander. *Stardom: The Hollywood Phenomenon.* New York: Stein and Day, 1970. Print.

Walker, Joseph, and Juanita Walker. *The Light on Her Face.* Hollywood: ASC Press, 1984. Print.

Weeks, Eric. "Where Is There? The Canadianization of the American Media Landscape." *International Journal of Canadian Studies/Revue international d'études canadiennes* 39–40 (2009): 83–108. Print.

Wells, Zachariah. "CC Says Everything's Cool." *Career Limiting Moves* 15 Oct. 2011. Web. 28 Feb. 2013.

———. "I'll Scratch Your Back: On Jurisimprudence and the GGs." *Maisonneuve.* Online Edition. 22 Nov. 2004. Web. 10 Jan. 2009.

Wendell, Susan. *The Rejected Body: Feminist Philosophical Reflections on Disability.* New York: Routledge, 1996. Print.

Weston, Greg. "Justin Trudeau Can Fill a Room but Can He Win an Election?" CBC 3 Oct. 2012. Transcript. 1 Dec 2012. Web. 13 Jan. 2013.

"What We're Looking For." *APTN.* Web. 23 July 2015.

Wheeler, Mark. "The Democratic Worth of Celebrity Politics in an Era of Late Modernity." *British Journal of Politics and International Relations* 14.3 (2012): 407–422. Print.

Whitfield, Eileen. *The Woman Who Made Hollywood.* Toronto: Macfarlane, Walter & Ross, 1997. Print.

The Who. "Behind Blue Eyes." *Who's Next.* Decca, 1971.

Winans, Richard M. "The Rhythm of Health: How Maud Allan, the World-Famous Canadian Dancer Keeps Body and Mind Vigorous by Nature Dancing." *Everywoman's World* June 1917: 12, 50. Print.

"Women's Sports Media Group Calls Don Cherry's Comments 'Sexist.'" *Globe and Mail* 28 Apr. 2013. Web. 17 Jan. 2014

Woodrow, Anna. "Why Are They Laughing? The Re-Formulation of Identity in Canadian Stand-Up Comedy." Diss. Concordia University, 2001. Print.

"Writers on Munro." Page Turner Blog, *The New Yorker.* 10 Oct. 2013. Web. 10 Oct. 2013.

York, Lorraine. *Literary Celebrity in Canada.* Toronto: U of Toronto P, 2007. Print.

———. *Margaret Atwood and the Labour of Literary Celebrity.* Toronto: U of Toronto P, 2013. Print.

Young, David. "Ethno-Racial Minorities and the Juno Awards." *Canadian Journal of Sociology.* 31.2 (2006): 183–210. Print.

Zdriluk, Beth. "'Mary Pickford and Questions of National Identity during WWI'." *KINEMA: a journal for film and audiovisual media* Spring 2005: n.p. Web. 30 Apr. 2013.

Contributors

Jennifer Bell received her PhD from the University of Alberta, where she specialized in Canadian memoir and political life writing. Her research interests include evolving forms of political communication and popular culture. She takes a special interest in representations of gender within political communication and the Canadian parliamentary system. Her most recent publication discusses changing representations of mothering in Canadian political and popular culture.

Liz Czach is Associate Professor in the Department of English and Film Studies at the University of Alberta. From 1995 to 2005 she was a programmer of Canadian and Québécois film at the Toronto International Film Festival. Her research interests encompass home movies and amateur films, film festivals, and star studies. Her publications on the latter include "Cinephilia, Stars, and Film Festivals" in *Cinema Journal* (2010), "Television, Film and the Canadian Star System" in *Canadian Television: Text and Context* (2011), and "The Transnational Career of Geneviève Bujold" in *Transnational Stardom: International Celebrity in Film and Popular Culture* (2013). Her current research project is a cultural history of postwar travel lecture filmmaking.

Danielle J. Deveau is a Lecturer at the University of Waterloo and the Managing Director of Pop Culture Lab. Her key areas of research include creative economies, fields of cultural production, cultural scenes, Canadian popular culture, and the politics of humour and laughter.

Katja Lee is a SSHRC post-doctoral fellow at Simon Fraser University in Burnaby and a member of the Persona, Celebrity, Publics research group at Deakin University in Melbourne. She has published essays on celebrity, public identity performance, and life writing, and is co-editor of *Contemporary Publics* (forthcoming). Her present research project traces how Canadian magazines fostered an emerging contemporary celebrity culture in Canada in the 1910–1930 period.

P. David Marshall holds a research professorship and personal chair in New Media, Communication and Cultural Studies at Deakin University, Melbourne, Australia, and is also a Distinguished High-End Visiting Foreign Expert at Central China University's School of Journalism and Communication in Wuhan, China. He is the author, co-author, editor, or co-editor of many books, including *Celebrity and Power* (2nd ed., 2014), *Companion to Celebrity* (2015), *Promotional Vistas* (2016), *Persona Studies* (2016), *New Media Cultures* (2004), *Celebrity Culture Reader* (2006), and *Fame Games* (2000). His current research is primarily focused on persona as a way to understand the presentation of the contemporary and online public self.

Valerie J. Millar is a former PhD student in the interdisciplinary graduate program, Faculty of Creative and Critical Studies at the University of British Columbia, Okanagan campus. An active member of the Canadian Disability Studies Association, Valerie interrogates constructions of chronic illness and disability, particular in Canadian and feminist contexts. Her present research seeks to redress the critical gaps in scholarly work on the disabled female voice in Canadian women's life writing.

Owen Percy is a Professor of Communication and Literary Studies at Sheridan College in Brampton, Ontario. He earned his PhD from the University of Calgary in 2010 where his dissertation focused on literary awards and prize culture in Canada. Dr. Percy has published essays, reviews, and interviews in several national and international scholarly publications such as *Canadian Literature, Canadian Poetry, ARIEL,* and the *British Journal of Canadian Studies.* He recently edited and introduced *The Order in Which We Do Things: The Poetry of Tom Wayman* (2014) for WLU Press's Laurier Poetry Series.

Julie Rak is a Professor in the Department of English and Film Studies at the University of Alberta. Her latest book is *Boom! Manufacturing Memoir for the Popular Market* (2013) and, with Anna Poletti, her latest edited collection is *Identity Technologies: Constructing the Self Online* (2014). She is the author of *Negotiated Memory* (2004), nominated for the Klibansky Prize for best book in the Humanities and has edited or co-edited many collections on auto/biography. She is presently writing a SSHRC-funded book manuscript called "Social Climbing: Gender in Mountaineering Writing." Until 2016, she played defence for the Edmonton hockey team The Booby Orrs.

Katherine Ann Roberts is an Associate Professor at Wilfrid Laurier University where she teaches in the French and North American Studies programs. She has published widely in scholarly journals on Québécois women's writing, Quebec nationalism, and, more recently, on Canadian western writing, masculinity in 1960s North American film, and cross-border culture in the Pacific Northwest. She is currently completing a book manuscript entitled "West/Border/Road: Nation and Genre in Canadian Narrative."

Amy Shore is Associate Professor of Cinema and Screen Studies at the State University of New York at Oswego. Her recent book, *Suffrage and the Silver Screen*, examines films made by and about the American woman suffrage movement and includes a chapter on how stardom was mobilized for the movement. She has also published articles and essays in *Camera Obscura*, *Afterimage*, and a collection on historiography, archival research, and feminist film criticism.

Ira Wagman is an Associate Professor of Communication Studies at Carleton University. He is the co-editor (with Peter Urquhart) of *Cultural industries.ca: Making Sense of Canadian Media in the Digital Age* (2012) and co-editor (with Will Straw and Sandra Gabriele) of *Intersections of Media and Communications: Concepts and Critical Frameworks* (2011). He has also published extensively on media history and cultural policy in Canada.

Lorraine York is Professor and Senator William McMaster Chair in Canadian Literature and Culture at McMaster University. She has published books on women's collaborative writing, Timothy Findley, photography in Canadian fiction, and has edited or co-edited books on Margaret Atwood and early Canadian literary culture. Her book *Literary Celebrity in Canada* (2007) was a finalist for the Canadian Federation for the Humanities' Raymond Klibansky Prize for the best Canadian book published in the Humanities. Her newest book, *Margaret Atwood and the Labour of Literary Celebrity*, appeared with the University of Toronto Press in 2013. A new project examines the phenomenon of the reluctant celebrity.

Index

ableism, 57–70, 71n2. *See also* disability

Aboriginal. *See* Indigenous

Aboriginal People's Television Network (APTN), 102–6, 109

achieved celebrity, 8, 204

Acland, Charles: on national spectatorship, 2, 150–51, 164n5, 154; on star-system-in-exile, 133, 147

administration. *See* bureaucracy

affect: and bureaucracy, 204, 212–13; and celebrity persona, 123, 126, 129; and fandom, 121–23, 125–26; and labour, 170; and nationalism, 12, 40, 51–52, 151; and sports, 113, 121; and television, 74, 80

Albani, Emma, 22, 38–53, 53n1, 53n5, 53n12, 55nn19–21

Allan, Maud, 22, 38–40, 44–48, 50–53, 54n8, 54n14, 55n19

American: citizenship, 42, 49–50; industry, 102, 115; influence, 16, 113–15, 118–21, 147–52; landscape, 27; markets, 2, 49–50, 114, 167–83; passing, 49–50, 172–73, 177; sameness, 148; xenophobia, 3. *See also* Canadian: export; star system: American

Anglo-Canadian. *See* Canadian; language

APTN. *See* Aboriginal People's Television Network (APTN)

artifact. *See* cultural heritage

ascribed celebrity, 8, 74, 86–87, 90

athleticism, viii, 24, 60, 62, 64, 69–71, 72n4, 81

Atwood, Margaret, 15, 65, 99, 153, 189–93, 205

audience: absence, 6, 150–51; constructions, 40, 43, 59–60, 81, 114, 132–33; studies, 6–7, 154, 159, 202, 216. *See also* Canadian: spectatorship; fandom

awards: Governor General (GG), 185–88, 191–95, 197–98; Griffin Poetry Prize, 187–88, 191–95, 197–98; Juno, 105–6, 110n4, 111, 179–80, 202; literary, 185–99; Montreal International Poetry Prize (MIPP), 187, 194–99; music, 105–6, 179–80, 202

Bell, Jennifer, 4, 9, 12, 146n10

Bennett, James, 9, 155

Berton, Pierre, 14, 38

Boorstin, Daniel, 5–6, 58–59, 75

border: American-Canadian, 16, 37, 136, 148–53, 158–63, 172–74, 182; crossing, 3–4, 10–13, 37–38, 44, 136, 140, 152–53, 162–63, 165n14; national, 11, 13, 16–17, 97; provincial, vii, 132–33, 136, 142

Boxer, Asa, 194–98

brand: advertising, 66; and commercial marketing, 34, 76, 86, 88, 90, 117, 206–7; consumption, 65, 86–88,